Idols and Celebrity in Japanese Media Culture

Idols and Celebrity in Japanese Media Culture

Edited by

Patrick W. Galbraith and Jason G. Karlin
University of Tokyo, Japan

First published 2012 by
PALGRAVE MACMILLAN

Palgrave Macmillan in the UK is an imprint of Macmillan Publishers Limited,
registered in England, company number 785998, of Houndmills, Basingstoke,
Hampshire RG21 6XS.

Palgrave Macmillan in the US is a division of St Martin's Press LLC,
175 Fifth Avenue, New York, NY 10010.

Palgrave Macmillan is the global academic imprint of the above companies
and has companies and representatives throughout the world.

Palgrave® and Macmillan® are registered trademarks in the United States,
the United Kingdom, Europe and other countries.

ISBN 978–0–230–29830–9

This book is printed on paper suitable for recycling and made from fully
managed and sustained forest sources. Logging, pulping and manufacturing
processes are expected to conform to the environmental regulations of the
country of origin.

A catalogue record for this book is available from the British Library.

A catalog record for this book is available from the Library of Congress.

10   9   8   7   6   5   4   3   2   1
21 20 19 18 17 16 15 14 13 12

Transferred to Digital Printing in 2012

Contents

Part III Difference

Part IV Image

Illustrations

Foreword: Revisiting "Idology"

It was back in 1988 that I decided to explore the conspicuous realm of popular cultural performance in contemporary urban Japan that was being represented by young media-promoted personalities called *aidoru* or "pop idols." As a novice of symbolic anthropology, I considered idols to be personified symbols that operated as tricksters in the public initiation of Japanese youngsters. My dissatisfaction with the fact that the few academic sources I could find on idols back then were all anecdotal statements by their authors about how the social meanings of idols could be interpreted led me to cultivate a new field of empirical studies on the idol phenomenon.

Naming this new field *gūzōgaku* or "idology," I spent the next ten years conducting fieldwork in Japan's entertainment industry and its surroundings, gathering concrete data on how young talents, their promoters, and supporting fans co-developed a domain in which idols were celebrated, commoditized, transformed into adolescent role models, and consumed. With many thanks to countless collaborators in Japan's entertainment world as well as in academia, my venture resulted in the publication of *Islands of Eight Million Smiles* in 2005.

This accomplishment was not free of shortcomings. In my book, I emphasized female idols, instead of male idols or queer icons, since it was the subject I knew best. My work has been criticized from time to time for its apparent focus on the aspects of conformity and its neglect of points of conflict—meaning that I had to open Pandora's box by highlighting the "behind the scene" underside of idol performance, including such issues as ethnic minorities and mobster politics. Perhaps, it was my sense of moral and ethical boundaries that configured the seriousness of the ethnographic approach and my inclination towards culturalism (i.e., my emphasis on the idea that enculturation is a compulsory praxis), which I inherited from anthropology, that prevented me from exposing these perspectives.

Idol performance has demonstrated new turns since I introduced its symbolic significance to the world, and changed in ways I would have never expected: instances are the growing popularity of Japanese pop idols alongside cutesy phenomena, manga and anime, as well as centers of "Cool Japan," such as Shibuya and Akihabara, among European and American audiences in a form that may be called neo-Orientalism; the influx of Korean idols, such as BoA, Jinki, Kara, and Shōjo Jidai, into Japan's pop idol scene; the transformation of idol imagery from cutesy to more sexy, classy, and/or hip personal configurations along-side emergent hybrid buzzwords, such as *erokawa* (sexy-cutesy), *kirekawa* (classy-cutesy), and *kawakakoii* (cutesy-trendy), as manifested in neo-idols, such as Amuro Namie, AYU, and Kōda Kumi; and the revival of cutesy idols in forms represented by Morning Musume and AKB48. For someone who expected that the clumsy representation of cutesy idols would fade away before long by becoming passé—and who com-missioned idology with the classical anthropological task of recording traditions, customs, and lifestyles that would never be rightly under-stood once lost or forgotten—these new changes in idol performance demand a new wave of extensive research on the idol phenomenon.

In this sense, this volume is something I was waiting to see for a long time: a set of case studies by the next generation of idologists who have managed to expose what I could not, carried theorization on idol-pop phenomena a step further, and achieved what many students who majored in media studies, cultural studies, and cultural anthro-pology could only touch on at the level of term papers and theses. I am convinced that this volume will provide an invaluable contribu-tion in our ongoing Baconian venture to deduce the mechanism of idol mystification.

Aoyagi Hiroshi

Acknowledgments

It's a little counterintuitive, but acknowledgments are perhaps the most difficult part of a book to write. They are written last, with much happening from the start to the finish of a project, meaning all sorts of loose ends to tie up. More importantly, the audience for this singular and strange genre is completely bifurcated: those who don't care at all and those who care a great deal. You seldom find people who just skim the acknowledgments. They either skip them entirely or pore carefully over every word looking for academic genealogies, strategic alliance-making (or breaking: the snub), and perhaps personal recognitions and resonances. In this most seemingly insignificant genre of writing, the stakes can be extremely high. It's hard to find a middle path and please everyone.

The logical conclusion is to thank everyone generally and no one specifically. Keep it short and offend no one! Indeed, such a set of acknowledgments makes a good deal of sense. To wax poetic, it seems to us that everyone we ever met and every conversation we ever had have deeply impacted the choices we have made and what we have written. More practically, in a book project that spanned many years from conception to completion, there are far too many people to thank individually and properly.

This book began with encounters at the University of Tokyo, Japan, in 2009, and then coalesced into a graduate seminar on celebrity and fandom. Many students in the Graduate School of Interdisciplinary Information Studies shared an interest in media and celebrity studies, and a few shared a more personal fascination with Japanese idols. It was hard for us not to notice the gap between the omnipresence of idols in everyday conversations in Tokyo and their absence in academic debates. In our readings on Japanese popular culture, we also found a surprising lack of dialogue and engagement with scholarship in the fields of media and celebrity studies outside Japan. As editors, Patrick, who was completing ethnographic fieldwork on Akihabara concurrently with the emergence of AKB48, brought a focus on female idols, and Jason, who had an abiding interest in Japanese masculinities in history, collected data on male idol groups. Seeing an opportunity to collaborate on a project that would address a dearth in the literature and be attentive to the gendered dimensions of Japanese idol culture, we jumped enthu-siastically (read: recklessly) into a publication project. Our sincerest gratitude goes to all those who saw potential in a few scribbled notes and joined or supported us on this journey.

We would also like to thank all the students in the Information, Technology, and Society in Asia (ITASIA) program at the University of Tokyo who participated in the seminar on celebrity and fandom and contributed to our dialogue on idols. We would especially like to acknowledge the assistance and participation of the students in host-ing a conference on idols at the University of Tokyo in December 2011. Aoyagi Hiroshi, Yoshimi Shun'ya, Gabriella Lukács, Anne Allison, David Slater and Brian Ashcraft offered their encouragement and advice at various stages of the book project.

Hirata Kaori and Tsurumaki Akihiko from *Asahi Shimbun* and Wachi Isao and Miyazaki Makoto from *Yomiuri Shimbun* generously agreed to the use of images for the book. Thanks also go to Nakashima Motoki and AKS Co Ltd for additional permissions. Kunda Nobuyuki from CEATEC Japan Management went out of his way to scan through thousands of archived images and liaise with Crypton Future Media, the National Institute of Advanced Industrial Science and Technology, and Yamaha Corporation concerning images in Daniel Black's chapter. Nishimura Keiko assisted in taking pictures in Akihabara for Patrick W. Galbraith's chapter. Also, Nakamura Jin shared his private collection of primary documents collected during AKB48's early career.

Our friends and family deserve special thanks. We suspect it means little to them to see their names in print at this point, and that they would just as soon not hear another word about this book. Issues of idols and celebrity in Japanese media culture have dominated our thoughts and conversations for quite long enough, they say. May they take some comfort in knowing that we will perhaps finally be able to talk about something else over coffee. Suffice it to say that without their great reserves of patience, input and well-timed wake-up calls we wouldn't have made it through this long and involved process.

And the process was long. While soliciting, writing, and editing chapters, we witnessed the rise and fall of many idols. The one we felt most acutely was the "graduation" in 2012 of Maeda Atsuko, whose image at the AKB48 General Election in 2011 is on the cover of this book. A book like this always risks being "untimely," in the sense of being out of its proper time. Reading from the individual chapters to the introduction to this set of acknowledgments reveals how the flow of time twists in on itself. What was new is now old, here made new again;

everything is out of order, but comes into clearer focus due to framing and juxtaposition. Following the lead of anthropologist George Marcus, we choose to embrace our untimeliness. The past returns, a recent past, a present that we once knew and don't want to know again. The unwelcome return of idols, their uncomfortable presence. It all seems "off" somehow, and so is open to interrogation.

Maeda Atsuko is gone, leaving behind only an image. But isn't that a fitting introduction to idols in Japanese media (and consumer) culture? We notice the arch of her career from start to finish—a series of mediated and marketed events, appearances, and disappearances—because of the untimeliness of academic publication. So, too, there is a revelation in untimely acknowledgments, directed not at the people we noted here, who have long since been personally thanked or have ceased to care, but rather aimed at others—the readers of this book. Why are these acknowledgments necessary? Who are we selling them to, and what are we selling them as? An image of earnest and experienced scholars? No: a moving image. Heart. Our own and one for the book. We have to thank idols for teaching us how to inscribe such a thing in commercial (re)production.

Patrick W. Galbraith and Jason G. Karlin
March 2012

Contributors

Daniel Black lectures in the School of English, Communications and Performance Studies at Monash University, Melbourne, Australia. He is the editor, with Stephen Epstein and Alison Tokita, of *Complicated Currents: Media Flows and Soft Power in East Asia* (2010) and writes on themes connected with the relationship between the human body and technology.

Patrick W. Galbraith holds a PhD in information studies from the University of Tokyo, Japan. He is the author of *The Otaku Encyclopedia* (2009), *Tokyo Realtime: Akihabara* (2010), and *Otaku Spaces* (2012). Academic publications include "*Moe*: Exploring Virtual Potential in Post-Millennial Japan" (2009), "Akihabara: Conditioning a Public 'Otaku' Image" (2010), and "*Fujoshi*: Fantasy Play and Transgressive Intimacy among 'Rotten Girls' in Contemporary Japan" (2011).

Lucy Glasspool is a PhD candidate in the Graduate School of Languages and Cultures at Nagoya University in Japan. Her research interests include gender in popular culture, male–male eroticism and female pleasure in contemporary Japanese women's media, and the links between globalization and fan culture. She is a graduate of the School of Oriental and African Studies in London, UK, where she completed her master's thesis entitled "Gender and the Body in Japanese *Shōjo* Pop Culture," focusing on performances of male homoeroticism. Her doctoral thesis will explore gender and Japaneseness in Western fandoms of Japanese roleplaying video games, a subject she has addressed at various international conferences.

Alexandra Hambleton is a PhD candidate in the Graduate School of Interdisciplinary Information Studies at the University of Tokyo, Japan. Her research interests include Japanese popular culture, nationalism, and gender. In her master's thesis, entitled "Flagging the Foreign: Non-Japanese Residents, Television and Cultural Nationalism in Japan," she focused on the use of foreign residents of Japan in popular culture as a medium through which to critique and re-evaluate Japanese traditional culture to achieve nationalistic ends. In her doctoral thesis she will explore the connection between media depictions of sex in television and magazines and sexual identities in contemporary Japanese society.

Aoyagi Hiroshi is a Phi Beta Kappa scholar and Professor of Asian Studies in the School of Asia 21 of Kokushikan University in Tokyo, Japan. He is a pioneer in the empirical study of Japanese pop idols, which he calls "idology," as described in *Islands of Eight Million Smiles: Idol Performance and Symbolic Production in Contemporary Japan* (2005). As a symbolic anthropologist, Aoyagi has been conducting a series of ethnographic investigations on roles played by personified symbols in the contemporary social settings of Asia. His wider research and pedagogical interests include popular cultural dissemination, civil movements in non-Western societies, the enculturation of youth, and ethno-iconographic research methods.

Jason G. Karlin is an associate professor in the Graduate School of Interdisciplinary Information Studies at the University of Tokyo, Japan, where he teaches gender and media studies. He received his PhD from the University of Illinois at Urbana-Champaign, USA, in 2002. Between 2003 and 2008, he served as managing editor of *Social Science Japan Journal*. He is the author of *The Eternal Return of History: Gender and Nation in Meiji Japan* (forthcoming).

Ho Swee Lin received her PhD in social anthropology from the University of Oxford, UK, and is currently an assistant professor in the Department of Sociology at the National University of Singapore. Her research and teaching interests include corporate culture, friendship, gender, global finance, global media, intimacy, migration, multiculturalism, popular culture, sexuality, and urban life in Asia. She worked for many years as auditor, financial journalist, and corporate executive in China, Hong Kong, Japan, and the UK before entering graduate school.

Jonathan D. Mackintosh is a lecturer in Japanese Studies at Birkbeck, University of London, UK. His research interests include gender/sexuality in postwar Japan, masculinities and the body, and historical East Asian diasporic identities. He recently published *Homosexuality and Manliness in Postwar Japan* (2009) and *Cultural Studies and Cultural Industries in Northeast Asia* (2009), a collected volume co-edited with C. Berry and N. Liscutin.

W. David Marx is Chief Editor of the web journal *Néojaponisme* (http://neojaponisme.com). He holds a BA from Harvard University, USA, in East Asian studies, and an MA from Keio University's Graduate School of Business and Commerce, Japan. His master's thesis looked at the effect of industrial organization on the Japanese music industry's rate of innovation. He has published widely on Japanese culture, including on CNN and in *Harper's*, *GQ*, and *Brutus*, as well as in *Best Music Writing 2009*.

Kazumi Nagaike is an associate professor at the Center for International Education and Research at Oita National University in Japan. Her scholarly interests include the analysis of female acts of fantasizing male–male eroticism in literary works and popular culture materials. Her most recent research focus is a methodological analysis of how Japanese popular culture is treated in the educational institutions of foreign countries. Her publications include "Perverse Sexuality, Pervasive Desires: Representations of Female Fantasies and Yaoi Manga as Pornography Directed at Women" (2003) and "Elegant Caucasians, Amorous Arabs, and Invisible Others: Signs and Images of Foreigners in Japanese BL Manga" (2009).

Igor Prusa is a PhD candidate in the Graduate School of Interdisciplinary Information Studies at the University of Tokyo, Japan. He is a graduate in Japanese and German philology from Palacky University, Czech Republic, and is simultaneously conducting research at the Institute of Communication Studies and Journalism, Charles University, Prague. His interest lies in Japanese media and the role of various mediation processes within Japanese society. He regularly publishes in Czech academic journals (*Prague Social Science Studies, Novy Orient, Pritomnost*) and is an active music composer/performer.

Introduction: The Mirror of Idols and Celebrity

Patrick W. Galbraith and Jason G. Karlin

The idol project

On 9 June 2011, news of nuclear contamination in earthquake-stricken Japan took a backseat to the AKB48 General Election in the mass media. The third election of its kind for the all-girl idol group formed in 2005, it was a massive promotion and marketing blitz. In addition to fan-club members, anyone who had purchased their 21st single, "Every-day, Kachūsha," could vote. In a week, it sold 1,334,000 copies, a new record for a single sold in Japan.[1] The results of the General Election were announced during a live ceremony at the Budōkan, where some of the most famous musical acts in the world have performed. The ceremony was also streamed live to 86 theaters (97 screens) in Japan, everywhere from Hokkaido in the north to Okinawa in the south, and in Hong Kong, Taiwan, and South Korea (Barks Global Media 2011a). Fans were desperate for a seat—be it at the actual venue or the theaters—but tickets sold out almost instantly. This was more than just fanaticism. It was a media event and a public spectacle.

The girls of AKB48 were pronounced "national idols" (*kokumin-teki aidoru*)—the performers "we" "Japanese" "all" know and love. The election was given prominent coverage by both print and television media, with as many as 150 outlets reporting on the event (Morita 2011). People were constantly updated on which of the members, nearly 200 by this point, would come out on top. They were kept up to speed on developments by online sites, cell phone news feeds, commercial and news spots on trains, and, of course, friends, family, coworkers, school-mates, and everyone else who was talking about it. On the day of the General Election, the streets of Tokyo were buzzing with the names of AKB48 members. It was hard not to be involved in some way, if not intimately so.

Such is the power of "idols," a word used in Japan to refer to highly produced and promoted singers, models, and media personalities. Idols can be male or female, and tend to be young, or present themselves as such; they appeal to various demographics, and often broad cross sections of society. Idols perform across genres and interconnected media platforms at the same time. They are not expected to be greatly talented at any one thing, for example singing, dancing, or acting; they are interchangeable and disposable commodities that "affiliate with the signifying processes of Japanese consumer capitalism" (Treat 1993, 364). From popular music and photo albums to fashion and accessories, idols are produced and packaged to maximize consumption. At the same time, they are the currency of exchange in the promotion and advertising of all manner of other products and services. For the Japanese consumer, immersed in a culture of celebrity, the idol is coterminous with consumption. In the Japanese media system, organized around idols, the consumer is positioned as a fan.[2] For the fan-consumer, the idol as an object of desire is a fantasy or ideal construct, a "mirror" reflection, which resonates with deep affective or emotional meaning.[3]

The "idol phenomenon" (*aidoru genshō*) in Japan, which began in the 1970s, has grown to the extent that one critic argues that the Japanese nation is ruled by the principles of idolatry (e.g., the emperor) and that its most important cultural products are idols (Nakamori 2007). Hyperbole aside, it is nearly impossible to grasp Japanese media culture without a substantial discussion of idols. Such a project is already underway in Japan, spearheaded by journalists, critics, and fans, but there is a growing awareness of a lack of academic organization and analytical rigor, leading to obsessive description of the "here and now" (Nakamori 2007, 115). Some scholars do analyze idols, but often without theoretical motivation or engagement.[4] Where discussion has occurred outside Japan, it has largely been a popular one; idols are embraced or dismissed, but either way go unproblematized. Despite sitting at the center of one of the biggest media markets in the world, idols have until recently for the most part been overlooked in scholarly debates about the Japanese mass media (Figure I.1).

This is unfortunate, as a discussion of Japanese idols has much to offer to the global and comparative analysis of media systems. With a uniquely dense, accelerated, and interconnected media market, centered on idols, Japan could be brought into productive dialogue with celebrity studies and media theory developing elsewhere. Japan has proven to be a place where CDs continue to sell despite music rental shops and digital file sharing, with a single customer buying multiple copies of the

Figure I.1 This article from the 6 September 2010 issue of *AERA*, a Japanese news magazine, says that AKB48 will "save the nation" (*Nihon o sukuu*).

same CD to obtain extra information on idols, goods featuring them, and access to them. In other words, idols stand at the center of the music industry, organizing and holding it together; the same is true for television and film. Indeed, the movement of commodities is also greatly influenced by the use of idols in advertisements (see Chapter 3, in this volume). Nowhere else in the world is celebrity such an integral, visible, and important part of the culture. Further, with abundant writings by insiders, journalists, critics, and fans, the rich literature in Japanese offers insights into the often-opaque workings of the media and entertainment industries.

This edited volume is a modest first step in exploring the significance of idols. The purpose of focusing on idols specifically, and celebrity more generally, is to understand the Japanese mass media by focusing on its most prominent characteristic. By situating the study of idols within the framework of media and cultural studies, we engage with debates in such areas of scholarship as stars in film theory, celebrity culture, audience studies, and fandom. This is the first book in English to feature work on both female and male idols, on issues of both production and consumption, and on the performances of idols and fans in economic, social, political, and cross-cultural perspective. Much of the existing English-language literature on idols, celebrity, and fandom is anthropological (Robertson 1998; Kelly 2004; Aoyagi 2005), and tends to tell us more about Japan than about the workings of idols in media and consumer society. These sorts of arguments keep the nation hermetically sealed,[5] and impede contributions to, and engagement with, broader academic debates outside the study of Japan. While sensitive to the local, the essays in this volume are by a group of interdisciplinary scholars who insist on the use of theory to challenge notions of Japanese uniqueness.

In what remains of this introduction, we will map out the discursive terrain of idols and celebrity in Japan. Rather than summarizing each of the chapters in the volume, we introduce some of the issues that they address, individually and collectively. We do not presume to speak from a position of authority or on behalf of all the contributors; many of the chapters challenge received notions about idols and celebrity, including those we are about to lay out, in whole or in part. However, we think that it is worthwhile at least to attempt to offer some touch points and orienting ideas to structure future debates and critiques, which we anticipate and welcome.

Idols in context

The word "idol" (*aidoru*) began to take hold in Japan after the French film *Cherchez l'idole* was released in 1963 under the title *Aidoru o Sagasu* (In Search of an Idol) (Aoyagi 2005, 4–5). Early movie stars aside,[6] the word idol is mostly associated in Japan with young performers who sing, pose for photographs, and appear frequently in the media. They are popular, and project themselves as clean, healthy, and energetic. The year 1971 is often remembered as the "first year of the idol era" (*aidoru gannen*) (Kimura 2007, 260). In that year, Minami Saori,[7] Amachi Mari and Koyangi Rumiko—"friendly looking" girls as opposed to incredibly beautiful and talented ones (idols not stars)—formed the group Three Young Girls (Sannin Musume); Minami was introduced as a "teen idol" (*tīn no aidoru*) at the 22nd NHK *Kōhaku Uta Gassen* (Red and White Song Battle); and idols began to be mass-produced on TV shows like *Sutā Tanjō!* (Birth of a Star!) (from 1971 to 1983).[8] Among male performers, the "new big three" (*shin-gosanke*)—Gō Hiromi, Saijō Hideki, and Noguchi Gorō—were referred to as idols, and the Four Leaves (Fō Rībusu) presented an early example of group idols produced by Johnny & Associates. It is estimated that between 1971 and 1975 some 700 idols debuted in Japan (Okiyama 2007, 260). An entire industry sprang up around the products associated with and endorsed by them.

The 1980s is popularly known as the "golden age of idols" (*aidoru no ōgon jidai*), when between 40 and 50 new idols could appear in a year.[9] The formation of a pool of local idols and celebrities helped to center the Japanese media on the domestic market.[10] In time, the cult of celebrity came to function as a defense against global media flows. Japanese local idols and celebrities indigenized television programming by inviting proximity and familiarity through their regular appearances in a variety of different programming and media outlets (Lukács 2010). The late 1980s was also the period of the bubble economy, when Japan became a post-industrial society organized around information and consumption. The idol system reached maturity amid intense changes in Japanese media and entertainment. Throughout the 1980s, celebrity was becoming an important means of organizing audiences and consumers in television, music, and advertising. The competition between commercial broadcast networks resulted in casting contracts to secure popular performers for serial drama (nine to 13 weekly episodes), which established the practice of broadcasting television dramas in four seasonal rotations (*kūru*). Even the genres of television changed, as "variety shows" (*baraeti bangumi*), talk shows, and music shows became popular for featuring idols. At the same time, tie-ups between pop songs and products in television advertising became widespread (Stevens 2011). Idols not only began appearing in commercials, but also provided the "image songs" (*imēji songu*) that played during commercials. Corporate sponsors began retaining popular idols and celebrities for advertising campaigns as a means of branding their products to achieve greater media exposure. The bubble period brought with it an emphasis on leisure, brand fashion, travel, and idols that formed a new ethos of everyday life. This formed the basis for the "affective turn" in lifestyle-oriented media in the 1990s centered on "talents" (*tarento*), when super idol groups like Morning Musume and SMAP took center stage in the media.

Idols and talents

In Japan, idols in many ways overlap with the category of *tarento*, or, as Gabriella Lukács (2010, 13) defines them, "celebrities who perform in various media genres simultaneously." Practically, *tarento* can refer to almost anyone, though it is typically reserved for those whose "talent" is not specifically singing, dancing, or acting. *Tarento* are mostly an interchangeable group of largely untalented celebrities. They epitomize what Daniel J. Boorstin (1992, 57) describes as "a person who is known for his well-knownness." Though in some ways similar in use to "star" or "celebrity" outside Japan, *tarento* has a very different valence. We therefore translate *tarento* as "celebrity performers," and in this sense see idols as overlapping, but with marked differences.

Tarento color the Japanese media landscape, obviating the need for ordinary people, whom they represent. They perform as a responsive audience for the media content that features them, talking to and about one another in shared or viewed media appearances (more on this point later). Despite the numerous genres of Japanese television, there is nothing identified as "reality television."[11] While one is unlikely to find reality TV featuring ordinary people in Japan, the same qualities that define reality TV are central to Japanese television programming and its celebrity system.[12] Celebrity voyeurism, scandalous behavior, reenactments, and unfiltered performances do not require their own category in the Japanese television landscape since these qualities are in abundance, particularly in variety TV. Japanese variety shows, with their endless parade of idols and celebrity guests and regulars, incorporate all the elements associated with reality TV. Like reality TV, the genre of variety TV in Japan is a hybrid format that combines factual and entertainment programming (Brunsdon *et al.* 2001). Much of Japanese television content, including even what is aired during "golden time" (prime time, 19:00–22:00), consists of "infotainment" on subjects that range from science and diet to current affairs and travel. Rather than being broadcast as straightforward factual television, these shows are often bifurcated into segments that involve a panel of celebrities (*hina-dana*) who discuss and interpret the informational content in an entertaining way. By cutting back and forth between factual and entertaining content, celebrities remain central to Japanese televisual discourse. As opposed to a continuum defined by fact and fiction, Japanese variety TV generally alternates between fact and celebrity. The *tarento* provide balance to variety TV as a way of attracting audiences and holding their attention.

As opposed to the category of *tarento* more generally, idols are first among equals in the Japanese entertainment industry. They organize the market into fan communities that allow predictable patterns of viewership and consumption. In addition to carrying the top billing on many shows, they often are the focus of the viewing experience. When appearing on talk and variety shows, idols are interviewed and their personal history is chronicled in detail. They will often sit at the center of the panel or studio set, whereas the hosts, typically comedians (*owarai geinin*), will be on the periphery. On music television shows, like TV Asahi's popular *Music Station*, the politics of the idol industry—not just the given groups' relative popularity—is reflected in the order of introducing guests, seating position, and the number of minutes guests are questioned by the host. On variety shows, the other performers, particularly comedians, are expected to inject humor but not steal the limelight from the idols. All of this indicates the important status of idols in the entertainment industry.

Idols are in most cases contracted to entertainment management companies, or "agencies" (*jimusho*), which produce and promote them, and in the process determine their degree of success in the industry. This is not to deny idols their own agency; idols can produce themselves and operate outside agencies (Lukács 2007; see Chapter 7 in this volume for a discussion of how an idol exercised her agency). However, the idol that enjoys the greatest popularity in Japan belongs to an agency and operates in a field crisscrossed with power relations that enable and disable movement. If a power struggle emerges, it is likely that the corporate agency trumps individual agency in creating and circulating the idol's image. This is certainly not without precedent. In his classic analysis of the Hollywood studio system, Richard Dyer (1979, 10–11) points out that stars were the studio's *capital*, represented a guaranteed return on studio *investment* in a film, had to be handled carefully as a major *outlay* for the film production, and were used to organize the *market*. This is still very much the case in what we might call the Japanese "agency system." Since the 1950s, production and advertising companies in Japan hire talent from agencies, which have a roster of celebrity performers kept on stipend and under control.[13] This is necessitated by the structure of the entertainment industry (see Chapter 1, in this volume). Mark D. West (2006, 186) argues that many dealings are based on reputation and informal ties, which creates an incentive to avoid bad publicity. Because much of the agency's revenue comes from idols appearing in commercials, it becomes even more important to provide a stable, safe image that is controlled so as not to damage the image of corporate sponsors and advertised products. The agency takes up this role, training and micromanaging its talents. This is especially true for female idols, who cannot drink alcohol, smoke, or be seen in the company of men.[14] West also notes that the value of Japanese media personalities is not talent, but rather personality; they need "to be accepted in the living room as one of the family, warts and all" (Ibid., 177). There is little distance between the performer and the audience in terms of ability, so an appealing image must be maintained so as not to betray the expectations of fans, who feel that they know the idol on a personal level (reinforced by near-constant media exposure).

In discussing the idol system in Japan, we tend to think of the idol as a performer who is produced by a talent agency and lends his/her image to the promotion of goods and services. However, as Bruno Latour (2005) argues, a better approach perhaps is to consider agency as distributed across a network of actors that all contribute to how interactions take place. That is, idols not only promote the sale of goods and services, but actually *are produced* by the goods and services that they sell. Rather than idols selling products, we have a system of commodities that is selling idols. By focusing on the idol alone, one loses sight of the network of relations that go into producing the idol. We falsely assume that agencies produce idols to perform on television or some other media stage, but the capitalist system too needs idols to advertise the products that it produces. The idol, then, is but a node in the network of the capitalist system of commodities that links producers to consumers.

Celebrity and media intimacy

With their cross-platform media ubiquity, an idol group like AKB48 or Arashi is integrated into everyday life in Japan today. On a morning "wide show,"[15] a news report discusses Arashi's recent concert. Billboards in train stations feature the members of AKB48 in advertisements for everything from computers to coffee. The magazine racks of convenience store and kiosks are crowded with magazines featuring members of these groups on their covers. On the subway, a hanging advertisement for a tabloid magazine features gossip about the groups' members.

On television, they star in dramas, host variety shows, and appear in commercials. Altogether, with no effort or intention, one might easily encounter countless images of AKB48 or Arashi in the course of a day. The frequency with which they and other idols and celebrities present themselves within Japan's media-saturated culture makes them not only identifiable but familiar. In the daily routine of life in contemporary Japan, one might have more contact with a particular idol or celebrity than with one's own family. This is the basis for feelings of intimacy.

The intimacy with idols in Japan derives largely from the central importance of television as a medium in postwar Japan. During the 1950s, due to the high price of television sets, there were few private owners, and audiences assembled in public spaces to watch television in the streets (*gaitō terebi*).[16] By 1960, more than half of all households owned a television (Yoshimi 2003, 37). As television moved from the public sphere to the private sphere of the home, it had an immense impact on the experience of celebrity. Once television was anchored in nearly every home by the 1970s, it became part of everyday life and a medium of greater intimacy. The experience of celebrity was no longer liminal and collective, but routine and personal. Television celebrities, mediated through their interjection into the cycles of everyday life, became part of the structure of the new television family in postwar Japan.

The medium of television is a technology of intimacy. T.J.M. Holden and Hakan Ergül (2006, 106) refer to the production strategy of Japanese television as a form of "intentionally engineered intimacy," and attribute its success to the form and content of its programming. Similarly, Andrew A. Painter (1996, 198) observes that intimacy is a result of Japanese television's construction of an "electronically created *uchi*" (in-group). He argues that Japanese producers and directors work to create intimacy by emphasizing themes related to unity and unanimity. The intimacy that is created through television is not unique to Japan—it is a function of the medium's capacity to form an emotional relationship between the viewer and the television performer—but it is arguably more pronounced in Japan due to the performance of idols and celebrities across media genres and platforms.

While recent scholarship has affirmed that intimacy is central to the structure of Japanese television, the agency of its audience in its affective relationship to celebrity is also important for understanding media intimacy. Though intimacy is structured in terms of rhetorical forms and patterns, the importance of affective intimacy in Japanese media culture demands greater attention to the forms of identification in star–audience relations (Stacey 1991). Intimacy revolves around the audience's establishment of affective emotional ties to particular celebrity performers. Lukács (2010, 29–31) argues that the "culture of intimate televisuality" in Japan is derived from its "*tarento* system." Celebrity performers in Japan make the programming more appealing to Japanese viewers, who take pleasure in accumulating knowledge about the *tarento*. Owing to the ubiquity of celebrity images across the Japanese media, even non-fans are familiar with most popular *tarento*. However, rather than focusing on the *tarento* system and its intertextuality, Lukács examines the genre of dramas as "vehicles for the transmission of information *about the tarento*" (Ibid., 31). Drama is but one node in the complex network of information about celebrities in Japan that includes wide shows, tabloid newspapers, weekly magazines, variety programs, social media, and so on. The intimacy of celebrity is not reducible to any particular genre or platform, but is rather a function of the complex intertextuality of the larger Japanese media system.

Celebrity and media intertextuality

Japan has one of the highest rates of media consumption in the world. With the intensity of its media culture, idols and celebrities create an intertextual web of meanings that link forms and contents together to produce new meanings. In film, television, music, and advertising, meaning is contained not within individual texts, but rather across a network of textual relations. As John Fiske (2011, 109) notes, "intertextuality exists [...] in the space *between* texts." The idol, as a multimedia performer, is always operating within a system of meanings and codes that are referencing other texts. The intertextuality of idols, through its potential to activate audiences, is fundamental to the structure of the Japanese media.

First, the intertextuality of the Japanese media is reflected in the way that idols perform across genres and platforms in the entertainment industry. From drama, game shows, music, travel, and sports programs, they mediate the television viewing experience. Moving freely between genres, they form the axis around which the media revolve and are the locus of audience identification. To understand Japanese television, the audience must draw on a vast cultural knowledge about celebrity. This intertextual knowledge activates the audience to produce meaning by tracing the relations to other texts or past performances. For example, when an idol appears on a variety show, the audience's knowledge of his/her roles in other programs, like dramas, will be an essential part of the interpretive process. While this form of horizontal intertextuality is common in the medium of television, the performers more than the genres are fundamental to the organization of intertextual relations in the Japanese media.

Second, idols appear in both fictional and nonfictional contexts, and their performances reference both their real and their onscreen lives. With the private lives of idols and celebrities forming a site of greater knowledge and truth, the journalistic discourse on celebrity creates new opportunities for the production of intertextual meanings. This form of intertextuality in the Japanese media necessitates a high degree of familiarity with the performances, as well as the gossip and trivia about idols and celebrity performers that circulates on wide shows and in weekly magazines, tabloids, and other media. Consequently, Japanese idols, even more than their counterparts in other countries, cannot escape their "real life" persona when they appear on the screen. Due to their sustained exposure, across genres and platforms of performance, they cannot help but appear as themselves in a drama or other fictional context; the perception is that they are not playing characters so much as they are playing themselves. As a result, the real world and the onscreen world cease to be different, and instead a deeply intertextual form of televisual pleasure is created between the performer and audience. The audience's desire for knowledge about the private lives of idols becomes the means for staging publicity.

Third, the idol is an intertextual commodity that circulates in the media landscape to link different media forms and to produce promotional discourse. An immense media industry exists in Japan for the purpose of promoting and selling other media, particularly through the idols and celebrities who provide the means of connecting disparate media texts. Often, celebrity performers appear on variety, talk, and game shows for the purpose of promoting other programs or products. While intertextuality describes how texts relate to other texts to produce meanings for the audience, the celebrity as an intertextual commodity engages with the interactive or fan audience by expanding promotional discourse across cultural forms and different media outlets (Marshall 1997). With the media industry's attempt to cultivate loyal audiences to engage in greater consumption, cultural commodities are endlessly cross-referenced between newspapers, magazines, online social media, and television. Through the audience's familiarity and knowledge of the idol, intertextuality seeks to create a deeper and more affective relationship to the audience that will facilitate promotional discourse.

Fourth, intertextuality in Japan is nostalgic. With intertextual knowledge based on a shared cultural framework of texts, it is historically rooted in the employment of past forms. As Linda Hutcheon (1989, 81) notes, "the past is only known to us today through its textualized traces." Hutcheon argues that intertextuality finds expression through parody. We can see this in the idol industry with, for example, Matsu'ura Aya, who came to prominence in the early 2000s during the revival of idols under Hello! Project. Matsu'ura cultivated a camp image that parodied, with a sense of irony, the female idols that dominated the 1980s.[17] With her cute songs and dress, she embodied nostalgia for the idol culture of an earlier time, before the economic stagnation of the 1990s. Indeed, the nostalgic production of intertexual knowledge is a staple of Japanese television programming. Music shows will often spend as much time featuring segments about the past (usually in the form of countdowns) as they do featuring performances of the latest artists. Idols, like other cultural forms in Japan, are nostalgic texts that link the past to the present through the intertextuality of their image and performance.

Intertextuality in the Japanese media sustains and nurtures a close relationship to its domestic audience, but limits its broader appeal. Since the popularity of Japanese idols in large part derives from the intertextuality of the Japanese media system, once removed from the Japanese media context, idols must appeal to audiences for reasons beyond the mere reproduction of their celebrity. Without the intertextual knowledge that comes from a shared understanding of the cultural codes that circulate across media forms within Japan, the idol is reduced merely to his/her ability as a singer, dancer, or actor, which is limited. As a result, Japanese popular culture does not translate well cross-culturally, since its forms are overdetermined by the self-referential structures of the domestic media landscape.[18] That said, idols have been relatively successful in Asia (Aoyagi 1996), and producers are increasingly considering how to expand into Asian markets and better serve fans there.

Celebrity and self-referentiality

Throughout the world, the mass media are becoming more market-oriented. As a result of increased competition, a vast entertainment-driven economy has formed for the purpose of expanding audiences and maximizing profits. One consequence of this shift has been a worldwide growth in the spectacle of celebrity. As Michael J. Wolf (1999, 28) notes, "in the entertainment economy, celebrity is the only currency." Celebrities are the nexus between producers and consumers that facilitates the circulation of media discourse. In Japan, the mass media have since around the 1980s turned towards the production of media spectacles centered on idols and celebrities to generate self-referential or autopoietic systems of media text reproduction or commentary. This system of self-referentiality in Japan has resulted in voluminous mass-media discourse about idols and celebrity.

The self-referentiality of the Japanese mass media operates within a closed circular system without origin (Figure I.2). As spectacle, the people, products, and events that are the focus of media attention are important only because they are the focus of media attention. In this definition of self-referentiality, the media refer to themselves or aspects of themselves as a way of reproducing greater media discourse.[19] On Japanese wide shows, the hosts will often display and read the headlines and relevant sections of articles about celebrities that have appeared in that day's newspapers. Displaying the pages of newsprint directly on the screen, Japanese television literally reads you the newspaper. When it is not referring to itself, it is circulating gossip and trivia about idols and celebrities. However, these performers are manufactured and promoted by the media, attaining their celebrity only as a consequence of their appearance in the media. Celebrity begets media spectacle in a self-generating system of media promotion.

For example, corporate press releases announcing new products or services in Japan often involve formal, staged press events that, in order to attract the media, employ idols and celebrities as "image characters" (*imēji kyarakutā*) or spokespersons. Typically, the image character will pose for photographers, who then print the celebrity's photos (along

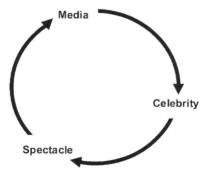

Figure I.2   The *wa* of Japanese mass media self-referentiality.

with articles) in newspapers and magazines. While ostensibly assembled to endorse a product, the celebrities will answer questions from reporters about their personal or professional lives. Television wide shows broadcast the celebrities' responses, noting their fashion and speculating on possible meanings. It may seem that the product is upstaged by the celebrities' own self-promotion, but for corporate sponsors these events offer an opportunity for their product's name and corporate logo to appear in the media, if only as a footnote to tabloid coverage. Products and corporate brands attract attention through their association with celebrities, whose public appearance provides the grist of tabloid journalism. This system serves the interests of all parties, who benefit from the celebrities' capacity to attract and hold public attention.

Even news coverage is not immune to celebrity spectacle (recall the AKB48 General Election). The films, movies, concerts, and even commercials featuring idols and celebrities are reported as if they were news. The appearance of "newsworthy" celebrities provides a faux justification for discussing celebrity. For example, on a morning wide show reporting about Arashi's 2010 summer concert in Tokyo, the broadcast adopts an objective news framework to report on the event.[20] This effect is achieved through an enumeration of data about the concert, beginning with the number of attendees, but extending to the height of the show's water cannons and the precise number of fireworks discharged. This inventory of the concert employs the rhetoric of hard news coverage in the telling of soft news. The story, which is interspersed with clips from the concert provided by the group's agency, Johnny & Associates, lacks any news value beyond the group's celebrity. Johnny's cooperation in providing high-quality footage from the event, which would later be used in the production of a concert DVD, created ready-to-air content that the television networks are only too eager to broadcast as "news;" the content is inexpensive and expedient, a major attraction for TV producers on tight budgets and schedules, and it is capable of attracting a wide audience of celebrity fan-consumers. This practice of preparing press release kits for the media is pervasive among Japanese agencies. By offering self-produced content to the networks, the agencies are promoting their own *tarento*.

Conditioning the codependent audience

The concentration of media institutions in postwar Japan has produced a self-referential system of representations that has remade everyday life in the image of consumer capitalism. The ethic of hard work and diligence that propelled Japan's postwar economic "miracle" reached a critical juncture during the 1970s (Yoshimi 2009). Tokyo became one of the most capital-saturated urban centers in the world, and an unprecedented amount was invested in advertising, packaging, design, and image production. During the 1980s, the rise of the bubble economy marked the excesses of the consumer-capitalist regime, embodied in the idol. As John Whittier Treat (1993, 361) explains: "Magazines, radio, above all television: in whatever direction one turns, the barely (and thus ambiguously) pubescent woman is there both to promote products and purchase them, to excite the consumer and herself be thrilled by the flurry of goods and services that circulate like toys around her." Of course, the idol phenomenon includes not only female idols, but also male idols, expanding the potential of Treat's critique.

Asada Akira (1989, 275), one of the most popular Japanese cultural critics of the 1980s, describes Japanese capitalism as "infantile." As he sees it, there is no transcendental value system or vertical system of control (external or internalized). Explaining Asada's now well-known position, Tomiko Yoda (2000) points out that, once everyone is embraced by and enfolded into a horizontal system of control, all that remains is relative competition and play with signs and symbols to establish categories and boundaries. The frantic pace of consumption and dense networks of information created around brands are indicative of this, as is the play of surfaces engaged in, with, and through idols.

While it is clear that Asada was being intentionally provocative (if not parodic) in his discussion of infantile capitalism, the infantilization of the consumer is itself not a new concept. Theodor W. Adorno (1991) argues that the "culture industry" shapes a passive and dependent consuming public. Standardized content contributes to a "regressive" audience that is "arrested at the infantile stage" (Ibid., 41–47). The culture industry approach has been roundly criticized for its dismissal of audience agency (see Chapters 5, 6, and 8 in this volume for examples of unexpected responses to and appropriations of idols), but to ignore it is to risk overlooking the processes that shape the production of mass culture.

In Japan, people interact with idols as soon as they are old enough to turn on the TV, and these interactions are ongoing. Further, audience demographics are collapsed together, with boys and men, and men and women, consuming the same idols. This, too, contributes to a sort of "infantile capitalism," whereby the consumptive pleasures one experiences as a child continue on through adult life. Further, these idols are in their cuteness—the aesthetic of *kawaii* (Treat 1993; Kinsella

1995)—associated with innocence and apolitical youth. In short, they are infantilized, even as the audience that organizes around and seeks comfort from them is infantilized. This is not unique to Japan, but rather is an example of the phenomenon that John Hartley (1998, 51) calls "juvenation," or "the creative practice of communicating [...] via the *medium* of youthfulness."

Organized around idols and celebrity, Japanese media culture, especially television, seeks a mode of address that is infantilizing as a function of its aim to reach a wide audience. It is structured in perpetual fear of losing the audience's attention, and as a result is constantly telling the viewer how to watch and interpret meaning. For example, during variety shows, the television screen is littered with text that accentuates the words and emotions of performers. Unlike closed captioning that displays a textual transcript of the audio portion of a program, Japanese captions (*tsukkomi terropu*) highlight certain words and phrases, adjusting the size, color, and appearance of the text for emotional effect. This practice began in the late 1980s and early 1990s with variety shows for the purpose of making the broadcast easier to understand and more entertaining.[21] Recently, when networks tried to eliminate or reduce the size of the captions, they found that their ratings declined (*Asahi Shinbun* 2005, 7). Another example is the practice of mediating the program content with a panel of idols and celebrities. Informational or educational programming will alternate between prerecorded footage (VTR) and a panel of celebrities assembled in the studio. As if watching the show together with the audience, the celebrity panel digests the informational content, often making humorous comments, asking questions, or being quizzed for answers. During the VTR, a picture-in-picture (*waipu*) of the in-studio celebrities' reactions is displayed in the corner of the screen, providing a visual cue to the audience as to how to emotionally interpret the content (Figure I.3). The image of celebrities onscreen (which is constant, regardless of content, due to the picture-in-picture) not only advertises the show for those who are channel surfing, but also creates a codependent relationship between celebrities watching one another, which makes the audience less active and productive in interpreting the meaning of the content being presented.

The nature of the Japanese entertainment industry is close to a form of "waste production" that fetishizes novelty. The low-budget, mass-volume production of Japanese popular culture results in a disposable mass culture. This metaphor extends even to the careers of idols and celebrities. The career of most idols in Japan is short-lived, especially for women: most female idols can expect their active careers to last no more

選抜総選挙開票直前
AKB48を2号が直撃

渡辺ﾏ

誰？ 誰ですか？

高橋みなみ

Figure I.3   Former Morning Musume idol Yaguchi Mari appears in inset (above left) during a VTR about the AKB48 General Election. The captions (bottom) highlight the words and emotions for the television audience.

than three years (*Nikkei Entertainment* 1999, 35–36). Since the maturation of the idol system in the 1980s, the careers of both male and female idols have become increasingly shorter.[22] Through the mass media, the awareness of a particular celebrity or idol permeates national consciousness until it collapses under the weight of its own self-referential reproduction. Very few celebrities have sustained long-term careers in the Japanese entertainment industry.

The abundance of media commentary on other media within Japan creates a social context wherein much of the knowledge that informs the act of media interpretation has been predigested. In this social context, the act of interpreting and evaluating media texts, such as idols, is never entirely independent, but rather intertextual. As one star fails to command public attention, a new one is immediately elevated in the media through the repetition of intertextual discourse. With each new celebrity performer, the media is invigorated with a new focus for further profiling, exposure, and gossip. As a result, the desire for novelty becomes engrained in Japanese media culture, guaranteeing stability and routinizing consumption.

The Japanese television industry is constantly struggling to produce new programming, and agencies to produce new celebrity performers. Commercial calculations play an essential role in every aspect of the production of television in Japan. Reruns or syndicated programs are rare on Japan's commercial broadcasting networks, particularly during golden time. In the period prior to the 1990s, the cost of videotapes made it too expensive to preserve old broadcasts. During the 1990s, commercial broadcasting networks often aired reruns of dramas on weekday afternoons, but have since largely abandoned the practice in favor of programming that will promote their regular evening shows and increase the number of viewers. In the relative absence of reruns or syndication (as well as with the limited availability of video-on-demand services), producers seek a return on investment solely from advertising revenue during the original broadcast. In Japan, rather than concentrating on finding alternate sources of revenue through retransmission, Japan's commercial broadcast networks emphasize the primacy of the original broadcast. The end result of low-cost television production in Japan with limited options for alternate sources of revenue or repackaging is that it must focus on topicality, trendiness, and word of mouth. These are the very factors that sustain Japan's idol and celebrity culture.

The prominence of celebrities within Japanese media culture also has resulted in an increasing loss of the distinction between the public and private spheres of everyday life. The media landscape of contemporary Japan is crowded with celebrities, whose images and private lives define publicness around simulacra of intertextual images devoid of political or moral meaning. The weak concept of the public sphere and inchoate journalistic ethics in Japan mean that the media primarily see their audience as consumers. Images of celebrities cultivate a media culture of voyeurism and tabloidization that collapse the distinction between the public and private such that publicness is based on the staging and appearance of idols and celebrities (see Chapter 2, in this volume). Kimura Takuya (2003, 8) of the male idol group SMAP once described himself as "public property" (*kōkyō-butsu*), saying of his celebrity persona that "anyone can enter and anyone can exit, like an empty public park without structures." The talent of Japanese idols often becomes less important than their private lives, which are commoditized as part of their persona or image.

Since celebrities are "newsworthy" as a function of their being well known, the emphasis in reporting often is on their private lives and relationships with other celebrities. Since Japanese celebrities spend an inordinate amount of time and energy engaged in promotion and publicity, the emphasis in interviews is on teasing the audience with information about some aspect of the celebrity's "hidden" or "unknown" private life. Generally, the form of expression in celebrity news aims to give impact to the story by revealing something unexpected or out of the ordinary.

Often this entails presenting a discrepancy between what the audience expects and what the news story actually specifies about the celebrity. Because the audience is already well acquainted with the overpromoted image, these teasers generate audience attention by promising greater knowledge, such as details about the personal life of the idol or celebrity.

Even in the physical space of urban Japan, saturated with advertising images, one becomes immersed in a culture of celebrity. The private space of media consumption in the home and the public space of the urban landscape converge to promote a constant diet of celebrity images. From television and magazines to outdoor digital screens and billboards, these images appear almost to return the gaze of the consumer. Walking the streets and other public spaces in Japan, one is always being watched—not in the Orwellian sense of surveillance society, but by the look of celebrities in a society of spectacle (Debord 1994). In Japan, the technologies of governmentality produce a citizenry to serve the policies of neoliberalism through the linking of the capitalist state and the ideology of consumerism. The state does not police these policies through the threat of force, but relies on corporations and the techniques of marketing and advertising to achieve disciplinary control and the subjugation of bodies. The biopolitics of this regime cultivates the mimetic desires of the masses by channeling their energies into ritualized forms of consumption. Celebrities are the enforcers of the regime of capitalism through their signification of the ideology of consumption. The mimetic desire to appropriate the image of the celebrity operates in the sphere of economic processes for the controlled insertion of bodies into the routinized repetition of the consumption of goods.

Cracks in the mirror and fan frustrations

In recent scholarship on fan cultures, efforts to avoid pathologizing fandom have given rise to a new orthodoxy that celebrates the active and productive agency of fans. Nearly two decades ago, Joli Jenson (1992) lamented how the literature on fandom was haunted by images of deviance; the fan was seen as an individual whose behavior was excessive and obsessive; the stereotype of the frenzied fan adhered around images of lonely, socially awkward men or hysterical women. In countering this image by considering fandom a "normal, everyday cultural or social phenomenon" (Ibid., 13), criticism of the culture industry's exploitation of fan communities has receded to the point of near obscurity. Though cultural studies originated as a critique of capitalist relations, today fan studies is almost complicit with the culture industry and the ideology of consumerism. Only recently have anti-fans and fan frustrations become the subject of cultural criticism.[23] Idols are not, however, beyond criticism, which is mounting in Japan along with the proliferation of fan discourse, which is not always positive or affirming.

From the late 1990s in Japan, CD sales, particularly sales of CD singles, have steadily declined (RIAJ 2011). While the transition to digital distribution gives us a partial explanation for this, which seems to hold true globally, the success of idol groups such as AKB48 and Arashi in Japan is extraordinary. Okajima Shinshi and Okada Yasuhiro (2011, 5) describe AKB48's success as a "paradigm shift." Namely, AKB48 developed a more intimate relationship with their fan community. According to Okajima and Okada, they were produced and promoted as "idols that you can meet" (*ai ni ikeru aidoru*) (Ibid., 14) through the establishment of the AKB48 Theater in Akihabara, where they perform live shows daily. The group's success originated in practices aimed at developing a loyal fan base. Many of these practices are not uncommon as sales techniques in Japan, but AKB48 brought them together in a way that cultivates the affective sensibility of fandom. The affective sensibility of fandom, argues Lawrence Grossberg (1992, 57), involves increases in both quantity and quality of meanings and pleasures. The quantity of the relationship is measured in terms of the frequency of its energy or volition, while the quality of the relationship is defined by the specific meanings affixed to experiences. In its relationship with its fans, AKB48 appeals to both in the structure of its business and marketing practices.

The longstanding practice of selling the same product multiple times has become closely associated with AKB48 (Okajima and Okada 2011, 16–17). For example, the group's eighth CD single, released in February 2008, came packaged with one of 44 distinct posters. Only those fans who collected all 44 versions would be allowed to attend a "special event" featuring the group. Like packets of trading cards or capsule toys sold to children in Japanese vending machines, the posters were randomly bundled with the CDs. The consumer did not know which of the posters was included with the CD and, in order to collect all 44, would likely need to buy far more than 44 separate CDs. As fans began complaining online, the special event offer was cancelled out of concern that it might be in violation of Japanese antitrust laws (*ITmedia News* 2008). In January 2011, on the occasion of the release of their new single, a three-day "handshake event" (*akushukai*) was held in Tokyo. For fans to experience the intimacy (relatively speaking) of a handshake with their favorite idol, they first needed to purchase a copy of the group's CD.

Fans wanting to shake hands with more than one member of the group were expected to buy additional copies of the CD.

Each event described above aimed at selling more CDs by harnessing the fans' energy, defined in terms of the quantity of consumption. At the same time, the fans' volition was exploited by the promise of an experience of greater qualitative intimacy and connection with the idol. In AKB48's business practices (AKB48 *shōhō*), the affective sensibility of fandom is commodified to generate greater CD sales. Fans are not purchasing CDs (music) so much as they are buying an experience that resonates with emotional meaning intensified through the frequency of their investment in the idol.

The fans of AKB48 typically describe themselves as "supporters" rather than "fans." AKB48's 12 latest consecutive singles have topped the charts in Japan, and they have sold nearly 11.8 million CDs, making them the most successful female group in Japanese history (as of January 2012). These sales figures attest to the group's commercial success, but, with fans purchasing multiple copies, CD sales may exaggerate their actual popularity. In other words, unlike in the past, CD sales are not an accurate measure of the number of people who listen to their music. These fan practices are in fact not uncommon in Japan's music industry. The male idol duo Kinki Kids have had 32 number one hit singles since their debut in 1997 (as of January 2012). Since their 11th single in February 2001, they have held the record for the most number one hit singles. Most music industry experts believe that this record is due to ardent fans purchasing multiple copies of their CDs, particularly within the first week of their release.[24]

While one might be inclined to describe the Japanese media industry as a system that integrates consumers from above, the audience arguably are empowered through their agency to decide which idol to devote themselves to. Okajima and Okada (2011, 21–26) argue that, unlike the idol group Morning Musume, whose popularity peaked in 1999–2004, AKB48 has been better at responding to fan needs. Though often at the price of a CD, AKB48 promotes greater opportunities for proximity and connection between fans and group members. As Franceso Alberoni (quoted in Dyer 1979, 19) writes, "the star system thus never creates the star, but it proposes the candidate for 'election,' and helps to retain the favor of the 'electors.' " While Alberoni sought to revise the view of the star system as a "narcotizing illusion" that manipulates and distracts its audience from the real conditions of their exploitation, the metaphor of the electorate becomes problematic in light of the dubious techniques of marketing and promotion aimed at fan communities.

AKB48 embraces this notion of the "elective" agency of its fans by literally organizing general elections, where fans vote to determine the most popular AKB48 member from among hundreds of girls. Roughly 1.16 million votes were cast in the election held on 9 June 2011. For the media and entertainment industries, the organization of fan activity aims to promote the belief that consumers are exercising agency and choice in their leisure activities. However, to vote in the election, fans must acquire a ticket included with the purchase of a CD single released by AKB48. Those fans who purchase more CDs receive more votes to cast for their favorite group member in the election. This system, by design, encourages fans to buy multiple CDs. During the 2011 election, reports in the Japanese media detailed stories about abuse of the system, including one claiming to have found 200 CDs in the trash that had been emptied of their voter tickets and another revealing that voter tickets were being sold in bulk online at auction sites. Amid a growing backlash against these practices, some fans have come to question the fairness of an election that allows one to purchase multiple votes. On online forums and blogs, some fans insist on the principle of "one man, one vote."[25]

However, if "votes are your love," as one AKB48 member put it (*Daily Sports* 2011), then the logic is clear that one man can have more love for an idol than another, and he expresses that through purchasing multiple CDs and casting a number of votes proportionate to his love. Since votes are acquired by purchasing CDs, this equation of votes with emotion is a form of commodity fetishism. It aims to conceal the material cost of voting in the rhetoric of love. The logic achieves the ideological effect of reinforcing the materialistic and commodified nature of human relations in capitalist societies: love is something bought and sold. Fans, for all their grumbling about fairness, are deeply embedded in an "asymmetrical" relationship (Yano 2004) with the idol (mass affection directed at the individual, who responds to an unindividuated mass) and are willing to settle for any sort of relationship over none.

Criticisms of AKB48's business practices have spread beyond fans to the Japanese entertainment industry. Media personality Ijūin Hikaru called the group's business practices "ruthless" (*akogi*) and greedy, and the comedian Okamura Takashi likened them to a kind of "reverse host club" (*gyaku hosuto*), by which he suggested that the members of AKB48 were exploiting their supporters by fostering patronage and competition (*Shūkan Shinchō* 2011, 43–44). If host clubs are premised on male hosts taking advantage of female clients, Okamura's analogy highlights how AKB48's male fans are manipulated (and "feminized," or placed in the imagined female role in relation to the host). Though these criticisms were directed mostly toward the group's producer, Akimoto Yasushi, Okamura later claimed that he intended to criticize only the group's most fervent fans (so-called "*otaku*"). In Japan's neoliberal media system, criticism of producers is almost always taboo. If fans are pathologized in the media, it is often because criticism of the media industry is strictly proscribed.

The role of the mass media in inflating the margins has created the effect of idols' perceived widespread popularity. Studies of the number of mentions of the group AKB48 in blogs have found an astounding discourse on idols within Japanese cyberspace. In the period between January and May 2011, there were 73,420 unique mentions on blogs of Maeda Atsuko alone, who is arguably the most popular member of the group (Barks Global Media 2011b).[26] However, not all of these mentions are from committed fans voicing their support. Many are from anti-fans, who are criticizing their relentless promotion and media hype. Moreover, Japanese idols are intertextual commodities; music is but one dimension of their popularity. There is much reason to be skeptical about the widespread popularity of groups like AKB48. Despite the Japanese media's relentless production of tabloid news and gossip about the group, AKB48's first variety program during golden time performed terribly in the ratings.[27] Dramas that have featured popular members of the group, such as Maeda Atsuko, have also had lukewarm receptions. From a rather cynical point of view, it seems that the success of these "national idols" is but an effect of the media.

Criticism of the business practices of idol groups is not limited to AKB48. In 2010, fan frustration with the ticket distribution system of Johnny & Associates reached the breaking point. Concert tickets for its idol group Arashi were parceled out according to a lottery system that required fans to pay in advance (*maekinsei*) for the chance to be awarded a ticket. With no assurance of receiving a ticket, fans had to pay the entire ¥7,000 ($88) price of the ticket.[28] Most had to wait at least a month before hearing the results of the lottery, but some waited for several months. In addition to paying a ¥500 ($6) application fee, those fans who were not awarded a ticket were required to pay a ¥700 ($9) fee in order to have the price of the ticket refunded. Even to enter the lottery, one needed to be a member of Arashi's official fan club, which costs ¥4,000 ($50) annually. All of this, in addition to many not being able to attend the concert, aggravated fans, including some who even lodged complaints with the Consumer Affairs Agency (*Shūkan Josei* 2010, 29–31).

Idol-ing Japan

Despite a sluggish period from the end of the 1980s to the early 1990s—known variably as the "idol ice age" (*aidoru hyōgaki*) or "winter time of idols" (*aidoru fuyu no jidai*)—the importance of idols has only grown in Japan. Without a doubt, there has been in recent years an enormous surge of interest in idols at all levels of society. In August 2010, Japan hosted what was heralded as its first idol festival, Tokyo Idol Festival 2010. This was the brainchild of a producer at Fuji TV who had been involved with the program *Idoling!!!* (2006–), and was intended to create (1) a stream of new idols in Tokyo, (2) a new relationship between idols and media, and (3) the world's largest "trade show" for idols. The first event featured 49 idol groups and attracted over 5,000 people (Oricon Inc. 2011). On the cover of every magazine are members of idol groups such as AKB48 and Arashi. But it goes beyond the everyday presence of idols, across gender and generational boundaries. *Weekly Josei*, a women's magazine, features the nostalgic roots of idols with a review of classic groups from the 1970s (*Shūkan Josei* 2011). *Weekly Playboy*, a men's magazine,[29] dedicates an issue to idols, in which it proclaims "society is amidst an unprecedented idol boom" and discusses the future of a variety of new and upcoming groups (*Shūkan Pureibōi* 2011a,b,c).

Even as hundreds of new idols are produced domestically, idols from overseas, especially South Korea, arrive, attracted to the rich sales market for CDs, DVDs, and goods (see Chapter 8 in this volume). As if this were not enough, physical idols must now compete with "virtual idols," a growing presence in the market (see Chapter 10 in this volume). This is no laughing matter; a virtual idol can enjoy immense popularity, perform "live" shows, and have endorsement deals with the likes of Toyota (*Flash* 2011). Given all this, it is perhaps fitting that people in Japan are increasingly talking about the "idol warring states period" (*aidoru sengoku jidai*), a crowded field without central authority, where competition is fierce and comes from all sides (e.g., *Shūkan Pureibōi* 2011a).[30] Everyone is struggling to find a niche: dance, foreignness, specific hobbies, connection to anime (e.g., voice actresses), and so on. At the same time, the number of members within idol groups continues to increase, adding internal variety. What is important, *Playboy* tells us, is for idols and groups to cultivate fans by giving them choices and allowing them to feel that they are directly involved in the process of producing and promoting their chosen idols and groups. They are empowered by the idol's successes (within the group and industry), willingly subjugate themselves to the idol, and do not get bored with interactions with the idol, interactions between members of the group, or interactions between groups (*Shūkan Pureibōi* 2011c).

Today, we are in what *Playboy* calls the "hyper idol age" (*chō aidoru jidai*) (*Shūkan Pureibōi* 2011b), when the presence of idols in Japanese media culture seems as inevitable as it does irredeemable. The "hyper" here also refers to "hypercapitalism" (Graham 2006), or a highly saturated media environment that produces celebrity spectacle for the purpose of promoting goods and services. Under hypercapitalism, notions of value become increasingly abstract as media companies seek to position consumers as fans (see Chapter 3 in this volume for a discussion of the "affective attunement" of audiences to idols). Fan behaviors, even those once attributed to hardcore fans (*otaku*, discussed in Chapter 9 of this volume), are spreading to all segments of society (see Chapter 8 in this volume about middle-aged and older women engaged in fantasy relationships with idols). Marketing to fan audiences in Japan today involves translating the sense of familiarity and intimacy with the idol into action. Hypercapitalism has extolled the myth of consumer agency to convince consumers that they are empowered to choose what they consume. However, as Arjun Appadurai (1996, 42) argues, this "fetishism of the consumer" is nothing more than a "mask for the real seat of agency, which is not the consumer but the producer." The power in the Japanese media of the idol producer specifically, and the entertainment management company (or agency) generally, demonstrates this. They create idols—literally, in the case of virtual idols (see Chapter 10 in this volume). Another rendering of the "hyper idol age" might be the "transcended idol age," when idols are no longer bound to any specific time, place, or body (see Chapter 9 in this volume for a discussion of female idols as images and Chapter 4 for a discussion of male idols as icons). It seems that potentially everyone can be an idol, and idols are potentially everywhere.

It is worth noting also that idols now seem to be "transcending" the limitations of their role promoting consumption. After the devastating earthquake and tsunami that struck northeast Japan on 11 March 2011 and the nuclear contamination that followed, idols and celebrity performers in Japan launched into charity activities that challenge the assumption that they are "simulacra of intertextual images devoid of political or moral meaning." For example, AKB48 postponed sales of their much anticipated third album (bringing the suffering of the earthquake, often experienced as far away from Tokyo, into the lives of fans); just days after the earthquake, their management company— AKS, along with Akimoto Yasushi and the members of all the groups he produces—pledged to donate ¥500 million ($6.25 million);[31] and they opened a bank account to solicit money from fans (announced as the "same one" used by the AKB48 members for their donations, opening a route to intimacy through shared action) (*Sankei News* 2011). They held multiple concerts and live events in (and in support of) northeast Japan; they even released a song commemorating the disasters (on 26 October 2011). In this way, Japanese idols joined the ranks of actors like Watanabe Ken and screenwriters like Koyama Kundō, musicians like Gackt and Yoshiki, athletes like Nakata Hidetoshi, television and radio personalities like Kume Hiroshi, and a slew of others from around the world (notably South Korea and the United States, which have highly developed entertainment industries with deep connections to Japan). Here, we really do see the emergence of "national idols," or idols who stand in for the people and catalyze the feelings of the nation. We also see the nation of Japan as idol—eerily actualizing recommendations by Nakamori Akio (2007, 16)—garnering far more sympathy on the global stage than equal or greater natural and human disasters of recent memory. It is difficult to say whether or not the activities of idols can ever be separated from their images,[32] when promotion of the cause becomes self-promotion (and a way to generate publicity and boost sales), but that is also not really the point. What is important is that idols can be political commodities in much the same way as they are economic commodities. They produce the issue and are produced by it; the audience consume the issue with and through idols. How explicitly political idols can be remains open to question. They tend to avoid deep meanings and lasting associations, which are divisive (and bad for business). Maybe idols can only express moral truisms (e.g., killing is evil, life is beautiful) and sufficiently general principles (e.g., we should help others). Maybe in order to secure mass appeal idols can only ever be conservative.[33] In any case, scholars will have to address idols if they want to make sense of the contemporary moment. As is the case with the "idol warring states period," the future is anything but clear, and the field is open for contestations.

Notes

1. It sold 942,475 copies on its release day alone. In the Oricon announcement of best-selling singles for the first half of 2011 (made 22 June), "Everyday, Kachūsha" was number one; number two was "Sakura no Ki ni Narō," an earlier AKB48 single. Holding both top spots was an achievement not seen since the idol group Pink Lady some 33 years before.

2. This is very much in line with what Henry Jenkins (2006, 61–62) calls "affective economics," but at a scale virtually unparalleled in the world.
3. These objects are internalized subjectively as images that are far from accurate representations of the actual, external others. Jacques Lacan related this idealized image of the external other to the concept of the "mirror stage." For the infant, the specular image of the self that is reflected in the mirror is perceived as an idealized figure of bodily integration and wholeness apart from the mother upon whom the infant still depends. The mirror image of the unified self is the first of a long process of imaginary identifications throughout our lives that are illusory and fictive.
4. See, most recently, Ōta (2011) and Okajima and Okada (2011).
5. In his critique of recent work in Japan Studies, Kōichi Iwabuchi (2010, 93) points out that the nation has emerged as the most marketable and significant local unit, not only for political, economic, and cultural exchange, but also for academic analysis. He is right to resist those forces that conspire to make us "methodological (inter)nationalists."
6. This includes people like Ishihara Yūjirō and Yoshinaga Sayuri, who were not called idols at the time, but are now remembered as having garnered "idol-like popularity" (*aidoru-teki ninki*). Stars are clearly different from idols in the former's possession of talents and skills that set them apart from the audience, whereas the latter are in close proximity with the audience, achieved through regular and simultaneous appearances in multiple media outlets.
7. Throughout the volume we use Japanese name order, family name followed by given name, unless the person publishes using reverse or "Western" name order or prefers it.
8. Candies got their start as the three female assistants on the *Kayō Gurando Shō* in 1972 (active until 1978). Pink Lady debuted on *Sutā Tanjō!* in 1976, and remained on top of the charts until 1979 (they disbanded in 1981, and reformed and broke up several times after).
9. Among them are superstars such as Matsuda Seiko and Kondō Masahiko.
10. We note as well a sort of "return to Japan" in the sounds of popular groups like Shibugaki-tai, which broke with the vaguely foreign sounding and styled male idols that had come before. They were contemporaneous with Hikaru Genji and Shōnen-tai.
11. One notable exception was the Fuji TV program *Ainori* (1999–2009), which featured the love lives of ordinary people traveling around the world. Though the show closely resembles the genre of reality TV, its own network categorized the show as "variety."
12. Generally speaking, the genre of reality TV is flexible and encompasses a broad range of formats. Some scholars define reality TV as blurring the boundaries between fact and fiction, while others locate it within the framework of documentary. Most viewers in the US and UK tend to equate reality TV with shows like *Big Brother* or *Survivor* that feature "real" people.
13. Gabriella Lukács (2010, 45) explains: "In the 1950s, television networks had to subcontract stars from the film industry, but the supply was cut off when cinema box office sales started dropping as a result of television's growing popularity. Television networks turned to theater—both kabuki and modern theater—for performers. Theater sources, however, could not satisfy the growing demand, and agencies were established to recruit new stars. Yet the

new actors could not be trained quickly enough to meet the demand. Thus, the growing number of actors without acting talent dates back to the rupture between the film and the television industries in Japan."

14. An idol can be ostracized for smoking (e.g., Kago Ai in 2007) or being in the company of men (e.g., Yaguchi Mari in 2005). See also Robertson (1998) for how women in Takarazuka are disciplined.

15. A "wide show" is something like a talk show, with a panel of hosts who discuss a wide range of topics. It is a genre of information and entertainment ("infotainment") programming that is often broadcast during the day, particularly in the morning, for a mostly female audience.

16. These TV sets were placed on the streets by manufacturers as a way to introduce people to television at a time when it was anything but familiar or popular.

17. Though many had pronounced the end of the age of female idols by the early 1990s, Matsu'ura cultivated a camp image of superficiality and excess (see Chapter 9 in this volume for a discussion of performing idol-ness). From her fashions to her way of singing, her performances embodied all aspects of idol culture to such a degree that she was often imitated by comedians, including the transsexual TV personality Haruna Ai.

18. There have been several famous examples of failed exports to the United States, including Pink Lady (resulting in the short-lived NBC variety show *Pink Lady* with comedian Jeff Altman in 1980) and Matsuda Seiko (resulting in the 1990 album *Seiko*, which included a duet with Donnie Wahlberg from the boy band New Kids on the Block). Even Utada Hikaru, lauded for her exceptional language and singing abilities, was unable to succeed in 2004.

19. For a discussion of media self-referentiality, see Luhmann (2000) and Nöth and Bishara (2007).

20. *Zoom In!! SUPER*, Nippon Television Network Corporation, originally aired 4 September 2010.

21. The first use of this technique was on the variety show *Tantei Knight Scoop* in 1988.

22. Though, of course, there are exceptions, namely the male idol group SMAP and especially its member Kimura Takuya, who rose to fame in the 1990s and was still popular during the first decade of the 2000s (see Chapter 4 in this volume).

23. See, for example, Gray (2003), Johnson (2007), and Alters (2007).

24. Their production company colludes with fans by releasing regular and limited edition versions of each of their CDs. In addition, the timing of the release of their singles is carefully calculated to avoid overlapping with the release date of other popular artists. Even more sinister, Rokusaisha Henshūbu (1998, 33–37) asserts that the agencies and their record companies purchase CDs in order to create number one hits.

25. Some also railed against "absentee" votes from overseas, claiming this was meant to be a national election.

26. The study analyzed more than 221 million pages of blogs.

27. The show, called *Naruhodo High School*, debuted on Nippon Television Network on 21 April 2011 and was receiving only a 4.5 percent share of the viewing audience by September 2011.

28. Throughout the volume, we use the conversion rate of ¥80 to $1, referring to US dollars.
29. As a magazine targeting men. *Playboy* in Japan is entirely different from the US version. Content is not necessarily pornographic, though idols in swimsuits and semi-nude models are a staple. In general, due to historical prohibitions on the depiction of genitals and pubic hair, and the longstanding need to develop large readerships (crossing gender and age divisions), most magazines in Japan avoid explicit content.
30. The expression *aidoru sengoku jidai* (idol warring states period) first appeared as a segment of NHK's program *MUSIC JAPAN* in May 2005.
31. Over the course of six months, they actually ended up donating some ¥668 million ($8.35 million) (Oricon Style 2011).
32. One compelling critique is offered by Lukács (2010, 49–50), who argues that production companies sending idols to witness and experience suffering (e.g., in Afghanistan or Africa), a common occurrence, is less about explicating politics or the situation itself and more about the idol being moved to tears. The audience, witnessing the suffering of both the people and the idol, cry along with him or her. The VTR of the experience is played during the TV show, and the idol featured in it watches along with a panel of celebrities, who cry as an audience (not only signaling the appropriate response to viewers, but also standing in for them, or crying in place of the viewers so that they do not have to).
33. The existence of subcultural and countercultural idols seems to suggest otherwise, though they obviously have smaller audiences and less influence.

Works Cited

Adorno, Theodor. 1991. *The Culture Industry: Selected Essays on Mass Culture*, edited by J.M. Bernstein. London: Routledge.

Alters, Diane F. 2007. "The Other Side of Fandom: Anti-Fans, Non-Fans, and the Hurts of History." In *Fandom: Identities and Communities in a Mediated World*, edited by Jonathan Gray, Cornell Sandvoss, and C. Lee Harrington, 344–356. New York: New York University Press.

Aoyagi, Hiroshi. 1996. "Pop Idols and the Asian Identity." In *Contemporary Japan and Popular Culture*, edited by John Whittier Treat, 197–234. Honolulu: University of Hawai'i Press.

———. 2005. *Islands of Eight Million Smiles: Idol Performance and Symbolic Production in Contemporary Japan*. Cambridge: Harvard University Asia Center.

Appadurai, Arjun. 1996. *Modernity at Large: Cultural Dimensions of Globalization*. Minneapolis: University of Minnesota Press.

Asada, Akira. 1989. "Infantile Capitalism and Japan's Postmodernity: A Fairytale." In *Postmodernism and Japan*, edited by Masao Miyoshi and H.D. Harootunian, 273–278. Durham: Duke University Press.

Asahi Shinbun. 2005. "Teroppu Nai to Sagaru Shichōritsu-tte Nan-no!" January 31.

Barks Global Media. 2011a. "Dai-3-kai AKB48 Senbatsu Sōsenkyo: Eigakan Nama-chūkei, Kokunai Eigakan Zen-97 Sukurīn Zenseki Kanbai." http://www.barks.jp/news/?id=1000070600 (accessed 10 June 2011).

————. 2011b "Shinki Fan Kakutoku no Kagi wa Yahari Sakano Yūmi? AKB48 menbā no Netto Kuchikomi Rankingu." http://www.barks.jp//news/? id=1000070251 (accessed 28 May 2011).

Boorstin, Daniel J. 1992 [1961]. *The Image: A Guide to Pseudo-Events in America.* New York: Vintage Books.

Brunsdon, Charlotte, Catherine Johnson, Rachel Moseley, and Helen Wheatley. 2001. "Factual Entertainment on British Television The Midlands TV Research Group's '8–9 Project'." *European Journal of Cultural Studies* 4, no. 1 (February): 29–62.

Daily Sports. 2011. "Oshima Yūko, Seken no Hihan o Aete Kuchi ni 'Tōhyō wa Mina-san no Ai.'" June 9. http://headlines.yahoo.co.jp/hl?a=20110609-00000064-dal-ent (accessed 11 June 2011).

Debord, Guy. 1994. *The Society of the Spectacle.* Trans. Donald Nicholson-Smith. New York: Zone Books.

Dyer, Richard. 1979. *Stars.* London: British Film Institute.

Fiske, John. 2011 [1987]. *Television Culture.* 2nd ed. London: Routledge.

Flash. 2011. "Amerika de Dai-senpū! 'Minna Miku Miku ni shite Ageru:' Nihon ga Hokoru Daininki Kashu Hatsune Miku no Rosanzerusu Hatsu-raibu o Dokusen Genchi Repōto." July 26.

Graham, Phil. 2006. *Hypercapitalism: New Media, Language, and Social Perceptions of Value.* New York: Peter Lang.

Gray, Jonathan. 2003. "New Audiences, New Textualities: Anti-fans and Non-fans." *International Journal of Cultural Studies* 6, no. 1 (March 1): 64–81.

Grossberg, Lawrence. 1992. "Is There a Fan in the House?: The Affective Sensibility of Fandom." In *The Adoring Audience: Fan Culture and Popular Media*, edited by Lisa A. Lewis, 50–65. London: Routledge.

Hartley, John. 1998. "Juvenation: News, Girls, and Power." In *News, Gender, and Power*, edited by Cynthia Carter, Gill Branston and Stuart Allan, 47–70. London: Routledge.

Holden, T.J.M. and Hakan Ergül. 2006. "Japan's Televisual Discourses: Infotainment, Intimacy, and the Construction of a Collective *Uchi*." In *Medi@sia: Global Media/tion in and Out of Context*, edited by T.J.M. Holden and Timothy J. Scrase, 105–127. London: Routledge.

Hutcheon, Linda. 1989. *The Politics of Postmodernism.* London: Routledge.

ITmedia News. 2008. "AKB48 'Posutā 44-shurui Konpu de Ibento Shōtai' Kikaku, 'Dokkinhō Ihan' no Osore de Chūshi." February 28. http://www.itmedia.co.jp/news/articles/0802/28/news120.html (accessed 2 November 2011).

Iwabuchi, Kōichi. 2010. "Undoing Inter-national Fandom in the Age of Brand Nationalism." In *Mechademia 5: Fanthropologies*, edited by Frenchy Lunning, 87–96. Minneapolis: University of Minnesota Press.

Jenkins, Henry. 2006. *Convergence Culture: Where Old and New Media Collide.* New York: New York University Press.

Jenson, Joli. 1992. "Fandom as Pathology: The Consequences of Characterization." In *The Adoring Audience: Fan Cultures and Popular Media*, edited by Lisa A. Lewis, 9–29. London and New York: Routledge.

Johnson, Derek. 2007. "Fan-tagonism: Factions, Institutions, and Constitutive Hegemonies of Fandom." In *Fandom: Identities and Communities in a Mediated World*, edited by Jonathan Gray, Cornell Sandvoss, and C. Lee Harrington, 285–300. New York: New York University Press.

Kelly, William W., ed. 2004. *Fanning the Flames: Fans and Consumer Culture in Contemporary Japan*. Albany: State University of New York Press.
Kilburn, David. 1998. "Star Power." *Adweek*, January 12.
Kimura, Tatsuya. 2007. "History of Japanese Idols: From the Silver Screen to the Internet Via the Living Room." Trans. Suda Takahisa. *High Fashion: Bimonthly Magazine for Women and Men*, no. 313, 259–260. February 1.
Kimura Takuya. 2003. *Kaihō-ku*. Tokyo: Shūeisha.
Kinsella, Sharon. 1995. "Cuties in Japan." In *Women, Media, and Consumption in Japan*, edited by Lise Skov and Brian Moeran, 220–254. Honolulu: University of Hawai'i Press.
Latour, Bruno. 2005. *Re-assembling the Social: An Introduction to Actor-Network Theory*. Oxford: Oxford University Press.
Luhmann, Niklas. 2000. *The Reality of the Mass Media*. Stanford: Stanford University Press.
Lukács, Gabriella. 2007. "The Net Idols: New Forms of Creative Employment and Neoliberal Labor Subjectivities in 1990s Japan." Paper presented at the annual meeting of the Association for Asian Studies, Boston, MA. March 24.
———. 2010. *Scripted Affects, Branded Selves: Television, Subjectivity, and Capitalism in 1990s Japan*. Durham: Duke University Press.
Marshall, P. David. 1997. *Celebrity and Power: Fame in Contemporary Culture*. Minneapolis: University of Minnesota Press.
Morita, Mutsumi. 2011. "No Stopping the AKB48 Juggernaut." *Daily Yomiuri Online*. June 24. http://www.yomiuri.co.jp/dy/features/arts/T110622002086.htm (accessed 26 June 2011).
Nakamori Akio. 2007. *Aidoru Nippon*. Tokyo: Shinchōsha.
Nikkei Entertainment. 1999. "Āteisuto no Jumyō." May.
Nöth, Winfried, and Nina Bishara, eds. 2007. *Self-Reference in the Media*. Berlin: Mouton de Gruyter.
Okajima Shinshi and Okada Yasuhiro. 2011. *Gurūpu Aidoru Shinka Ron: "Aidoru Sengoku Jidai" ga Yatte-kita!* Tokyo: Mainichi Komyunikēshonzu.
Okiyama Sumihisa. 2007. "The Story of Dreams and Yearnings: The 'Promide' Pictures of Marubelldo." Trans. Lawrence Pruor. *High Fashion: Bimonthly Magazine for Women and Men*, no. 313, 260. February 1.
Oricon Inc. 2011. "Kokunai Saidai no Aidoru Fest 'Tokyo Idol Festival 2011.'" *Web De-View*. July 4. http://www.oricon.co.jp/news/deview/89516/ (accessed 5 July 2011).
Oricon Style. 2011. "AKB48, Hantoshi de Gienkin 6 oku 6800 man en: Shien Katsudō Keizoku o Hyōmei." *Oricon Style*. September 16. http://www.oricon.co.jp/news/confidence/2001849/full/ (accessed 17 September 2011).
Ōta Shōichi. 2011. *Aidoru Shinka Ron: Minami Saori kara Hatsune Miku, AKB48 made*. Tokyo: Chikuma Shobō.
Painter, Andrew A. 1996. "Japanese Daytime Television, Popular Culture, and Ideology." In *Contemporary Japan and Popular Culture*, edited by John Whittier Treat, 197–234. Honolulu: University of Hawai'i Press.
Recording Industry Association of Japan (RIAJ). 2011. "Kakushu Tōkei." http://www.riaj.or.jp/data/quantity/index.html (accessed 20 August 2011).
Robertson, Jennifer. 1998. *Takarazuka: Sexual Politics and Popular Culture in Modern Japan*. Berkeley: University of California Press.

Rokusaisha Henshūbu, ed. 1998. *Jyanīzu no Yokubō: Aidoru Shihonshugi no Senryaku to Kōzō*. Nishinomiya: Rokusaisha.
Sankei News. 2011. "AKB48 ga 5-oku-en o Kifu: Gienkin Kōza mo Kaisetsu." March 15. http://sankei.jp.msn.com/entertainments/news/110315/ent11031520540015-n1.htm (accessed 18 March 2011).
Shūkan Josei. 2011. "Mō Ichido 'Kyandīzu' kara Furikaeru: 70s Aidoru Purēbakku." June 7.
———. 2010. "Shōgeki Shinsō Kyacchi: Arashi 'Chiketto Daikin Kaise' Daisōdō." October 26.
Shūkan Pureibōi. 2011a. "Aidoru Dai-sengoku Jidai: Aidoru Ibento Tokusōtai." July 11.
———. 2011b. " 'Chō Aidoru Jidai.' " July 11.
———. 2011c. "Ima, Gurūpu Aidoru ga Dai-būmu no Wake wa?" July 11.
Shūkan Shinchō. 2011. "Ijūin Hikaru to Okamura Takashi ga Iron o Tonaeta AKB48 Sōsenkyo." June 30.
Stacey, Jackie. 1991. "Feminine Fascinations: Forms of Identification in Star-Audience Relations." In *Stardom: Industry of Desire*, edited by Christine Gledhill. London: Routledge.
Stevens, Carolyn S. 2011. "Touching the Audience: Music and Television Advertising in Japan." *Japanese Studies* 31, no. 1: 37–51.
Treat, John Whittier. 1993. "Yoshimoto Banana Writes Home: *Shōjo* Culture and the Nostalgic Subject." *Journal of Japanese Studies* 19, no. 2: 353–387.
West, Mark D. 2006. *Secrets, Sex, and Spectacle: The Rule of Scandal in Japan and the United States*. Chicago: The University of Chicago Press.
Wolf, Michael J. 1999. *The Entertainment Economy: How Mega-media Forces Are Transforming Our Lives*. New York: Three Rivers Press.
Yano, Christine R. 2004. "Letters from the Heart: Negotiating Fan-Star Relationships in Japanese Popular Music." In *Fanning the Flames: Fans and Consumer Culture in Contemporary Japan*, edited by William W. Kelly, 41–58. New York: State University of New York Press.
Yoda, Tomiko. 2000. "The Rise and Fall of Maternal Society: Gender, Labor, and Capital in Contemporary Japan." *South Atlantic Quarterly* 99, no. 4: 865–902.
Yoshimi Shun'ya. 2003. "Terebi ga Ie ni Yatte-kita: Terebi no Kūkan, Terebi no Jikan." *Shisō* 956 (December): 26–48.
———. 2009. *Posuto Sengo Shakai*. Tokyo: Iwanami Shinsho.

Part I
Systems

1

The *Jimusho* System: Understanding the Production Logic of the Japanese Entertainment Industry

W. David Marx

Artistic works produced in the field of popular culture act as symbolic goods, shaping the way we understand our own lives and our place in society. The human interaction with these goods, however, often ignores the fact that, since the twentieth century, the vast majority of popular culture enters society in the form of commercial products, and is therefore subject to the shaping of a wider production system. In the early 1970s, the Production of Culture school brought this understanding into its analysis of popular culture, viewing cultural objects within the organization of their production: creative processes, audience reception, industrial frameworks, and institutional positions. One of the primary figures of this new approach, Richard A. Peterson, explains this so-called "Production of Culture" school as research that assumes that "the social arrangements used in making symbolic elements of culture affect the nature and content of the elements of culture that are produced" (Peterson 1994, 163). Acknowledging that the public cultural sphere is mainly constructed of products enabled a wider application of economic market analysis to the field of popular culture. As Paul DiMaggio (1977, 437) writes:

> Economic and organizational factors as how a popular culture form is distributed and how the market for it is segmented may determine in large part the level of independence granted creators and the degree of innovation and diversity in the products themselves.

Specific circumstances of the cultural industries—unpredictable demand, unlimited creative inputs, high sunk costs—shape the organization of the market, and the changes in the market structure invariably lead to changes in the emerging products' form and content. Furthermore, wide audience reception of those products depends greatly upon the goods' favorably guided movement through highly competitive distribution channels (Hirsch 1972). The nature cf a national popular culture, therefore, is not only a product of creator ingenuity and wider social norms but also of the relative market power of institutions in the market system.

In applying this analytical framework to the field of Japanese popular entertainment we find the question—how does the industrial organization of the Japanese cultural market thus impact the dominant style of performance and artistic creation? Unfortunately, there has been no significant research in pursuit of the answer. As Hugh De Ferranti (2002) notes, academics have written very little scholarly work on the Japanese entertainment industry either in Japanese or in other languages. In the last two decades, there have been many works providing descriptive analysis of the Japanese music industry in English—such as Herd (1984), Kawabata (1991), Kimura (1991), and Kitagawa (1991)—but there still remains little research taking up the specific perspective of looking at the market's industrial organization.

Anthropological work on the field of *enka* and idols provides a crucial hint, however, that Japan's performer management companies—colloquially known as *jimusho* (meaning "office")—are most responsible for the content of the entertainment world. *Enka* artists and idols rarely write their own music. The *jimusho* create performers of these genres from scratch and control every aspect of the performers' public image and career. Christine Yano's examination of *enka*, the quintessentially "Japanese" twentieth-century pop music style, reveals that the genre's singers have traditionally not been self-guided musicians, but "something created by those around them" (*mawari no tsukutta mono*), in a Nippon Columbia director's words (Yano 2002, 54). In this dominant mode of *enka* production, the management company sets the image and character of the new artist to match its perceptions of market conditions (Ibid., 63). Hiroshi Aoyagi (2005) also finds this approach common in the world of idols. Aoyagi's portrait of the idol *jimusho*, many of which dominate the Japanese entertainment scene overall, gives important clues to the dominant modes of production praxis in the industry: creating performers from zero, full coordination of artistic content by company employees, long-term market planning, and demands to control all media content pertaining to the idol. Aoyagi sees management company staff not just shaping the personalities, repertoire, and visual appearances of their idols, but then forcefully pushing their talent out into the wider popular culture. One idol manager even labeled his work "mass control" (*taishū sōsa*)" due to the ability to shape the zeitgeist through the popularity of its idols (Aoyagi 2003, 145). If we take up Aoyagi's assertion that idols create socially understood meanings of adolescence and identity, then the production companies are hence directly responsible for crafting those social meanings (Aoyagi 2005, 32).

With these *jimusho* being so critical to the shaping of the performers who become the faces and personalities of the expansive Japanese media world, it is imperative that we understand their organization and production logic. The *jimusho* are responsible for performer creation, management, and overall production. Despite their small size and limited access to capital, they exert strong control over the entertainment market, even compared with other firms in the industry. This *jimusho* power often stems from less-than-transparent characteristics of their business—from secretive organization into larger *keiretsu* structures as well as strong control over their performers and associated copyrights. Their organizational power allows *jimusho* to direct performers' careers completely, and, in pursuit of profit, they maximize entertainers' incomes through a wide variety of activities, most deeply focused on product sponsorship. The economic incentive that follows from the *jimusho's* institutional organization thus strongly influences the *jimusho's* preferred type of performers to "create." Idols are products of their *jimusho*, and the *jimusho* work to create idols who have the greatest economic potential.

With the *jimusho* under-analyzed within academic literature and even avoided in the mainstream Japanese press,[1] research on this field required two critical sources: the testimony of Japanese entertainment industry insiders, and publicly available industry data. Japanese entertainment insiders, whom I interviewed through 2003 to 2006, affirmed and clarified many of the *jimusho's* business practices that are often exposed in Japan's weekly magazines (*shūkanshi*) and monthly tabloid magazines like *Cyzo*. This information, however, worked best as a starting point, as the (relatively cohesive) narratives that emerged needed external verification. Most information about specific *jimusho keiretsu* composition and market power could be found in three sets of data: the Oricon ("Original Confidence") music charts from 1988 to 2004; performer appearance lists for the top three primetime music shows *Music Station* (TV Asahi), *Hey! Hey! Hey! Music Champ* (Fuji TV), and *Utaban* (TBS) for the same time period; and the Japanese Society for Rights of Authors, Composers and Publishers (JASRAC) online copyright database.[2] These three data resources will be referred to henceforth as the "research set." This data focuses primarily cn music, which admittedly is only one slice of the Japanese entertainment business, but the three databases offer detailed information on which artists belong to which *jimusho*, which *jimusho* artists appear on TV most often, and which *jimusho* give their publishing rights to other *jimusho*—the primary way of discovering undisclosed *keiretsu* membership.

General descriptions of the *jimusho* system

While the industry structure of the Japanese entertainment culture closely resembles that of other equally sized markets in terms of media output (TV, music, film), the most fundamentally distinctive institutional variation is the degree to which *jimusho* hold power within the market system. The best-known companies in this *jimusho* category are Johnny & Associates, Yoshimoto Kōgyō, Horipro, Watanabe Production, Tanabe Agency, Up Front Agency, Sun Music, and Amuse Inc. Two record labels, Sony Music and Avex, also have subsidiaries or internal departments that exclusively manage talent. The *jimusho* have a wide spectrum of responsibilities: scouting new performers/models; training them in singing, dancing, and other skills; scheduling performers' daily activities; booking television appearances; negotiating contracts with record labels and other media institutions; organizing fan clubs; doing public relations work to enhance the performers' image; and coordinating live performances and concert tours. For musicians and idols with musical careers, the management company works very closely with the performer on day-to-day tasks, while record companies are left to organize the financial resources. Ian Condry (2006, 232) quotes an employee of management company Amuse explaining that the *jimusho*, for musicians, is like the artist's "mother" and the record company is the "father." For performers without a musical career, the *jimusho* becomes the sole authority in their careers.

Despite their dominance over the entertainment market, *jimusho* in Japan are relatively small, private companies with limited capital resources and staff. For example, moderately sized record label EMI Music Japan (formerly Toshiba-EMI) has over ¥1.667 billion ($20.8 million) in capital. Meanwhile, Burning Production—the management company run by Suhō Ikuo, a man understood to be the "Don" of the wider Japanese entertainment industry—only publicly claims ¥20 million ($250,000) in capital. Another key characteristic of *jimusho* is that almost all are privately held companies, with the exception of

Avex, Horipro, and Amuse.[3] Without being publicly traded on stock exchanges, most companies have no legal impetus to reveal information about earnings, and thus we have no way of knowing the specifics about their financial transactions and profit/losses. The result is that *jimusho* are often highly profitable and hold great institutional power, yet there are few public indications of this situation. For example, despite decades-long domination of the pop charts and television dramas, young male idol purveyor Johnny & Associates maintains a public image of being a family-run, privacy-obsessed small enterprise with only the slightest presence as a "business" (i.e., a company engaged in pursuing growth, collecting investment for further expansions, and acquiring subsidiaries).

The relatively low entry costs of managing and developing human capital in the music business have created a very large number of firms in the field. Aoyagi (2005, 39) estimates that 1,600 *jimusho* exist in Tokyo alone. The *Oricon Nenkan* (2005) industry registry, however, lists only around 975 operating within Eastern Japan. These numbers, too, may be slightly misleading. In the research set, only around 400 *jimusho* had performers with a top 100 yearly hit or appeared on one of the three largest music programs from 1988 to 2004. Theoretically the supply of performers should massively exceed the demand for their usage in media—a "buyer's market" that would give media companies a strong negotiating position with the *jimusho*. We will see, however, that these numbers are misleading as measures of market concentration, since only a few *jimusho* wield effective levels of institutional power.

Organization of *jimusho* into *keiretsu*

Although there appear to be hundreds of independent *jimusho* operating in Japan, the top companies are mostly organized into loose but very hierarchical *keiretsu*-type organizations.[4] The *keiretsu* are the key to understanding the *jimusho* system, but, unfortunately, this is also the most oblique characteristic of the field to measure and observe. Some *jimusho* openly admit formal subsidiaries. The agency Topcoat, for example, is part of Watanabe Productions. Up Front Agency at one time split up its talent under a host of companies: A-dash, Coolie Promotion, Endebar Promotion, Fab Promotion, Galaxy Promotion, and Harmony Promotion. For some of the top *jimusho* groups, however, like Burning Production, K-Dash, and those under the auspices of Nagara Production, there is no official or otherwise publicly revealed relation between companies in the same *keiretsu*. The dozens and dozens of firms within the alleged Burning Production *keiretsu* do not reveal affiliations, and these relations are only known to deep insiders. Tabloid publications like *Cyzo* often mention certain talent agencies as being part of the Burning *keiretsu* ("*Bā-kei*" in industry lingo), but there are no easily procured public documents or public pronouncements from Burning itself that this corporate group exists.[5] Most surprisingly, many performers within the subsidiary agencies often have no idea that their *jimusho* answers to a larger one. Without this knowledge of the *keiretsu*, which is mostly hidden from the general public, all of these small firms look to be independent, and, therefore, in heavy competition. The real structure, however, is that the head at the *jimusho* at the top of the *keiretsu* doles out work to each of the subsidiaries and makes final decisions about which talents get what projects. In other words, we should understand the *jimusho* in a *keiretsu* as a single corporate unit in terms of competitive measure.

According to industry contacts, membership of a *keiretsu* can also be set by a simple phone call: the "boss" of the parent company calls a new management company and asks whether the new *jimusho* is in the group or out. Most *keiretsu* subsidiaries, however, are formed by veteran managers inside the group branching out and opening up their own agency. The larger agency may even provide funding to start the new agency, although this is done in such a way as to avoid public indications of ownership or shareholding. What does a small company get in return for being a part of the *keiretsu*? Essentially, the use of the larger company's network and power. Without any formal capital relations, and with all financial transactions private, we can only speculate on the nature of "payback" to the parent company. Insider accounts suggest anything from complicated "consulting service" schemes to cash in envelopes.[6]

One of the most common payback methods, however, is the transfer of publishing rights for musical performers. This practice also is convenient as a method of identifying *keiretsu* memberships. Many small companies alleged to be part of a larger organization will give their performers' publishing rights to the "parent" company. For example, the Oricon charts from the 1980s show evidence that most alleged members of the Burning *keiretsu* gave Burning's subsidiary Burning Publishing their publishing rights.[7] While this practice became less transparent within the Oricon charts in the 1990s, a new JASRAC database of copyright holdings clarified ownership between Burning and these subsidiaries. Many were shocked to discover that Avex Trax, the incredibly popular, publicly traded record label with a *jimusho* wing, would give a massive number of copyrights for its hit artists, such as Hamasaki

Ayumi and Every Little Thing, to Burning Publishing. Avex, despite its size and stature, should be considered part of the Burning Production *keiretsu* based on this measure. From a purely rational business perspective, Avex should have no reason to give up its lucrative publishing rights, since the company owns its own highly profitable publishing subsidiary. These transfers of rights make most sense as a "tributary" payment to the top company in the *keiretsu* hierarchy.

Having this structure of loosely related small companies helps the main company avoid paying excessive tax or attracting too much attention from authorities for its size. This structure also allows the major *jimusho* to wield control over the industry without audiences having any idea of power being centralized. For example, the three main models of magazine *CanCam* during its peak years around 2007 all came from the *keiretsu* headed by *jimusho* K-Dash, but technically Ebihara Yuri and Oshikiri Moe were from the agency Pearl while Yamada Yū was from K-Dash proper. This arrangement made it look more diversified to the general public as well as less knowledgeable people in the industry.

The dissolution into small, distinct firms also fits with the unique *jimusho* culture of avoiding the public eye. In general, the giants of the industry, who sit atop the *keiretsu* structure, rarely give interviews to the media, show up in front of the camera, or otherwise leave traces of their existence. There are basically no public photographs of Suhō Ikuo, the head of Burning Production, despite the fact that he is considered the most powerful man in Japanese entertainment. The same goes for Taira Tetsuo, once of Rising Production (now Vision Factory), who spent some years in prison for tax evasion. Johnny Kitagawa, founder of Johnny & Associates, is also famously reclusive and has only been photographed by paparazzi. These business leaders tend to fit the image of the *kuromaku* (the man behind-the-curtain) in stark contrast to Hollywood's extravagant industry moguls like David Geffen. Or, for a more regional comparison, the Japanese bosses are even reclusive compared with their Korean counterparts—like Kim Young Min, CEO of top management company SM Entertainment—who frequently appear in media interviews and win accolades from the Korean government.

These *keiretsu* groups explain how there can be heavy oligopoly in the Japanese entertainment industry even when it technically contains a large number of firms. Only the top *jimusho* groups—such as Burning Production, K-Dash, Kenon, Johnny & Associates, Stardust Promotion, Horipro, Yoshimoto Kōgyō—are able to place talent on major TV shows, in commercials, and in other high-profile work. The entertainment industry does not really have an "open casting" system, and, in many cases, the top powerbrokers of about a dozen groups essentially dictate to the media and advertising agencies which members of their *keiretsu* they want used.[8] The *keiretsu* arrangement allows the *jimusho* to control access to hundreds of celebrities, which in turn gives them market power in transactional relationships between themselves and the media. If the media do not want to use a new star, the boss can then threaten to withdraw all of his talents from use by those media. This system ultimately favors the management companies.

Sources of *jimusho* power

Within the Japanese entertainment industry, the *jimusho* wield an enormous amount of power, with which they dominate other institutions and influence overall decision-making processes. This power originates from three sources: possession of master and publishing rights, mass media dependence upon star talent, and perceptions of extralegal activity.

With so much of the entertainment world operating within the sphere of musical performance, the *jimusho* create solid revenue streams and have ultimate authority on business transactions through their possession of master rights and publishing rights. The larger *jimusho* take full responsibility for investment into the recording process and songwriting coordination for their artists, which rewards them with the master rights to the recording—a legally recognized right that endows the owner with control over the work's mechanical duplication and third-party use. In the traditional market model, record companies pay for their artists' recording fees and subsequently receive the master rights. Since the 1960s, however, the larger *jimusho* have invested in recording and coordination themselves, entitling them to all consequent privileges. At the time this practice began, Japanese record labels were accustomed to making licensing deals with American record labels, and so the idea of leasing master recordings from outside parties was easily extended to domestic companies (Azami 2004). Today, *jimusho* often hold master rights exclusively or share the rights with other organizations, like record companies and publishing companies. This is a significant source of revenue in itself and means artist management companies are directly entitled to profits from record sales—something that is not true of most other music markets. In the case of Johnny & Associates and Up Front Agency, the *jimusho* have even gone as far to create their own record labels (J-Storm and Zetima, respectively), further cutting out the large record labels from profiting from their musical artists.

In addition to master recording rights, *jimusho* that organize the song-writing process for their talent often lay claim to the songs' publishing rights, which control copyrights for individual songs. These rights allow the collection of mechanical royalties on the duplication of CDs, including owned songs (around 6 percent of the price of the CD), performance royalties for public usage of the song (collected by JASRAC), and variably priced synchronization licenses for media usages (Caves 2000, 299). Publishing has the most potential for long-term revenue streams, because songs may be rerecorded by future artists or used in other media long after CD sales have dried up (Cahoon 2005). This also creates revenue streams from the lucrative karaoke business. In Japan, artists almost never hold their own publishing rights; these are often split between multiple parties, including the management company, its parent management company, the record label, and television networks (especially if the song was used in a television tie-up).

Holding both master rights and publishing rights gives management companies ultimate decision-making power about a song's media usage, and other parties looking to utilize the song in a new context must win approval from the *jimusho*. Featuring a song in a TV commercial, for example, requires permission of both the master rights holder and the publisher. With *jimusho* normally holding one or both of these rights, they generally keep control over a large portion of musical content, and therefore make themselves a major player in the music-driven entertainment market overall.

The second source of the *jimusho*'s industry power emanates from media companies' structural dependence on management companies for access to performers. Television networks and magazine publishers create content for the specific purpose of attracting audiences to sell to advertisers, and common to this process is the casting of celebrities and well-known talent. In Japan, decision-making authority over appearance and performance lies squarely with the *jimusho*, and therefore media outlets must negotiate with the management company for access privileges. This may be generally true in other music markets as well, but in Japan performers' inability to exit these firms (see section below on labor relations) creates large-sized *jimusho* with a sizable and permanent "stock" of in-demand talent in the fields of acting, modeling, music, sports, and comedy. The *jimusho*'s total negotiating power is proportional to all its stars' cachet, which means that the top companies in this field benefit from a compounded star power.

Negotiations on the use of one star have implications for the use of other *jimusho* members. Often large *jimusho* require networks to take smaller or newer talent on the network's other television shows in exchange for use of well-known celebrities (called "barter" in industry lingo). Of course, management companies rely on media exposure to sell their talent, but healthy competition between the five major TV networks and the firms' ability to limit access to a large pool of talent means management firms have the upper hand: they can threaten to give better treatment to other stations if demands are not met. Using established celebrities as leverage, large firms are therefore able to get more of their new talent into the media, which, in turn, creates more overall popularity for their performers. Celebrity stature thus directly shapes market power for *jimusho*, and networks are beholden to the firms for access to creative inputs. Networks may be able to forgo the use of one specific performer, but the *jimusho* system raises the stakes of negotiation to *all* performers under a company's auspices. This arrangement ultimately makes the *jimusho* the central authority when media are putting together programming. A member of the production team for a network music television program explained that he calls the top *jimusho* each week and asks which of their stars they want to put on the show, rather than the TV station picking the talent and asking for his/her participation.

Finally, large *jimusho* obtain market power through industry perceptions that they may carry out actions outside legal and commercial barriers. Although there has been very little public information on the topic, many of the oldest and most powerful *jimusho* in Japan are believed to be connected in some capacity to the world of organized crime. Aoyagi (2005, 50) writes of friends warning that "some agencies might be acquainted with the underworld." In the early half of the twentieth century, crime syndicates openly managed and coordinated performances in various creative fields, and, while since 1964 police have actively fought to keep the *yakuza* from working in the entertainment industry, links dating from the prewar era are still alleged to exist (Suzuki 2005). Kaplan and Dubro (2003, 183) note in their survey of the Japanese *yakuza* that the Yamaguchi-gumi was directly responsible for managing the career of iconic *enka* singer Misora Hibari. Ugaya (2005, 226) notes that this "dark side" of the industry remains strong in the Japanese music industry despite its absence from contemporary film and video game production fields. In the last decade, many *jimusho* heads have been arrested and jailed for tax evasion, including Taira Tetsuo from the market leader Rising Production (now Vision Factory) and Yamada Eiji from AG Communication. Tax evasion should not necessarily imply organized crime, but consider the case of Rising's Taira: at his trial, he begged for leniency from the courts, citing the necessity of "underground" (*urashakai*) financial measures in the music business (Ugaya 2005).

The best concrete evidence of links between top *jimusho* and organized crime comes from the Tokyo Metropolitan Police Department—although not intentionally. In 2007, a police officer leaked a host of confidential files to the Internet, including a spreadsheet outlining companies related to the Gōtō crime family. As reported in Jake Adelstein's *Tokyo Vice* (2009, 297) and reported at the time obliquely in many Japanese insider tabloids, the file lists top *jimusho* Burning Production as a "client business." A footnote in McNeill and Adelstein (2008) mentions: "In December of 2007, the National Police Agency sent out a formal request to the Federation of Civilian Broadcasters asking them to sever ties with organized crime groups." If there were no organized crime in entertainment, the National Police Agency would clearly not need to make such a request. In general, the tendency of *jimusho* to keep financial information private, change official firm names on a frequent basis, and splinter into informal groupings creates an industry environment in which improper financial transactions can go easily undetected. In America, as well, organized crime has been associated with independent radio promotion firms, but the US government has been more active over the last five decades in investigating and prosecuting these connections than has been the case in Japan (Dannen 1991).

While direct links between the *jimusho* and organized crime are murky at best, industry actors do behave under the assumption that these rumors are true. Threats of extralegal punishment for noncooperation would certainly guide actors towards the avoidance of unnecessary conflicts with *jimusho* alleged to be allied with the underworld. Suggestions of criminal connections cannot explain the majority of the *jimusho*'s power, but the possibility of these connections most likely increases smaller firms' deference to the larger management companies rumored to be dangerous. Organized crime presence creates market distortions, as conflicts are solved outside legal frameworks and decisions are often made for reasons other than rational market logic. The producer of the network music television program mentioned above commented to me that one of the most powerful *jimusho* received preferred treatment in casting because it was *kowai* (scary).

Jimusho power through television

Television has been the most powerful and influential medium in Japan for introducing new entertainers and performers to the wider public. Stars who appear on variety shows on a constant basis are the ones broadly understood to be "popular." In the case of music as well, TV has been mostly responsible for directly driving sales. In the Recording Industry Association of Japan's 2004 music media user survey, the top four "information sources leading to purchase" were, in order, network TV programs, TV dramas, TV commercial songs, and TV commercials for music. During the market peak in the 1990s especially, songs repeatedly heard on TV became hits. While the decline of the music market has changed this to a certain degree, *jimusho* still greatly depend upon TV stations in order to turn unknown performers into profitable stars.

Theoretically this would create a symbiotic relationship between television and management companies, but *jimusho* retain the decision-making power about which performers appear on which TV programs. This is mainly due to their ability to leverage access to their most popular stars. Use of established performers becomes conditional on TV station support of new and upcoming ones. This reaches a point where there is basically no "open casting" in Japan, and top stars such as Johnny & Associates' Kimura Takuya have shows built around them.[9]

A survey of the research set finds that the majority of stars appearing on top network music programs *Music Station* (TV Asahi), *Hey Hey Hey Music Champ* (Fuji TV), and *Utaban* (TBS) came from the top *jimusho keiretsu*. Competition should be fierce for appearance slots (only four to six per week, depending on the program) since the music programs have traditionally been the number one driver of sales. The TV stations, however, need actors, models, and performers to appear on their other programming, so the larger *jimusho* have leverage in demanding appearances for their new and less popular artists. In the case of *Music Station* from 1988 to 2004, the top five *jimusho keiretsu* (in this case, Johnny & Associates, Burning Productions including Avex and Rising, Up Front Agency, Sony Music Artists, and Nagara Production Group including Being) made up around 50 percent of all appearances (2,692 of total 5,212 slots). This level of concentration generally held true for the other two shows *Hey! Hey! Hey Music Champ* and *Utaban* as well. In other words, over half of TV appearances on music shows are doled out semi-automatically to the most dominant players and the vast majority are doled out to the top dozen *jimusho* groups.

Labor relations between performer and *jimusho*

Most agencies, especially the major idol firms, very strictly control their performers and give them little freedom to control the direction of their own careers. Unlike the American talent system, whereby performers freely hire managers or agents as employees and retain the power to fire them for underperformance, Japanese performers tend to become contracted employees of their management companies. The standard labor relation for aspiring performers is the "management contract," which gives the firms full rights to guide performers' careers and privilege to all earnings (including songwriting royalties). This contractual condition essentially makes performers into full employees of the *jimusho*, for which they receive a monthly stipend regardless of temporary profitability. These stipends traditionally start at ¥200,000 per month ($2,500). Firms cut loose performers who are unable to show long-term potential within the contract period, while successful performers can renegotiate for higher payment at the expiration of the contract once they have attained a moderate level of success. *Jimusho* thus invest money into performers without immediate returns, and this wage-like payment strategy only pays off when performers make it big. However, with full possession of all copyrights and access to all guarantees for performance and promotional duties, the *jimusho* can make enormous sums of money with a hit performer.

Even though these standard management contracts give *jimusho* great potential for high earnings, most performers do not become profitable. Aoyagi (2005, 166) notes that the price of producing an idol can cost upwards of ¥30 to ¥40 million, which should be considered an extremely high investment for a product with unpredictable earning potential. Especially in cases of creating performers from the "raw stock" of young teenagers with limited natural talent, development costs are sunk and fixed.

Jimusho hence face a great threat from expensive "trained" talent with widespread recognition leaving the firm and joining other management groups. The business model requires long-term "ownership" of the performer in order to be profitable. Back in the 1950s and 1960s, the production company could control labor movement by owning a singer's entire song catalog, thus making exit impossible for most established singers hoping to maintain a career based on past success and well-known songs (Fujie 1989). The diversification of publishing in the 1970s helped alleviate this barrier (Ibid.), but the danger of *jimusho* switching still exists, prompting management companies to use a variety of legal and extralegal methods to ensure talent do not freely move throughout the market. Contracts, for example, contain strong financial penalties for early dissolution.

More widespread, however, is the use of unofficial blacklisting. Performers who leave their initial management company can often find themselves unwelcome within the entertainment industry as a whole—"left out to dry" (*hosareta*) in industry jargon. Although tabloids have hinted at blacklisting for years, the practice first became highly conspicuous when the industry-leading female idol Suzuki Ami sued to dissolve her contract with *jimusho* AG Communication after that firm's chief executive, Yamada Eiji, was arrested for tax evasion (McClure 2001). Although courts ruled her contract termination to be legally sound, Suzuki immediately lost her recording contract with Sony and was then unable to secure promotion and distribution through the traditional channels for her self-created music and goods. Although she was a top female talent at the time, her entertainment career completely evaporated until she re-signed with Avex Music (a member of the same Burning *keiretsu* group as AG) in 2005.[10] The blacklisting system is a taboo topic in the Japanese mainstream media and is not well documented, but it appears that the *jimusho* demands that all partners cease working with the rogue. This keeps other management companies from picking up loose talent, and perhaps, in an act of sympathy, other firms respect the blacklisting decision for fear of encouraging the possibility of *jimusho*-switching among their own performers. Tokyo-based English magazine *Metropolis* hosted allegations from YouTube-based American talent Magibon that her former *jimusho* would call up and offer her clients a pick of the agency's stable of famous stars to work in her place (Galbraith 2010). This case could be considered a "positively reinforced" blacklist.

As a result of this practice, very few artists in the Japanese music industry have changed management companies, and those who do generally move "up" into a larger, more powerful agency, leave on amicable terms, or put their careers on hold for several years as self-punishment for leaving. Popular actress Kanno Miho, for example, was easily able to leave the small Tani Promotion to enter larger *jimusho* Kenon. More recently, voice talent and singer Hirano Aya left her agency Space Craft and moved to Grick, a member of the Burning Production *keiretsu*. Of the artists appearing in the research set, only a handful left their management companies and started their own independent *jimusho*. With many idol performers being total products of their companies and not self-made creations, the inability to leave creators is a rational extension of the industry structure. Performers who are responsible for their own work, however, may be equally susceptible to these harsh industry penalties. The rock band Glay, once a top musical act in Japan, saw their career go on hold for four years when they had a management dispute with two different powerful *jimusho* groups.

Jimusho's preferred performer style

As stated above, the *jimusho* create idols and *tarento* (celebrity perform-ers) rather than simply managing successful performers. In the most common pattern, *jimusho* scout unknowns and then "debut" them to the public with an intentionally crafted look, personality, and style. Half-Japanese model Marie, for example, was positioned as a "model from a rich family" like Paris Hilton, while doctor Nishikawa Ayako debuted as the "cosmetic surgeon *tarento.*" *Jimusho* also play a big role in determining the kind of performers who are tolerated in the market. Johnny & Associates has been able to effectively stop any other com-pany from producing male idol groups through pulling its stars from any program that uses rival talent. Even the major *jimusho* Rising Pro-duction (now Vision Factory) found difficulty in making their male idol acts Da Pump and w-inds successful in face of the Johnny's boycott.

The *jimusho* system is a closed world of small firms, most of which have long-standing position within the entertainment world. In fact, most of the senior people working within today's management compa-nies helped produce *enka* and *kayokyoku* singers in the 1960s and 1970s. The general industrial structure of the *jimusho* world, especially the fact that new firms have a hard time entering it, essentially means that the same people have been responsible for crafting new stars decade after decade. The consistency of output in Japanese pop is perhaps related to the consistency of personnel behind these idols. Johnny Kitagawa, who is 79 years old, still plays a hands-on role in the output of his Johnny & Associates acts. Recent idol group AKB48 is incredibly close in concept and lyrical nature to 1980s idols Onyanko Club, mostly because they have the same creator, Akimoto Yasushi.

Nonetheless, there is a stronger economic logic at work in the indus-try's preference for "created idols" rather than managing more indepen-dently minded stars. Most *jimusho* prefer multi-field performers, ones who are likely to put out music, appear in bikinis on the cover of *Weekly Playboy* or *Shonen Jump*, banter on variety shows, and act in the occa-sional TV drama or film. The fees from these activities can add up to significant income, and, in the case of music, a million-seller can be extremely lucrative. Yet none of these particular activities tops the greatest income stream: corporate/product sponsorship and promotion. Appearing in a single ad campaign for a major corporation or retail chain will guarantee a high source of revenue for the *jimusho* through a rel-atively small amount of work. Compare this with the hard-to-obtain music hit: promoting singles takes millions of dollars in marketing to the public. An ad sponsorship, meanwhile, only takes a smaller campaign of winning over the ad men of Dentsu and Hakuhodo and a few key corporate executives. The rate of return for an ad campaign is much higher than for other activities.

In recent years, the crash of the music market and decline of TV viewership means that *jimusho* have more reason to pursue advertising work over payment for actual "performance." In most cases, the actual performances should be understood as promotion for the star to eventually secure advertising deals; an act usually has to prove popular before becoming a viable spokesperson for a consumer brand.[11] The aforementioned AKB48, for example, finally reached peak profitability in 2010 as they moved beyond an income stream based on a theater in Akihabara and limited record sales into a broader income from dozens of product sponsorships. As the *jimusho* makes almost all its money from the star's total body of work, rather than just a single field of artistic endeavor, the industry as a result moves towards explicitly commercialized pursuits rather than artistic ones. When performers are able to hire the managers rather than *vice versa*, the performer often finds it easier to concentrate his/her career solely on being a performer in the preferred field.

If the ultimate economic goal is a constant line-up of promotional deals, what kind of performers do *jimusho* prefer? The *jimusho* have a logical reason to push stars who lack any barriers to becoming national spokespeople for other corporations. This obviously tilts the balance towards "nice" female idols. And, when making a decision on which newcomers to push, the *jimusho* will not particularly value inherent or learned talent—a strong voice, skillful dancing, acting chops—as these are only indirectly related to the most profitable work of corporate promotion. Conversely, when a singer is only a singer, promotional work can get in the way of his/her reputation. While plenty of talented musical performers end up doing ads—for example, Shiina Ringo, Southern All-Stars and Oyamada Keigo—they are much less likely to do every ad the *jimusho* requests and may get in trouble with advertising clients for including too much personal opinion/attitude into their artistic body of work. Their appeal is also limited to a smaller audience directly interested in their musical or cultural output rather than their fame itself. Talented performers are generally not "pretty faces" pleasant to a wide audience. Most idols and models, on the other hand, can be effective tools for promotion to consumers who might not even enjoy their particular cultural output.

General *tarento* are expected to do this kind of advertising work, and it is most lucrative for the *jimusho* to focus on performers who are not too specialized. For the music market, the main TV shows such as *Music Station* spend as much time interviewing the stars and probing their personalities as actually seeing them perform their songs. The end result is that the *jimusho* allow big stars to be poor actors, bad singers, and unskilled dancers, but they can certainly not be controversial, unattractive, or otherwise disruptive. *Jimusho* face major repercussions when their stars get in trouble for personal scandal—first and foremost because companies have invested in using their "clean" image to promote their products. This is why "uncontrollable" *tarento* such as Sawajiri Erika quickly lose their contracts and have a difficult time moving back into the industry (Poole 2010). Sakai Noriko's recent drug scandal put the industry's reputation seriously at stake. *Jimusho* supply Japanese corporations with promotional vehicles, and Sakai turned out to be highly defective (see Chapter 2, this volume).

Even when stars do possess respectable levels of talent, *jimusho* schedule their activities disproportionately towards promotional work rather than the artistic side of their duties. For example, most TV dramas are shot in a "one-take" style as performers do not have time to dedicate their full schedule to the filming. As long as there are no major mistakes, dramas take only one cut of every scene as a way to finish the work in the shortest amount of time. The business logic is solid: the performers' time should be spent on pursuing promotional work for major companies. The overall "craft," however, becomes an afterthought for entertainment related to the major *jimusho*.

Conclusion

In the search for stable profits within the Japanese entertainment industry framework, the *jimusho* work to create performers who can create revenue streams from a wide range of activities—of which corporate promotion is the most central. The end result is that these firms: (1) promote "created" idols over self-motivated performers, (2) emphasize pleasant looks and demeanor over artistic talent, and (3) invest most time and resources into securing advertising deals rather than creating entertainment content itself. Every pop culture market ultimately focuses on commercialized culture—in other words, crafting pop songs with the greatest chance of broad audience and high sales—but the Japanese system, due to *jimusho* business logic of holding individual performers organized inside broader companies from which they cannot easily exit, goes one step further in emphasizing direct commercialization (advertising) over creative works (the culture itself).

The missing factor in this equation, however, is the audience. With thousands of independent musicians and entertainers, Japanese consumers have every right to reject this model and demand culture that is more "cultural." This has indeed happened many times in Japanese history, when the public loses interest in "idols" and yearns for something more "real." The most famous period of this consumer revolt was the Band Boom of the late 1980s, when *Music Station* and other prime-time music shows lost their audiences to live houses around the country. Many amateur bands gained mass popularity after performing on the late-night show *Ikaten* (short for *Heisei Meibutsu Ikasu Bando Tengoku*) (De Launcey 1995). Unfortunately for musicians, television stations started to reduce the number of music programs in the 1990s, and many performers found themselves needing to be guests on non-music shows to keep up exposure (Yano 2002, 74). While this was ultimately good for sales and diversity of content in the music market, this change in tastes threatened the *jimusho* business model—bands were less suited to media saturation and product promotion than idols. The industry, however, adapted towards the more "real" style to win back the audience, as well as co-opting smaller successful *jimusho* and arranging them into their *keiretsu*. This then allowed *jimusho* to move popular talent back to the same media points such as *Music Station*, and, once audiences returned in the 1990s, the *jimusho* slowly moved the audience back to idol-like performers. There are likely sociocultural reasons why the Japanese audience prefer "what is popular" over "what is unpopular but well-crafted,"[12] and the *jimusho*'s control of the overall entertainment system means that they have very strong influence on the long-term state of Japanese cultural tastes.

Yet in the 2010s, as the music market implodes, TV viewership becomes marginal, fashion magazine readership declines, and youth-oriented "popular culture" generally loses its influence among an increasingly graying Japanese public, the *jimusho* are likely to face an existential threat. That being said, small firms are most likely to be first to take a major hit. TV stations will cut budgets on shows, but make up for it with more variety programming—which, of course, need famous *tarento* from the large *jimusho*. Most importantly, the idea of sponsoring products with celebrities is deeply ingrained within corporate culture in Japan, and, whatever its cost, few decision-makers are likely to take the risk of trying a different approach. Marketers will not be fired for doing a campaign with AKB48 or other top stars, but may get fired for trying something radically new. At least for the next decade the *jimusho* structure is set, and structural inertia will keep the top *jimusho* afloat.

Notes

1. The Japanese media depend upon the *jimusho* for access to stars, and therefore writing about the more controversial parts of the *jimusho* system could result in reduced access. The end result is that these "intra-industry" topics are often not discussed in the mainstream press but relegated to tabloids.

2. The Japanese Society for Rights of Authors, Composers and Publishers (JASRAC) online copyright database can be found at http://www2.jasrac.or.jp/eJwid/.

3. Although these three public companies are some of the larger *jimusho* in Japan, they are by no means the most powerful. Being public does not exempt the companies from having to pay "tribute" to more powerful industry players. Avex, for example, gives a significant amount of publishing rights to the small private *jimusho* Burning Production.

4. *Keiretsu* is the term for these arrangements used within Japanese industry circles, but does not exactly mirror the corporate structure of Japan's other famed *keiretsu* as defined in works such as Miwa and Ramseyer (2006).

5. With no public information, the "Burning *keiretsu*" often resides in an area between myth and reality. Wikipedia Japan in the past had a long internal debate over whether or not to acknowledge the mythic "Burning *keiretsu*" in an entry. Insiders, however, do not hesitate to frame the companies around Burning as a *keiretsu*.

6. In the case of fashion brand A Bathing Ape and its sister Ura-Harajuku, they were fined in 2005 by the Japanese tax authorities for running a tax evasion scheme that used dummy orders to pay consulting companies, as reported in the 27 May 2005 issue of *Shukan Post*.

7. Although companies continued to give Burning Publishing their rights throughout the 1990s, the practice became less transparent within the pages of Oricon starting in the mid-1990s. For example, Burning is never listed as a publishing rights holder for Every Little Thing and Hamasaki Ayumi in the pages of Oricon, but these relations were revealed with the debut of JASRAC's publishing rights database in the early 2000s.

8. Even the bit roles in Japanese TV shows are usually fleshed out by junior members of the stars' agency.

9. Advertisers also have influence over which stars appear in TV shows; see Chapter 3 in this volume.

10. AG Communication can be understood to have been a member of the Burning *keiretsu* in that its former artists' publishing is currently owned by Burning Publishing. This relation, however, was not transparent to the public at the peak of AG's success in the late 1990s.

11. The larger *jimusho*, however, have an amazing track record of securing promotional deals with large firms for their brand new talent. An example would be Avex singer Iconiq, who promoted Shiseido products as part of her debut campaign. Her singles, despite widespread promotion, failed to produce serious sales.

12. See Condry's remark, "Absent any gesture of intimacy towards the artists, we are left with a kind of consumption that is above all concerned with

riding the wave of what is popular and communicating with one's friends via these items" and his quote of a record store employee saying "Only about 20 percent of [the customers] care about the music" (1999, 167, 178).

Works Cited

Adelstein, Jake. 2009. *Tokyo Vice*. New York: Pantheon Books.

Aoyagi, Hiroshi. 2005. *Islands of Eight Million Smiles: Idol Performance and Symbolic Production in Contemporary Japan*. Cambridge: Harvard University Press.

———. 2003. "Pop Idols and Gender Construction." In *Japan at the Millennium: Joining Past & Future*, edited by David W. Edgington, 144–167. Vancouver: University of British Columbia Press.

Azami Toshio. 2004. *Popyurā Ongaku wa Dare ga Tsuru no ka*. Tokyo: Keisō Shobō.

Cahoon, Keith. 2005. Interview by author. July 26.

Caves, Richard E. 2000. *Creative Industries: Contracts between Art and Commerce*. Cambridge: Harvard University Press.

Condry, Ian. 1999. "Japanese Rap Music: An Ethnography of Globalization in Popular Culture." PhD diss., Yale University.

———. 2006. *Hip-Hop Japan: Rap and the Paths of Cultural Globalization*. Durham: Duke University Press.

Dannen, Fredric. 1991. *Hit Men*. New York: Vintage Books.

De Ferranti, Hugh. 2002. "'Japanese Music' Can Be Popular." *Popular Music* 21, no. 2: 195–208.

De Launcey, Guy. 1995. "Not-so-big in Japan: Western Pop Music in the Japanese Market." *Popular Music* 14, no. 2: 203–225.

DiMaggio, Paul. 1977. "Market Structure, the Creative Process, and Popular Culture: Towards an Organizational Reinterpretation of Mass Culture Theory." *Journal of Popular Culture*: 11, no. 22: 436–452.

Fujie, Linda. 1989. "Popular Music." In *The Handbook of Japanese Popular Culture*, edited by Richard Gid Powers, Hidetoshi Kato and Bruce Stronach, 197–220. New York: Greenwood Press.

Galbraith, Patrick. 2010. "Magibon: Internet Sensation." *Metropolis*, March 11. http://metropolis.co.jp/features/upfront2/q-a/magibon/ (accessed 2 April 2010).

Herd, Judith Ann. 1984. "Trends and Taste in Japanese Popular Music: A Case-Study of the 1982 Yamaha World Popular Music Festival." *Popular Music* 4: 75–96.

Hirsch, Paul M. 1972. "Processing Fads and Fashions: An Organization-Set Analysis of Cultural Industry Systems." *American Journal of Sociology* 77, no. 4: 639–659.

Kaplan, David E. and Alec Dubro. 2003. *Yakuza: Japan's Criminal Underworld*. Berkeley: University of California Press.

Kawabata, Shigeru. 1991. "The Japanese Record Industry." *Popular Music* 10, no. 3: 327–345.

Kimura, Atsuko. 1991. "Japanese Corporations and Popular Music." *Popular Music* 10, no. 3: 317–326.

Kitagawa, Junko. 1991. "Some Aspects of Japanese Popular Music." *Popular Music* 10, no. 3: 305–315.

McClure, Steve. 2001. "Teen Idol's 'Disappearance' Spotlights Japanese Practice." *Billboard*, December 8.

McNeill, David and Jake Adelstein. 2008. "Yakuza Wars." *Japan Focus*, September 29. http://www.japanfocus.org/site/view/2911 (accessed 2 April 2009).

Miwa, Yoshiro and J. Mark Ramseyer. 2006. *The Fable of the Keiretsu*. Chicago: The University of Chicago Press.

Oricon Nenkan. 2005. Tokyo: Oricon Entertainment, Inc.

Peterson, Richard A. 1994. "Culture Studies Through the Production Perspective: Progress and Prospects." In *The Sociology of Culture: Emerging Theoretical Perspectives*, edited by Diana Crane, 163–189. Cambridge: Blackwell, 1994.

Poole, Robert Michael. 2010. "Erika Sawajiri: Inside the Head of Japan's Outspoken Star." *CNNGo*, September 19. http://www.cnngo.com/tokyo/life/erika-sawajiri-548777 (accessed 21 September 2011).

Suzuki Tomohiko. 2005. "Enka Kōgyō, V Cinema, Burning Hidan Jiken.... Geinōkai ni Tsukimatou 'Kuroi Kōsai' no Uwasa o Kenshō suru!" In *Jitsuroku! Heisei Nihon Tabū Taizen*, edited by Ichinomiya Mitsunari, Benjamin Fulford, and Terasawa Yū, 50–60. Tokyo: Takarajimasha.

Ugaya Hiromichi. 2005. *J-Poppu to wa Nanika? Kyodaika suru Ongaku Sangyō*. Tokyo: Iwanami Shinsho.

Yano, Christine. 2002. *Tears of Longing: Nostalgia and the Nation in the Japanese Popular Song*. Cambridge: Harvard University Press.

2
Megaspectacle and Celebrity Transgression in Japan: The Sakai Noriko Media Scandal

Igor Prusa

Introduction

Immediately after Takasō Yūichi was arrested in central Tokyo in August 2009 for possession of illegal stimulants, his wife, the popular Japanese actress and former idol Sakai Noriko, suddenly disappeared from the city.[1] Media speculation ran rampant. An arrest warrant was issued for Sakai, based on a minute quantity of drugs found in her apartment. Six days after her disappearance, in the middle of unprecedented media frenzy, Sakai returned to Tokyo, surrendered to police and admitted to the charges against her. Following the police search and arrest that made the front page of all the national dailies, Sakai's management company, Sun Music, publicly condemned her actions, suspended sales of all products related to her, and eventually cancelled her contract (she simultaneously lost all commercial contracts). After spending a few weeks in a detention center, Sakai was indicted and released on bail. She publicly apologized during a closely scrutinized press conference, and was sentenced in November 2009 to a suspended 18-month prison term for violating the Stimulants Control Act. In the 2010 aftermath of the scandal, the fallen celebrity divorced her husband, started attending university courses (in social welfare and nursing), and wrote an autobiography titled *Shokuzai* (Atonement). According to some sources, Sakai's comeback is being planned in China and Taiwan, where she has been gaining popularity since the 1990s.

Despite the relative banality of the described events within their given contexts, Sakai's story became a national obsession—a major media spectacle and the biggest Japanese celebrity scandal in years. In August

2009, Sakai's case received three times as many hours of TV coverage as the national election that lead to a regime change in Japan; although media coverage of celebrity scandals in Japan usually lasts about a week, Sakai's case was extensively covered for months. The scandal was picked by the editors of *The Japan Times* as one of the top domestic news stories of 2009, along with the shift in political power, swine flu, and introduction of the jury system. At the time of writing, three books about the scandal have been published, and one of them (Nashimoto 2009) has even been adapted for the screen.

The main aim of this chapter is to offer critical perspectives to illuminate what shaped Sakai's (morality) tale into a mediated megaspectacle. Due to limitations of space, I only refer to the theoretical framework of scandal mediation in Japan, which I analyze elsewhere (Prusa 2010). While partly following Jean Baudrillard (1988) and Douglas Kellner (2003), I will argue that there was nothing really "scandalous" about Sakai's transgression itself. Rather, it is corporate media under capitalism that are often ferocious, cruel, immoral, and inherently scandalous in their obsession with celebrity. This in turn renders the whole capital-oriented celebrity culture to be one big "scandal," while the entertainment world occasionally reveals itself to be corrupt, inauthentic, and impure. Sakai, herself conflicted by the perceived gap between her "authentic" self and "inauthentic" image,[2] accidentally became an internal enemy and temporarily ostracized victim of the social system, caught in the discursive web of commercial media spectacularity, anti-drug policy and celebrity fetishism. While paying homage to laws and conventions, Sakai was made to serve as a scapegoat for various strategic (both commercial and political) interests in the symbolic process that regenerates the reality principle in distress and masks the very core of the scandalous system.

Socioculturally located meanings in celebrity scandal discourse

The intimacy of Japanese television culture (Holden and Ergül 2006; Lukács 2010) shapes specific ties and inherently asymmetrical relationships between fans and stars. Many observers assert a higher degree of affective involvement in audiences and identification with stars; Japanese stars tend to publicly position themselves as fans' servants rather than superstars (Yano 2004), and Japanese fans (through active public support and becoming "surrogates" for stars) tend to conceive themselves as participants rather than mere observers of celebrity

discourse (West 2006). Given this, problems of authenticity, conflation, and distinction between image and reality may arise, impacting
on how celebrity scandals are approached. In Japan, a prescribed form
of celebrity conscience is required. Celebrities, "social phenomena"
within "social practices," are symbolic commodities with unstable values and carriers of information that stimulate consumption. They are
assigned significant cultural authority connected with huge symbolic
influence, but simultaneously tend to be approached as public property
with certain obligations, duties, and socially created values that are ide-
ologically designated as "virtues." Moreover, this public is defined in
national terms, thus turning these obligations and values into "national
virtues." It is not easy to determine whether Japanese society naturally leans towards consuming scandals and enjoying gossip (i.e., the
notion of "gossip society"), or whether this desire is simply always
already inculcated by the Japanese tabloid machinery that feeds audiences what it believes they crave.[3] In any case, the media in Japan can
and often do put celebrities' careers on hold (if not ruining them completely) by turning audiences with the way scandals are presented and
framed.

Symbolic transgression and expectancy violation

The transgression and disapproval of Sakai Noriko occurred simultaneously on two levels: legal and symbolic. Within the legal frame,
prosecutors, police, and the court criminalized Sakai's actions by indict-
ing and sentencing her, but, more importantly for initiating a spectacle,
the media—operating within the symbolic frame—mediated her transgression and triggered public discussion. The same media that colluded
to fabricate, maintain, and profit from Sakai's celebrity image now
caught her violating what Daniel J. Boorstin (1992, 51) calls "the laws
of social illusions." Since they could not reintegrate her transgression
into any comfortable worldview, they were "allowed" to construct what
Kellner (2003) refers to as a "megaspectacle."[4]

The expectancy violation theory asserts that, when certain social
actors (and above all those who appear frequently in the media) violate our expectations, we tend to evaluate them far more harshly than
other people who might be doing exactly the same thing (Hinton 2000).
Despite entertainment management companies' expectations that the
private lives of their stars will not be in serious moral contradiction to
their public images, subtle discrepancies (like the gaps that occur when
sliding between different registers of reality and fiction on various TV

programs) are actually essential for stardom (deCordova 1991; Lukács 2010). In processes of both "making" and "breaking" a star, the basic narratological pattern is initial uncertainty advancing towards climactic certainty, and the elementary unit is "knowledge." The news in general makes use of our inherent desire for knowledge (i.e., decoding moments and disclosing concealments), whereas tabloids go as far as combining the general search for knowledge about on- and off-screen discontinuities with the search for knowledge as a practical imposition on life itself (i.e., "we *must* know"). Stardom is necessarily structured by this concealment–revelation discourse.

However, the discrepancy in Sakai's case was far from subtle: she fatally offended her constructed "remarkability" and sparked tremendous expectancy violations on multiple levels. First, Sakai, known by the nickname *Noripii*, debuted as a "cute young idol" (*seijunha aidoru*) and eventually became a "national idol" (*kokumin-teki aidoru*) embodying certain virtues. She was unspoiled, virginal, and pure, becoming a role model for many girls. During this initial idolization process, Sakai, with her innocent girl-next-door image, was molded into "Japan's little sister" (West 2006, 178). She even introduced her own speech style (*Noripii-go*), which was widely emulated. A decade later, based on new circumstances (i.e., marriage, childbirth, aging) and due to her management company's strategy, her pure image was transformed into "mother idol" (*mamadoru*), still unspoiled but not virginal anymore. She adjusted to live as a symbolic reincarnation of the "good wife, wise mother" (*ryōsai kenbo*) ideology, thus serving as a role model for many women within the Japanese framework of socially and culturally defined femininity.[5] Contrary to other grown-up sweet-divas such as Matsuda Seiko, Nakamori Akina, or Miyazawa Rie, Sakai was throughout her career never involved in a big scandal—an element that contributed to the massive expectancy violation. Finally, throughout her acting career she played certain types and characters that made the gap between the "real self" uncovered in the scandal (drug addict running from the law) and past "reel selves" even more earthshaking. Apart from many mother roles, perhaps the most significant ones in terms of expectancy violation were the gentle character who is eventually diagnosed with leukemia in the TV series *Hitotsu Yane no Shita* (1993, 1997), the deaf and mute orphan in the TV series *Hoshi no Kinka* (1995),[6] and the leading role in a film (2009) to promote the new jury system in Japan.[7]

While observing and judging the (in)coherence between the star and her non-star self, the Japanese media both retrospectively and concurrently monitored the gap between the signs that Sakai was "giving and giving off" (Goffman 1959), and went on alert each time certain signs appeared to be outside what Roland Barthes calls the proper "circuit of signification" (quoted in Langer 1998, 59). The media organized a narrative of pursuing the "truth," which started with the general assumption that "something is wrong and we will find out what it is" (Altheide 2002, 49). Roughly at that point in time the narrative became what Kellner (2003, 100) calls the "media-mediated spectacle": the media itself became part of the story, with both mainstream and tabloid journalists following the traces left by Sakai after her flight from Tokyo, occupying the press conferences and infiltrating the courtroom during trial proceedings.[8] In this and other similar cases there is a sort of ironic dialectic "for its own sake" at work: the media "make" a celebrity (i.e., create the "unreal" social illusion) just to "unmake" him/her (i.e., negatively re-examine and rediscover "realness"). Similarly, the media make audiences feel worried, surprised, afraid, and outraged just to make them feel safe again (agitation followed by pacification).

The narrative background

In high-profile scandal cases, in Japan and elsewhere, media create an intertextual universe of information (numbers, facts, observations, images, sounds) that are mediated on multiple discursive levels (mainstream media, tabloids, everyday gossip). Our perceptions of a star and scandal are based on the sum total of all our mediated experiences. Further, due to the fact that Sakai was a fully fledged member of what John Langer (1998) describes as the powerless cultural elite, the media already had plenty of sensitive material on hand (mostly from past tabloid investigations) and was able to piece fragments together immediately into an impressive, "telegenic," narratological body of knowledge. Also, due to the overall *zeitgeist*, Sakai's mass-mediated (a)morality tale fitted neatly into general cultural prescriptions ("drugs are evil") and particular problem frames ("celebrity crime"). Thus Sakai's use of drugs, itself just the tip of the iceberg, came to be considered the boiling point of the 2009 super-scandal series in the Japanese entertainment world (most notably Suzuki Shigeru, Kusanagi Tsuyoshi, and Oshio Manabu).

Sakai's disappearance from the scene in order to avoid a drug test might have caused such an outcry because it gave rise to real "action." Sakai's initial uncooperative and unpredictable nature greatly contributed to the agenda of uncertainty and speculation. Along with the police that attempted to locate Sakai and searched for clues to her whereabouts, the media, performing "cultural police" work, raised speculations and ethical questions, compiled and analyzed detailed maps of her escape route, and immersed themselves in a serious in-depth investigation.

The narrative development and "search for truth"

Scandals are in principle never born but always "given." In Sakai's case, it was the arrest of her husband that accidentally triggered the scandal narrative by initiating disequilibrium. This scandal was initially not based on gossip or leaked by a whistleblower to some tabloid (as is usually the case), but came in the form of hard news reporting, grounded by certain confirmed facts, and therefore having immediate nationwide impact. Only afterwards did associations and speculations (in the form of "soft news" reporting) emerge, though these were still only precursors of the real spectacle.

After setting the initial discursive agenda of confusion and uncertainty (proclaiming that the situation is "out of control" and Sakai's family, fans, and agency are concerned for her safety, all the while securing great audience ratings), the media proceeded to set the sleaze agenda. The protagonist was now associated with concrete images representing transgression and crime, and the key term of the narrative, "stimulants" (*kakuseizai*), was constantly repeated to create firm symbolic linkages. Sakai's husband, Takasō Yūichi (framed as a bogus pro-surfer, spoiled slacker), took on the role of the "main villain," serving as a potential target for Sakai's confused fans' negative projection. The media frame of the main character, Sakai, was in flux. She was initially rendered as a "tragic" figure, generating feelings of sympathy. However, in a very short time her disappearance was recognized as "contemptible," and her acts were reframed as irresponsible and antisocial. The media tended to reveal and emphasize only negative aspects while critically re-examining the transgressor's past: the gossip stories surrounding Sakai were "backlighted" by failure and the pitfalls of success and the entertainment industry.[9]

Simultaneously, Sakai's celebrity/social status began to shift. "Organic intellectuals," public figures, and (in Japan not surprisingly) her fellow celebrities felt that powerful words were needed. Among many others, the producer Itō Terry, veteran singer Wada Akiko, major entertainment reporter Nashimoto Masaru, and then Chief Cabinet Secretary Kawamura Takeo vehemently condemned Sakai and refused to accept her as a worthy celebrity. (The occasional person-in-the-street interviews, themselves obviously under the spell of the spiral of silence, further reinforced the impression of a unified collective subjectivity and public opinion.) These self-appointed (informal) agents of social order were simultaneously reaffirming their own positions within the entertainment industry and purifying the symbolic elements that underlined the corruptness and inauthenticity of that world. The transgressor was temporarily "muted," or only allowed to "say the right thing" during scripted performances, for example in the courtroom and at press conferences.

Sakai's fan base, however, did not always share the mainstream point of view. Many fans in Japan and China were loud in their support of Sakai, condemning the arrest itself. Moreover, many individuals urged the police to let them volunteer to take her place in the detention center; supporters gathered in front of the police station, screaming "*Noripii!*" and greeting their idol after her release with a banner that read, "Congratulations" (*omedetō*). One fan (Kanbara Masami), at the end of August, even demanded the immediate release of Sakai from the Tokyo Wangan detention center under the threat of a firebomb attack.

Somewhat parasitizing on the instinctive human pleasure derived from the misfortunes of others, the media degrade and humiliate (not only) celebrities, and Sakai was no exception. The media even retrospectively reframed objects, events, and actions related to Sakai in a negative way. Past interviews were "re-examined" and doubted in terms of trustworthiness. Sakai's body tattoos did not mean anything prior to the scandal, but now they were regarded as symbolic referents of "crime" and signifiers of incoherence between the star and her non-star self. Similarly, Sakai's interest in clubbing, and her DJ activities, were closely associated with drug culture. Captions in news broadcasts were inserted to indicate preferred readings. The media also employed linguistic devices, which are central to the construction of frames. For example, the suffix attached to Sakai's name underwent a spectacular "round trip" during the scandal: "Ms Sakai" (*-san*) or "actress" (*-joyū*) became in turn "suspect" (*-yōgisha*), "defendant" (*-hikoku*), "former defendant" (*-moto hikoku*), "former actress" (*-moto joyū*) and once again reached the initial neutral status of "Ms Sakai" (*-san*). In addition, the nickname *Noripii*, which always connoted familiarity and intimacy, was temporarily dismissed or mentioned somewhat sarcastically. While combining visual and linguistic frames and anchorages, the media often represented and superseded the audience by utilizing the personal pronoun "we" (*watashitachi* or *wareware*). The media spoke on behalf of the nation when they uttered laments such as, "This behavior of the suspect Sakai

Noriko is so far apart from how we used to know her," or, "Where on earth did the pure idol, as we knew her, go?" (Nashimoto 2009, 75).

The morality tale and hegemony in action

Determined by their logic and format, the print media simultaneously proceeded with the scandal coverage on two levels: the dailies were rather focused on synchronic analysis of the latest events related to Sakai's case (investigation results, trial proceedings, press conferences), whereas the tabloids were more often engaged in diachronic analysis of Sakai's past. The latter usually prevailed, simply because there were not always any new major developments, but the media were still determined to focus on Sakai. Besides, now representing both agents of social control and sources for institutionalized crime news, police/detectives updated the main narrative by leaking to the media private information that they gained while interrogating the detained celebrity (Sakai 2010, 53). Since "infotainment" in Japan and elsewhere merges news/journalism and entertainment/business (enabling, among other things, the national news media to transmit tabloid investigative reports), the final output was informed by both synchronic and diachronic aspects, and crystallized into a morality tale that conflated structural factors (Sakai's transgression was more or less caused by her celebrity/family lifestyle) and personal failure.

It should be also be noted that Sakai's transgression occurred in a "drugophobic" country (to borrow Thomas Szasz's term) that cooperates with prosecutors, police, and media in setting the agenda of a moral system that designates people who take the "wrong" drugs as "addicts." At the same time, illegal drugs are and always have been widespread in the Japanese entertainment industry, with plenty of celebrities past and present involved in drug-related scandals.[10] As is usually the case in drug-related scandals, the excessive media coverage inserts the event into more or less closely related problem frames, determining the kind of discourse that will follow (i.e., illegal drug use as an issue of "public health," "criminal justice," "celebrity crime," or "foreign crime"). Many Japanese celebrities involved in drug scandals claim that they bought them from foreigners (Takasō and Sakai's personal dealer was allegedly of Iranian descent). Apart from other "issues" arbitrarily linked to the Sakai scandal, the case triggered mediated debate on foreign crime, eventually reinforcing the stereotype of foreigners selling drugs in central Tokyo. The most widely circulated Japanese daily even linked the issue of foreigners staying illegally in Japan, via a Korean illegal immigrant who was also tried for possession of stimulants concurrently with Sakai (*Yomiuri Shinbun* 2009). As usual, the media and police were reactionary and superficial in focusing on easy-to-target individuals, while avoiding the well-known taboo of Japanese organized crime (*yakuza*), which is deeply involved in the drug business and outsources its activities to foreigners.

As well as trying to connect the particular case with larger issues, the Japanese media simultaneously focused national attention on absurd minutiae. By putting on display anything related in any way to Sakai, the tabloids and TV news programs managed to give the emptiness an appealing variety. Typically exhaustive was the media's inquiry into transformations of Sakai's appearance (how and why did the length and color of her hair change, how do the color and style of her clothes reflect the nature of a given public event). There was also a "prison discourse" (how many meals is she receiving a day in the detention center, what does her prison toilet look like?). The information also usually displayed the (Barthesian) feature of the "surprise of quantity": the media were obsessed with recording and providing the audience with accurate numerical data, often transforming trivia into seemingly important news (the police found 0.008 grams of stimulants in Sakai's apartment, her escape route was 481 kilometers long).

More importantly, certain minutiae may have contributed to the hegemonic strengthening of (or awareness of) the electronic panopticon. While reporting exactly what Sakai was buying (the nation was informed that she purchased underwear, cosmetics, and instant noodles prior to her flight), how much money she withdrew and where she was and had been, there was an implicit but clear message being sent to the public: everybody who lives in the media-saturated postmodern symbolic environment ruled by the "discourse of fear" (Altheide 2002) is permanently monitored. Personal data is processed and stored in databases for future reference. Furthermore, since mediated displays of deviance and its punishment serve to reinforce social norms, the media as self-appointed agents of social control are legitimately making use of these databases to publicly shame, persecute, and stigmatize anybody who happens to defy given conventions.

Sakai's transgression was not grounded in deliberate subversion of the status quo, nor was she struggling to disrupt or transform the "artistic" field of process, where J-pop has maintained its hegemonic position since the 1990s. However, Sakai did virtually defy both cultural conventions and legislative rules, and not punishing her "adequately" would represent an actual threat to the integrity of the system.

Orchestrated patterns of repentance: the press conference

One important feature of media societies is that the public is fascinated by the trials and tribulations of celebrities (including various depictions of them being degraded, humiliated, and persecuted), while the media in turn focus on such representations (Kellner 2003). The real climax and spectacle of the Sakai scandal came in the form of a press conference attended by the transgressor herself. The staged pseudo-event, which took place immediately after Sakai's release on bail in September 2009, attracted phenomenal attention (43.3 percent of the national viewing audience in Japan), caused a traffic jam around the conference venue, and was called "a moment of history" (Nashimoto 2009, 14). Distinct from previous public appearances during the scandal (leaving or entering the detention center or courtroom), the press conference placed Sakai front and center, providing audiences with observable physiological evidence of her suffering. This sort of emotional public apology is, as Nick Smith writes, "sadistic" (Smith 2008, 104). In the spirit of what Smith calls "reform and redress," the sobbing Sakai repeatedly demonstrated her commitment never to use drugs again, promising to resist temptation while skillfully conflating apologies for causing "inconvenience" (*meiwaku*) with expressions of gratitude. During the ten-minute ritual, witnessed by 500 rabid reporters, the media recorded 22 large teardrops rolling down Sakai's cheeks, though their authenticity was doubted (cf., Nashimoto 2009). In this and other similar cases, media commentators (sometimes joined by "expert" panelists) do not impartially report the event, but rather passionately judge it, focusing on every detail of the performance (the degree of sorrow and guilt expressed by sobbing, blushing, sweating and shaking, frequency and duration of bows, physical appearance including makeup and clothing, word choice and usage, etc.). It is a standard obsession of Japanese media covering such events to somewhat "playfully" attempt to discover what has been carelessly violated or, more importantly, deliberately concealed for the sake of the performance (e.g., Sakai's "problematic" tattoos were again a topic of discussion, since they were concealed with foundation for the press conference). Apart from moralizing etiquette, the media more often try to discredit the "realness" of the apology by attacking the very essence of performing. Here is the paradox: the media expect the transgressor to perform the repentant role during the conference, making use of all the devices at hand (including waterproof makeup to increase the visibility of tears), but at the same time criticizes the skillfully delivered dramatic act (Sakai's tears only prove that she is an experienced actress).

The media observed, analyzed, and finally judged Sakai's performed "coherence of front" (Goffman 1959), her readiness to feel guilty, and the degree of her moral transformation (i.e., the honesty and seriousness of the "conforming self" as opposed to the lies and cynicism of the "rebellious self"). At any rate, caught in the coerced act of apology, the former actress was required and expected to perform that she was not performing, while the audience was more or less kept aware that the only mysterious aspect of this theater was that there really was no mystery.

The aftermath: purification, destigmatization, and reintegration

A sufficiently "painful" apology postulates, "I will never do it again" rather than just "I am sorry," and is ideally followed by moral reconciliation (Smith 2008). This has to be an act of both humility and humiliation. At the aforementioned apologetic press conference, Sakai already started the process, which was meant to publicly dissociate her management company (and celebrities they contract) and sponsors from her stigmatized image, but also to restore her reputation and lay the groundwork for a possible future comeback. As the first step, Sakai was transported immediately after the press conference to the Tokyo Medical University Hospital to undergo drug rehabilitation.[11] Later, during her trial, Sakai was asked how she planned to "return to society" (implying that she was virtually ostracized and outside the social realm), and, although her contract had been cancelled, it was her former management company's director, Aizawa Masahisa, who laid out the process: the former singer and actress announced that she would enter Sōzō Gakuen University in Gunma prefecture and study welfare in order to become a social worker.[12]

Meanwhile, Sakai proceeded with her own purification. She had already given up her luxury condominium in Tokyo,[13] but she also decided to "sacrifice" her marriage to further disassociate herself from drugs (divorced in July 2010), and devoted herself to anti-drug campaigning based on her own experiences. The "manifest" of her endeavor (along with well-known facts about her life and dull elaborations of her autocue answers from press conferences and trial proceedings) was published as the autobiographical text *Shokuzai* (Atonement) (Sakai 2010). This publication can also be understood as the final stage of her purification, concluding the previous orchestrated events of her "positive expectancy violation": Sakai aimed, under experienced supervision, to recursively violate expectations of a convicted drug user, and attempted to close the scandal narrative by re-establishing representational equilibrium.

The stigma of her "deviance" will gradually vanish, although perhaps not altogether, since the scandal entered into the realms of both social memory and popular culture (due mostly to the film adaptation). Needless to say, Sakai's potential comeback will be the result of a variety of economic, political, and societal pressures. It is very likely that her purified image, no matter how radically reshaped and geographically relocated, will soon find its way back onto TV screens and magazine covers.[14] Indeed, in some ways Sakai never left the entertainment world, though she did shift from "good" to "bad" roles, all the while generating high audience ratings and profits for corporate media.

Conclusion: contradictory effects of transgressive media

While gaining legitimation as the defender of fundamental moral values and simultaneously maximizing profits, the media often construct and mediate social controversies and transgressions. These mediations in principle serve as tools of pacification and social integration, and may reinforce public definitions of morality. Nonetheless, they also may have contradictory effects, paradoxically delegitimizing the social system (Kellner 2003, 117). Sakai's transgression was indeed presented as "scandalous," but it seems to me that at the center of the scandal were the Japanese media, themselves entering the mode of transgression on many levels—excessive, sensational coverage out of proportion with the events, and multiple violations of norms of privacy and decency. This scandal illustrates that in contemporary Japan mainstream journalism is being irrecoverably supplanted by tabloid journalism. This is characterized by an aggressive shift away from covering important social issues to gossipy infotainment and celebrity triviality. More importantly, the effects of the Sakai megaspectacle were received in opposing ways. The mainstream media not only failed to put the case into proper context, but also did not analyze why the use, manufacture, and distribution of drugs is bad. The impact is alarming: the Japanese Broadcasting Ethics and Program Improvement Organization (BPO) announced in early November 2009 that the overheated coverage of Sakai's case actually aroused interest in drugs among Japanese youth.[15] It also aroused interest in Sakai's music: though her label, Victor Entertainment, responded to the scandal by withdrawing her music from circulation, after the scandal her single "Aoi Usagi" from 1995 was for a brief time in the fall of 2009 the best-selling song in the iTunes Store in Japan.

Even after the legal action against Sakai was formally concluded, partly due to various media sources that were simultaneously working within different frames, overall frame conflicts hinder any final resolution. More importantly, the symbolic "struggle" for meaning also still continues at the level of audience reception. No matter how firmly the media set the agenda and framed the events, there will always be a quantitative discrepancy between the people who knew about the scandal and those who actually believed it. Despite all the efforts of the Japanese cultural and political hegemony, Sakai did gain some sympathy for both her "conforming self" and "rebellious self." Regarding the former, the key moment was Sakai's decision to give herself up to police and face the court, which may in turn transform her into a "good person" again. Regarding the latter group (and seen from the psychoanalytical perspective), Sakai demonstrated and projected the irrational "mass-id" (i.e., the desire to go beyond the limits of "normality," to transgress and revolt) and temporarily bypassed the collective super-ego (civilization and rules of the everyday). Her "great" transgression might have fed into desires for escape, distracting the audience in a cathartic way from the frustrations and pressures of everyday life.

Notes

1. Born in 1971 and known by the nickname *Noripii*, Sakai Noriko was an idol who appeared in TV dramas, advertisements, popular entertainment programs and magazines. Signed to a minor management company called Sun Music, Sakai rose to fame in the 1980s after releasing her debut single a few days before her 16th birthday. Sakai belongs to the "Golden Age of Idols" in Japan, along with other sweet-girl divas such as Matsuda Seiko and Nakamori Akina, establishing a female singer/actress celebrity that builds on previous markers of distinction and differentiation within the "*kawaii*" (cute) system of that period. In the1990s, when young, good-looking singers were striving to become artists instead of idols, and right after she got married and gave birth to her son, Sun Music transformed Sakai's original good girl image to that of the good mother. In the meantime, she appeared in anti-drug campaigns (1993) and released a song called "Aoi Usagi" (Blue Rabbit) in 1995, considered her only real smash hit. While maintaining her image throughout the beginning of the new millennium, Sakai was also actively engaged in some significant international and domestic public events, including the Japan–China sports–culture exchange event (2007) and the promotional campaign for Japan's new jury system (2009). For a more detailed biography, and an in-depth description of the scandal, see Nashimoto (2009) or Sakai (2010).

2. The stressful internal conflict was grounded in the gap between professional image and private self. Sakai initially found this dual nature of her persona "stunning," but later it became the main reason for her physical and mental exhaustion (Sakai 2010). Linking these obstacles with drug use, Philip Brasor (2009) ironically but aptly remarks that, if someone like Sakai wants to cope with an image (agency-constructed, advertiser-sponsored) that has nothing to do with reality, one would really "have to be stoned to think you could get away with it forever."
3. Evidence suggests the latter. For example, the enormous crowd waiting for Sakai's trial on 26 October 2009 did not reflect public interest. According to media reports, there were 6,615 people waiting in the rain to possibly get one of the 20 public gallery seats at the Tokyo District Court. However, apart from hardcore fans (who even spent the night in a park), the majority of people waiting in line were actually part-time "extras" hired by media companies in order to increase their chances of getting into the courtroom. (The author received this information from Esaki Hajime, a researcher at The University of Tokyo who conducted a poll at the venue.) In short, the media reported on a crowd and excitement of its own making.
4. Kellner's notion of megaspectacle is based on Guy Debord (1994), whose theorizing about commodity spectacles in capitalist societies as illusory representations of life was also partly validated by Sakai's case. In spectacles, "see-worthiness" (the politics or aesthetics of phenomena that are promoted) gives way to "seen-ness" (the representational aspects of the phenomena, organization of appearances), whereby people acquire (falsified) knowledge of certain general aspects of life.
5. The ideology and discourse of popular music in Japan actually did come to play an important role in the construction and maintenance of femininity in the 1990s. See Stevenson (2008).
6. The impact of this story was intensified by the fact that Sakai herself was abandoned at birth.
7. The immediate countermeasure to dissociate these representations from Sakai-the-transgressor was the cancellation of a rerun of *Hoshi no Kinka* just a few days after her arrest in August. This was followed by the withdrawal of about 190,000 copies of the jury system promotional video from regional courtrooms and legal offices nationwide.
8. It was not only the presence of cameras and journalists that modeled the scandal flow: the very medium of TV itself contributed to the main narrative twist. Sakai surrendered to police after she saw the breaking news about herself on television (Sakai 2010).
9. The tabloids, followed by TV and other media commentators, came to the conclusion that the key to explaining Sakai's drug "addiction" was her past, absurdly claiming that her "real essence" had been misunderstood since the very beginning of her career (cf., Nashimoto 2009, 85). In order to support their assumptions, the tabloids went as far as to interview Sakai's former classmates.
10. For detailed accounts, see West (2006) and Nashimoto (2009).
11. During this transfer, somewhat resembling the notorious 1995 freeway flight of O.J. Simpson, her car was followed by a TV helicopter (another essential

signifier of any megaspectacle), so that this whole pseudo-event *par excellence* could be transmitted live from a bird's-eye view.

12. Perhaps both the stigma of transgression and her "remarkability" made Sakai initially proceed only with the e-learning course so as not to "disrupt" campus life. In the meantime, Sakai actually appeared in a video promoting the university in question.

13. This, however, was due to her having to pay various damages and losing her annual income of ¥100 million ($1.25 million).

14. The preparations for her comeback, although initially not on Japanese soil, seem to have been underway since the end of 2009. Sakai's field of study, social welfare and nursing, is linked with musical therapeutics. There seems to be a real chance for her in China, where methods of healing through relaxing music are common, and Sakai the actress is said to be well-known among people in their 30s and 40s.

15. Moreover, reporting on drug scandals such as Sakai's does not influence the popularity of drugs in general. On the one hand, the Japanese media rarely specified the drug in question—usually using abstract terms such as "stimulants" (*kakuseizai*) or "chemical substances" (*yakubutsu*). On the other hand, they actually often provided detailed instructions on how to use it. There exists some evidence of deviance amplification at work. Although state authorities and social commentators were throughout the scandal emphasizing the drug crisis in Japan, police data show that arrests for stimulants have been declining since a peak in 1984, dropping to less than half in 2008 (Kyodo News 2009). Over half of the people recently arrested for alleged possession of stimulants were gang members (Fukue 2009).

Works Cited

Altheide, David. 2002. *Creating Fear: News and the Construction of Crisis*. New York: Walter de Gruyter, Inc.

Baudrillard, Jean. 1988. *Jean Baudrillard: Selected Writings*, edited by Mark Poster. Stanford: University of Stanford Press.

Boorstin, Daniel J. 1992. *The Image: A Guide to Pseudo-events in America*. New York: Vintage Books.

Brasor, Philip. 2009. "Sakai's Twin Personalities Were Falling Apart Before Bust." *The Japan Times Online*, August 16. http://www.japantimes.co.jp/text/fd20090816pb.html (accessed 23 January 2011).

Debord, Guy. 1994. *The Society of the Spectacle*. New York: Zone Books.

deCordova, Richard. 1991. "The Emergence of the Star System in America." In *Stardom: Industry of Desire*, edited by Christine Gledhill, 17–29. London: Routledge.

Fukue, Natsuko. 2009. "Sakai Bust Puts Spotlight on Narcotics Evil." *Japan Times Online*, August 13. http://www.japantimes.co.jp/text/nn20090813a2.html (accessed 23 January 2011).

Goffman, Erving. 1959. *The Presentation of Self in Everyday Life*. New York: Doubleday Anchor.

Hinton, Perry R. 2000. *Stereotypes, Cognition and Culture*. East Sussex: Psychology Press.

Holden, T.J.M. and Hakan Ergül. 2006. "Japan's Televisual Discourses. Infotainment, Intimacy, and the Construction of a Collective Uchi." In *Medi@sia: Global Media/tion in and out of Context*, edited by T.J.M. Holden and Timothy J. Scrase, 105–127. London: Routledge.

Kellner, Douglas. 2003. *Media Spectacle*. London: Routledge.

Kyodo News. 2009. "Arrest, Drugs Shatter Sakai's 'pure' Image." *Japan Times Online*, August 9. http://www.japantimes.co.jp/text/nn20090809a2.html (accessed 23 January 2011).

Langer, John. 1998. *Tabloid Television: Popular Journalism and the 'Other News.'* London: Routledge.

Lukács, Gabriella. 2010. *Scripted Affects, Branded Selves: Television, Subjectivity, and Capitalism in 1990s Japan*. Durham: Duke University Press.

Nashimoto Masaru. 2009. *Sakai Noriko: Kakusareta Sugao: "Aoi Usagi" wa Naze Mayotta no ka?* Tokyo: Iisuto Puresu.

Prusa, Igor. 2010. "Scandals and Their Mediations: Theorizing the Case of Japan." *Electronic Journal of Contemporary Japanese Studies* March 10. http://www.japanesestudies.org.uk/discussionpapers/2010/Prusa.html (accessed 2 April 2010).

Sakai Noriko. 2010. *Shokuzai*. Tokyo: Asahi Shinbun Shuppan.

Smith, Nick. 2008. *I Was Wrong: The Meanings of Apologies*. New York: Cambridge University Press.

Stevenson, Carolyn. 2008. *Japanese Popular Music: Culture, Authenticity and Power*. London: Routledge.

West, Mark D. 2006. *Secrets, Sex, and Spectacle: The Rules of Scandal in Japan and the United States*. Chicago: The University of Chicago Press.

Yano, Christine R. 2004. "Letters from the Heart: Negotiating Fan-Star Relationships in Japanese Popular Music." In *Fanning the Flames: Fans and Consumer Culture in Contemporary Japan*, edited by William W. Kelly, 41–58. New York: SUNY Press.

Yomiuri Shinbun. 2009. "Fuhō Taizai no Ue Tōbō 1-nen-chō no Onna Kakuseizaihan." November 3.

3
Through a Looking Glass Darkly: Television Advertising, Idols, and the Making of Fan Audiences

Jason G. Karlin

The five members of the popular idol group Arashi are playing Nintendo Wii on television. The "boys," who are mostly in their late 20s, sit across a coffee table on a couch flanked by two chairs.[1] In a scene that looks like any living room, they hold Wii controllers while looking back at you through the television as they play. In an instant, your television set has become a looking glass into the living room of these idols, collapsing the distance between the space of their living room and yours. Though a TV commercial,[2] the voyeuristic experience of watching them play conveys intimacy and familiarity.

Later, on a segment of one of their television shows, they are again playing Wii—this time, before a studio audience of young women who cheer and applaud as they play.[3] Like a game show, the program's guest—a popular actress—plays against the members of Arashi in mock competition. The focus, as well as the camera, never leaves Arashi: they are the stars. Their spontaneous reactions and easy familiarity are as evident here as in the commercial. Though nearly concurrent, the broadcasting of the commercial and the show converges in the land-scape of Japanese commercial television. Evaluated solely in terms of their iconography, the commercial and the show are nearly identical. Which one is the commercial? And which is the content?

For the Japanese television audience, the basic codes for under-standing the medium demand a lesser distinction between advertising and programming content. To describe Japanese television as program-ming content broken up by brief advertising spots misrepresents the way that the content is highly promotional. Indeed, when viewed through the lens of celebrity, the whole of Japanese television is branded

Figure 3.1 Which one is the commercial? The members of the idol group Arashi play Nintendo Wii in a television commercial (top) and on one of their regular variety shows (bottom).

entertainment. The celebrities who are featured in the programming appear throughout Japanese television commercials, and their celebrity images feature prominently in advertising, such that the intertextuality between the programming and advertisement is predicated on the exchange value of the celebrity performer (*tarento*). Just as the broadcast programs are intertextually implicated in the logic of commercial advertising, the television commercials function as advertisements for products as well as vehicles for the promotion of the idols they feature.

This chapter examines the role of idols and celebrities in reproducing the television audience as fans. With the declining effectiveness of television advertising in recent years, advertisers have found that they need to reach fan audiences who are more receptive to their message. Advertising to fan audiences involves translating the sense of identification and intimacy with the celebrity to action that promotes brand loyalty. As the targets of the affective economics of advertising, Japan's largely female audience are watching (and even recording) television commercials today as fans texts that feature their favorite idols. Through an analysis of fan communication on women's blogs and other social media, this chapter will assess the effectiveness of celebrity in mobilizing fan audiences to purchase goods and services in Japan.

Television advertising in Japan

Celebrities and idols are ubiquitous in Japanese television advertising. Kaji Yusuke (2001, 106), who worked in advertising for more than 40 years, describes Japanese television advertising as suffering from a "dependence on celebrity" (*yūmei tarento izonshō*). Though there has been no recent systematic content analysis of celebrities in contemporary Japanese advertising, about 50–70 percent of all Japanese commercials feature a celebrity.[4] Generally, the production of commercials in Japan begins with a discussion of what celebrity is to be featured (Kawashima 2006, 398). In casting a celebrity to feature in an ad, marketing managers consider the status of the celebrity that their budget can afford and the image of the celebrity that they hope to project for their brand. A one-year contract for a top idol or celebrity generally runs at ¥50–100 million ($625,000–1.25 million) (Takano 2009, 50). When the idea for a commercial is pitched, the initial presentation is prepared with a particular *tarento* in mind.[5] The production of a commercial is not cast so much as it is designed around a certain celebrity.

The celebrities who appear in advertisements for particular goods and services are referred to in the Japanese media as "image characters" (*imēji kyarakutā*). This pseudo-Anglicism was coined around the mid-1980s as idols were increasingly being employed to improve the image of brands. While television performers had been used to market products in the past, the earliest image characters during the early 1980s were female idols and models who signed contracts to represent a particular cosmetic or fashion brand. Instead of being hired for a single one-time advertisement, image characters signed contracts with a brand to appear in cross-media advertising campaigns. During the period of the bubble economy in Japan, the idol system reached its maturity at the same moment when brand consciousness defined consumer practices. Identity was becoming defined in terms of fashions, particularly the brands one consumed (Hara 2006, 184). Through new technologies of marketing and advertising, idols and celebrities became closely connected to the structure of commodity culture, as consumers looked to idols as models for fashioning their identity. Since idols had become postmodern performers whose image cultivated media spectacle and self-referentiality for the purpose of commercial promotion, they were a natural fit for advertisers hoping to connect their products to the image of popular performers.

For advertisers, an image character is intended to create an association between the star image of the performer and the brand. Compared with not using celebrities, one study suggests that commercials featuring celebrities in Japan have about a 20 percent greater degree of brand recognition (Takano 2009, 52). Unlike celebrities in the US, Japanese *tarento* do not endorse products. Instead, image characters lend their star image to the brand, but without implying any direct endorsement or testimonial. The Japanese celebrity is not making any claims or representations for the product. Indeed, in most commercials, the celebrity never even mentions the name of the product. In general, image characters are chosen because their star image complements the brand's image through their mutual association. Those celebrities with the most commercial endorsements are deemed "commercial (CM) queens" or "kings" in Japan's media culture. In 2009, the male celebrity with the highest commercial exposure was Kimura Takuya, an idol affiliated with the talent agency Johnny & Associates (hereafter Johnny's). He appeared in 68 different commercials for 15 separate companies, and his commercials were broadcast more than 12,000 times (CM Sōgō Kenkyūjo 2010, 118–119). In Japan's celebrity culture, becoming the image character for a mobile phone company is considered the pinnacle of prestige and success. The three largest mobile phone providers in Japan (i.e., KDDI/au, SoftBank, and NTT Docomo) account for more than half of all broadcast television commercials (CM Sōgō Kenkyūjo 2011). Each has contracts with the most popular idols or television performers. Celebrity advertising contracts in Japan specify that the performer will not engage in any activities or behavior that might damage the "company's image" (*kigyō imēji*) (*Shūkan Josei* 1988, 180–182). Many companies place restrictions on their image characters to ensure that they do not appear in dramas or programs that are sponsored by their competitors (Tanimura 2005, 27–33). In addition, they may insist with the networks that their image character appears in the drama they sponsor. In this way, brands cultivate and benefit from their exclusive association with celebrity. The term "image character," then, expresses a relationship between an advertiser and a celebrity that seeks to transfer the associative values and identification of the celebrity performer to the brand.

Compared with television advertising in the US, Japanese commercials tend to rely more on emotion and image rather than product comparisons, testimonials, or persuasion. The emotional or soft-sell focus of Japanese advertising, with its seeming disregard for the product, has been much discussed in the literature on Japanese advertising.[6] This emphasis on emotion and image can be understood to be a function of the intertextuality of celebrity image. Commercials in Japan featuring celebrity are interpreted by the audience in relation to other programs, news, and gossip about the celebrity. With this emphasis on the audience's preexisting cultural knowledge of the celebrity, most television commercials are short. In the 1950s and 1960s, the average commercial's length was one minute. As the years passed, and with the shift from program sponsorship to spot advertising, the average length shrank to 15 seconds. Today, the vast majority of advertisements in Japan run in 15-second increments.[7] The shorter length of ads favors celebrities as quick devices for raising awareness of new products.

In addition to their short length, commercials in Japan generally are broadcast for a short period of time and are rapidly replaced with new ones. In fiscal year 2009, Tokyo's five commercial broadcast networks aired 17,519 different commercials a total of 1.45 million times (CM Sōgō Kenkyūjo 2010). Japanese companies are constantly launching new products each year (*shin-hatsubai*). While the brands, and often the products themselves, remain mostly the same, they are launched with great fanfare and spectacle. The conventional wisdom is that the emphasis on market-share as opposed to profitability is what drives this tendency. Nonetheless, the result is immense advertising and promotional campaigns, often employing idols and celebrities, to raise awareness of the new product. About ¥1.7 trillion ($21.3 billion) is spent on television advertising in Japan every year (Dentsu 2011).[8] The industries that spend the most on advertising, and thus rely most greatly on idols and celebrities to promote their products, are mobile phone providers, food, cosmetics, toiletries, and home electronic appliances.

With 89 percent of all people tuning in every day, television is undoubtedly the most important daily form of mass media in Japan (NHK Hōsō Bunka Kenkyūjo 2011, 8).[9] The average Japanese watches television for 3.6 hours each day (Ibid., 9).[10] Daily viewership has recently started to decline among some younger viewers as the Internet and other forms of digital media compete for the audience's attention. In terms of gender, women in Japan generally watch more television than men. In fact, women in their 40s watch about one hour more of television daily. Even among young Japanese (16–24 years of age), women watch about 23 percent more television every day (Broadcasting Ethics & Program Improvement Organization (BPO) 2009, 6). For advertisers, celebrities attract attention, particularly for female viewers who are steeped in a media culture saturated with tabloids and celebrity gossip.

For television advertisers, the female audience is the primary target, particularly due to their important role as consumers in Japanese society. Compared with other approaches to getting the viewer's attention, the emphasis on celebrity performers in Japanese television advertising is largely a function of its female audience. While explicit sexual images are one means of getting the audience's attention, sexually themed ads are rare in Japan. For most popular commercials in Japan, due to the large female audience, sex appeal is almost never a significant factor.[11] As studies have shown in the US, women on average exhibit a marked negative reaction to explicit sexual content in advertising.[12] In Japanese marketing studies of the effectiveness of advertising, the term "likability" (*kōkando*) is used to assess the audience's favorable response to a commercial.[13] Among the criteria for measuring the likability of a commercial, the celebrity performer is considered to be the most important factor for audiences in Japan (Sekine 2002, 13).

Intimacy and identification in television advertising

The medium of television is defined by its intimacy within the space of the home. The context of consumption of television means that public figures, such as idols, are as near as family members. Television creates intimacy through both the quantity and the quality of images of public figures. As John Langer (2006, 187) writes about television personalities, "Each repeated appearance, even though it may not elicit 'personal data'... nonetheless tends to build what is perceived to be a knowable and known 'television self.'" Through close-up shots, it allows greater intimacy, which has only increased with the introduction of high-definition digital broadcasting. The clarity and detail of digital television creates a lifelike representation that permits a close reading of every facial detail. The number of hours of daily television viewing in Japan impresses celebrities into the routine of everyday life, making them as recognizable and familiar as anyone in real life.

The celebrities who are most effective in appealing to the female audience include not only male idols, but also female entertainers whose image resonates positively with women. Aimed at young, working women (office ladies, OL) seeking to relieve the stress of a long workday, a 2010 commercial for Glico ice cream features actress Ayase Haruka lounging on a couch at home eating an ice cream cone.[14] Dressed as if she had just taken a bath at the end of a long hot day, the camera cuts between medium shots of Ayase's outstretched body on the couch and close-ups of her consuming the product. Ayase is a popular actress, who has appeared in many successful Japanese TV dramas. Like many performers, she often appears in several commercials for different products at the same time. In this commercial, Ayase's on-screen and off-screen personas are conflated by depicting her in what appears to be a private moment in a setting that is meant to resemble her home. As one news article writing about the new commercial observed, "Is this what Ayase Haruka is like during her off-time?" (*Sankei News* 2010). In the medium shots, the camera is positioned in front of the couch in the place where one would expect the television (Figure 3.2). As a result, the audience's television becomes a window into Ayase's living room. The television collapses the distance between the audience and the star, such that private and public merge to form a space defined

Figure 3.2   Ayase Haruka "at home" enjoying ice cream after a long workday in this 2010 Ezaki Glico commercial.

entirely by the celebrity. In short, the intimacy of television constructs the experience of celebrity as a form of mediated voyeurism.

Due to the importance of achieving affective identification in a short 15-second commercial, the production aims to naturalize the effect of spontaneity and authenticity. Generally, commercials are edited from a large amount of footage shot over several hours. The *tarento* is expected to perform certain scenes in the commercial according to the close instruction of the commercial's director. To maximize audience affect, the director provides detailed instruction about how to hold the product, what pose to strike, and which facial expression or gesture is desirable. In many cases, a scene or shot lasting no more than a few seconds is the result of as many as 20–30 takes.[15]

In Japanese television advertising, the celebrity not only gets attention, but also arouses desire. The celebrity functions to get the attention of the viewer, and advertising relies then on the role of the star to shape audience behavior through the desire to become closer to or more like the star. Through imitation and modeling, which express the desire for greater proximity and connection, "stars serve a normative function to the extent that they are often read as role models" (Stacey 1991, 151). In many Japanese commercials, the image of the idol or celebrity becomes a source of pleasure achieved through identification. The successful 15-second commercial is structured so as to achieve affective identification. Often, such moments of affective identification appear in the final few seconds or final frames of the commercial (before the product's name or logo), and are encapsulated in a particular image, look, or gesture. These moments of affective identification cannot appear to be artificial or performed, but trade on the revelation of the true, authentic self of the star. The intertextual pleasure that arises from these moments may be productive of desire, thereby initiating new fans into a process of deeper identification and intimacy with the idol or celebrity.

The motherly gaze of the female fan

Married with school-aged children, many female fans—particularly fans of Johnny's idols—describe how they often look upon their idols with a "motherly" gaze, which derives pleasure from supporting and encouraging the success of their idol. As mothers, often stressed with the responsibilities of caring for their children and husbands, it is difficult to understand why female fans would not seek instead to escape from the burdens of domesticity. Instead, their lives defined entirely in terms of their roles as mother and wife, they fantasize about their lost youth and project feelings of maternal satisfaction towards male idols.[16] Matsumoto Mika (2007, 48–58), who authored a book about her experience as a Johnny's *otaku*, described the role of the female Johnny's fan as being like a "virtual mom" (*bācharu okan*). Since Johnny's fans self-identify in term of which idol they support (*tantō*), fans will often talk about their idol as if he were a member of their own family. They will boast about his achievements and take pride in his successes. The image of Johnny's idols, especially Arashi, is not of indolent and delinquent boys, but, rather, hard-working and successful models of male adolescence. They represent youth, energy and the promise of success in a way that resonates strongly in the post-bubble period of economic stagnation and sexual lethargy.

Johnny's idols are produced with the aim of achieving affective identification by appealing to the female audience's desire to support and to foster the success of their favorite male idol. The system of Johnny's idol production begins by recruiting young boys, and teaching them to sing and dance. After completing training, they will become members of "Johnny's Jr," who serve mostly as back dancers for the older groups in the Johnny's family. The members of Johnny's Jr are mostly boys in their early teens who have not yet debuted in a group or as a solo act. In many cases, the groups will perform (often in theater productions) before they have their official debut. Once a new group has officially debuted, it will regularly release singles and receive the full support of its production company in promoting its success. Throughout this process, the production company is closely attuned to the fan community and organizes those members of Johnny's Jr into groups based on the support of the idol's fans. This system creates a relationship of sponsorship and support at an early stage with the fan community that fosters a sense of propriety that is akin to a mother's rearing of her own child.

Johnny's fans reject the view of the artificial or produced star image, and strongly insist upon knowing the true self of the idol. As one Johnny's fan states in a magazine interview, "they don't have two sides" (*uraomote ga nai*) (*Grazia* 2011, 210–211). These fans reject the distinction between the front stage and backstage behavior, and if they encounter scandalous information, such as the gossip reported in weekly magazines, they dismiss it as lies fabricated to generate tabloid sales. Much like a parent, Johnny's fans defend the actions of their idol and take pleasure in knowing his true self.

For the fan, pleasure derives not merely from familiarity, but rather a close attunement to the idol that permits these moments of identification to resonate deeply with meaning that is not easily recognizable by non-fans who lack a similar close sense of mediated intimacy.

Similar to what is called *moe* in Japan's *otaku* subculture,[17] affective identification here is a system written on the body or the representation of
the body that is decoded through the cultivation of familiarity and intimacy (i.e., fan knowledge). Meaning is entirely contingent upon the fan
or viewer, who interprets the star's performance by reading deep meanings into each image, look, or gesture. For the fan with a high degree
of familiarity and intimacy, each expression or movement in the idol's
performance serves as a mass of references to a database of fan knowledge about both the idol's on-screen and off-screen lives. This database
of fan knowledge is highly intertextual, drawing on a level of familiarity
with idols and celebrities that is only possible through the autopoietic
machine of the Japanese media system.

The use of idols in television commercials exploits the audience's
over-familiarity, verging on preoccupation, with the stars whose actions,
gestures, and expressions are perceived as deeply meaningful opportunities for pleasure through the repetition of viewing and consumption.
Japanese audiences are so completely absorbed in the news, gossip, and
minutiae of celebrities, particularly idols, that every nuance of their
expression, smile, or gesture becomes an opportunity for pleasure and
affective identification. Indeed, the lives of idols and celebrities have
become so closely and intuitively identifiable by today's media-saturated
audience that the emotional needs of the viewer are mirrored in the
smallest nuances of the idol's behavior.

This form of distinctly feminine identificatory pleasure is gendered
differently from the male experience of visual pleasure. For women,
this desire perhaps is closely related to psychoanalyst D.W. Winnicott's
notion of "primary maternal preoccupation," wherein the mother is
able to closely identify with the emotional state of her infant child.
According to Winnicott (1987), the mother relates to her infant child
through non-verbal communication of feeling states. Her intimate identification with the infant allows the mother to read and adapt to her
baby's needs. The "good-enough mother" is attentive to the smallest gesture of her child in a gaze that is empathic and nurturing. This motherly
gaze structures female desire toward male idols, looking at their bodies
not sexually, but in the way of a mother who is attentive to her child.
Unlike men, whose pleasure is scopophilic, the female gaze is asexual.
Just as the mother communicates with her pre-linguistic infant child
by reading deep meaning into every smile, gesture, or expression, the
female fan achieves a deep bond and sense of intimacy with the idol.

If the male gaze scrutinizes the female body through a controlling
or disavowing look, the maternal gaze seeks "mutuality" (Winnicott
1992). The experience of mutuality describes a form of emotional or

affective attunement between the mother and infant. According to psychologist Daniel Stern (1998, 142), "affective attunement is the performance of behaviors that express the quality of feeling of a shared affect state." For example, in the mother's reading of the infant's feeling state, she will express a similar response generated through an experience of intersubjective sharing of affect. If the infant expresses surprise, the mother will echo the infant's reaction through a shared feeling state, such as raising the pitch of her voice or widening her eyes. Affect attunement is not mere imitation of the infant's behavior, but rather an expression of the sharing of affective states. On television shows and other performances featuring male idols, the assembled audience of Japanese female fans often will collectively call out *"kawaii"* (cute) in response to an idol's anecdote, action, or expression. For the audience, these verbalizations arise unconsciously as expressions of emotional states, similar to saying "ouch" when experiencing something painful. In these idol–fan relations, like the infant–mother relationship, the expressions and emotional states of the idol are intersubjectively exchanged and communicated through the fan's close identification with the idol.

For the non-fan, this form of unconscious communication and pleasure is difficult to understand. In Japanese blog postings by fans of Arashi, many comment that watching their reactions and expressions "makes them feel good" (*genki ga deru*) or is "comforting" (*iyasareru*).[18] The source of pleasure here cannot be shared with others who lack the degree of intimacy and knowledge that is specific to fan audiences. Japanese fans often watch their idol's commercials, as well as concerts and television shows, repeatedly or in a focused or attuned way that derives pleasure from reading the emotional states and knowing the true self. For example, fans will often favorably comment online about how a particular commercial expressed the "true" (e.g., *su no Arashi*) side of the idol.[19] Seeing glimpses of the authentic idol in these commercials is contingent upon the familiarity and knowledge to differentiate between the true and the unscripted self. Often fan comments focus closely on reading the idol's facial expressions or interpreting the intertextual meanings of the idol's performance.

A female blogger, who describes herself as an OL (female office worker), posts about a new Japan Airlines (JAL) commercial featuring Arashi:[20]

In the morning, I suddenly first saw the commercial. Without even thinking, I accessed JAL's website . . . As it played several times,

I thought "Wow!" But then, sure enough, my eyes go to Matsumoto Jun. For me, the opening of the 30-second version just hit the spot. I watched it several times in slow motion!...The silhouette of Matsumoto Jun sitting with his legs crossed—it just totally hits the spot.[21]

On another blog, a housewife living in Yamaguchi prefecture writes:

I saw the JAL commercial yesterday, but I wasn't able to record it. Today, I was able to get it. I watched the JAL commercial frame-by-frame (*koma okuri*). I noticed that when they jump only [Ōno] Satoshi's face appears to be jumping really hard and on the airplane [Matsumoto] Jun seems to be looking in a different direction from the rest.[22]

For these fans, pleasure arises from the articulation of the body. Their heightened reading of the signifiers within the commercial are not concerned with the meaning of language, but rather the way in which pleasure is materialized and embodied.[23]

The appearance of idols in commercials generates fan activity on blogs, fan websites, and social media. Fans also will obligingly visit the websites of companies to watch the commercials and peruse the other content about the company's image character. Moreover, evidence from blog postings indicates that fans do purchase products to support their idols. Among female fans, in particular, for whom the idol is perceived in a maternal way, buying the products they endorse is a way to help foster and nurture the success of their idol's career. Female fans take pleasure in the success of their idols, boasting about them almost as if they were their own children. In general, fans are highly invested in promoting the success of the object of their affection, but for female fans, especially in Japan, fandom goes further in reproducing gender identities and naturalizing women's roles as nurturing and supportive.

Indeed, much fan communication on blogs and social media revolves around sharing and discussing media with other fans, who understand the nuanced meanings that are exclusive to the fan community. The ineffable quality of affective identification with idols or celebrities compels the fan to want to convey the experience to others. Moreover, since it is a system written on the body, it is visual in the way that a look or expression can convey multitudinous and complex meanings. With the spread of online video sharing, including commercials, these experiences can now be collected, shared, and discussed by fans in a way that was not possible earlier. Unable to watch all the commercials that feature their favorite idols on TV, fans now have recourse to online websites where they can repeatedly and carefully watch and study their idols. The pleasure arising from this over-familiarity is thus closely linked to the spectacle of celebrity, but operates with special attention to the fan, as a committed consumer with whom the message of the commercial is expected to resonate strongly.

The affective economics of celebrity

In recent years, marketing analysts in Japan have expressed concern about the growing ineffectiveness of television advertising (Tominaga 2011). The diversity of media platforms, particularly mobile phones and the Internet, have reduced the relative effectiveness of TV commercials; and blogs and social media have replaced traditional forms of media in sharing trusted information about products. In the past, TV advertising was generally considered to be the most effective means of raising the awareness of new products. Overwhelmed with information, audiences risk becoming cynical and indifferent to media messages. Today, with media convergence, consumers are more active in their relationship with media companies. As Henry Jenkins (2008, 18) notes, "[media] convergence requires media companies to rethink old assumptions about what it means to consume media." With media convergence, there is not only a change in technology but also a shift in the relationship between the producer and the consumer. The consumers under the old media system were predictable and stationary, but new consumers are seeking greater interaction and connection.

Audiences in Japan, however, are not abandoning television, but rather developing a digital lifestyle of new social practices. Television viewers are increasingly multitasking or watching while engaged in other activities (*nagara shichō*), particularly while accessing the Internet on PCs or mobile devices (Mizushima 2008, 152). The key search terms for popular search engines, and the trending topics on social network sites and blogs in Japan often closely reflect what is on TV. As a result, television and the Internet are not evolving as mutually exclusive domains, but, rather, have become closely intertwined. Hirai Tomohisa (2009), who has written about the relationship between television and the Internet, argues that net users in Japan are not only familiar with television, but are always conscious of television in what they discuss, share, and consume online. Television is becoming an increasingly interactive and participatory experience. The practice of using the Internet (including mobile devices) while watching television has become much more common in everyday life. Even after broadcasts, viewers in Japan will share and watch television video content online at websites, such as GyaO!, YouTube, and Nico Nico Douga.[24] Many more are recording shows that feature their favorite celebrities.

The recording of television for either concentrated or repeated viewing outside the original broadcast schedule is closely linked to fan consumer practices that are organized around particular celebrity performers. Nearly 73 percent of all Japanese households in 2010 have a digital recording device (Economic and Social Research Institute (ESRI) 2011). In 2004, as digital hard drive recorders were becoming popular, the National Association of Commercial Broadcasters in Japan (Minpōren) became concerned about viewers skipping commercials (Ogino 2004, 4). A study in 2005 estimated that viewers skipping commercials was costing the industry ¥54 billion ($675 million) in revenue (Nomura Sōgō Kenkyūjo 2005). Among Japanese youth (16–24 years of age), during regular broadcasts only 31.6 percent skip the commercials by either changing the channel or engaging in other activities; however, when watching recorded programming (i.e., digital video recorders (DVRs)), 93.8 percent either skip or cut the commercials (BPO 2009, 17). The shows that are recorded the most tend to be dramas, since viewers report that they do not want to miss an episode (Ibid., 92–97).[25] Among young viewers in particular, when they record other kinds of programming, such as variety or music shows, the guest or featured celebrity is the primary consideration in deciding to record these genres of television. Even for commercials, most fast forward through commercials while watching recorded television, but will watch commercials if they are interesting, such as when they feature idols or celebrities they like (Ibid., 97).

The renewed focus on idols and celebrities in Japanese television and advertising in recent years is related to the growing importance of marketing to fans through what Henry Jenkins (2008, 61) calls "affective economics." Loyal viewers of certain cult television shows in the US are emerging in marketing discourse as valuable consumers due to their strong emotional investment in certain shows. Fans, as loyal viewers, tend to watch television in a more focused and deliberate manner, typically at the time of the original broadcast. In addition, they are more receptive to targeted advertising, due to the affective power of the fan's identification with the show. By building a long-term relationship with a fan community, advertisers and marketers are branding their products as a means of establishing consumer loyalty. Jenkins describes affective economics as a solution to the crisis in American broadcasting resulting from changes in media technology that have allowed consumers greater control over the flow of media into their homes. Japanese advertisers, as in the US, have also been appealing to fan audiences, but by focusing on the audience's affective identification with idols and celebrities. Affective economics, through celebrity, has been an important means of organizing the media market and producing the fan audience in Japan since at least the 1980s. In Japan, celebrity advertising provides assurances that a product marketed to its fan audience will be watched. Moreover, fans are more receptive and likely to seek further involvement with the product as a way of showing support for their favorite celebrity performer. By building a prolonged relationship with a particular idol or celebrity through a process of branding, the consumer/fan seeks greater engagement across media platforms, including the watching of commercials.

On 27 January 2011, KDDI's campaign for its new Android smartphones epitomized the new interactive approach of television advertising that appeals to and reproduces the fan audience. Marshaling Arashi as its image character, KDDI released 60 commercials on the same day. This campaign set records for the most commercials for the same product broadcast within 24 hours, the most aired within eight hours on one commercial network, and the most broadcast for the same product during one 30-minute program.[26] In addition, KDDI made all 60 commercials available to view on its company webpage.[27] Fans of the group were overwhelmed and delighted by the wealth of new content. Many recorded the commercials off live television in order to keep permanent copies of this valuable content. On some blogs, fans even kept a journal to log each of the commercials they collected.[28] In the quantity of commercials that were produced and the frequency with which they were broadcast and discussed in the wider media, this advertising campaign demonstrates the affective economics of celebrity in contemporary Japan.

Conclusion

Consumption, as fan activity, allows an imagined relationship of proximity to the star. The branding of products around celebrity image seeks to conflate the desire for the idol with the desire for the product. This dimension of celebrity in branding and product marketing relates to the emergence of a media-saturated culture that allows constant mediated access to celebrity, through video, blogs, corporate websites, and social networking. The initial broadcasting of a commercial featuring a prominent idol or celebrity results in an explosion of fan activity. On fan websites, social media and blogs, fans post announcements or reactions about the new commercial that briefly increase the visibility of the product in online media; and blogs, tweets, and other social media often direct fans to company websites or online videos of the commercials.[29] Many companies that employ celebrities in their commercials have targeted fan audiences by creating webpages, where the product's image character is prominently featured in a variety of media content. These corporate websites typically feature commercials, a video of the making of the commercial, downloadable PC wallpaper, and—in some cases—web games, all featuring the celebrity. In one case, a website featuring Arashi member Ninomiya Kazunari even included a recipe for the dish he eats in the commercial, so that fans can experience intimacy and connection with the star by consuming the same foods (Nisshin Corp. 2011). Ultimately, this appeal to fans drives traffic to the company's webpage and further solidifies brand identification with the celebrity.

For many fans, the appeal of these corporate websites is that they feature not only videos of the broadcast commercials, including extended versions, but also videos about the making of the commercials. These videos purport to show the unscripted performer behind the scenes, but are highly edited for promotional purposes. For fans seeking greater intimacy, including fan knowledge and authority, the watching of these videos offers the pleasure of glimpsing the unscripted or "true" self of the celebrity. Though described as videos about the making of the commercial, they are completely structured around the role of the celebrity in the making of the commercial. Typically, these videos conclude with the celebrity answering questions about the making of the commercial as well as the product. The proliferation of information about the making of the cultural commodity, such as the extras included on DVDs, appeals to active audiences who seek greater fan knowledge through what Jonathan Gray (2010) calls "media paratexts." Television commercials, then, are as much celebrity media texts as any other show, movie, or song produced by the idol.

How effective are Japanese celebrities in mobilizing fan audiences to purchase the goods and services they endorse? When idol group Arashi was selected to appear in commercials for Nintendo's "Wii Party" video game, fans were influential in promoting its sales. Although the game did not go on sale until 8 July 2010, commercials featuring Arashi first appeared online at the company's webpage from 24 June. According to sales rankings for video games at Amazon Japan, the game was ranked as low as #68 on the day before the commercials debuted. By the end of the day on 24 June, after the commercials had appeared online, the game had climbed to #15 in sales rankings. On 30 June, when the commercials were first broadcast nationally on television, the game climbed even higher to #5 on the sales chart.[30] The day the game went on sale, it was ranked #2. The close correlation between increases in pre-orders for the game and the appearance of these commercials, first online and then broadcast, suggests that idols and celebrity are highly effective at generating attention and mobilizing fans to consume.

Idols and celebrity are central to the Japanese media's strategy of attracting audiences. With its huge newspaper circulations, large number of magazines, and daily television viewing, Japan has a high degree of media saturation. For the mass media, celebrities offer the means of organizing the audience to consume the products of their sponsors. However, with the rise of digital communications, media fragmentation has further intensified competition for the audience's attention, which is now more divided around various taste communities than a single national audience. In the past, television advertising provided the means of assembling the national audience in order to raise awareness of products. Today, advertising must harness the energy of fan audiences to consume and promote its products.

Idols are the means for connecting producers to consumers in a media landscape where our identities are increasingly being defined by what we consume. With celebrities functioning as intertextual commodities, the mass media in Japan is now producing promotional discourse across cultural forms and different media outlets.[31] In responding to the promotional discourse of idols, the audience adopts the subject position of its celebrity-saturated media culture. As a result, the audience is being hailed or interpellated as fans rather than consumers. The media's construction of the subjectivity of the audience as fans (e.g., Johnny's *otaku*) has sought to erode the critical function of rational consumers by seeking affective identification. Today, the mass media, supported by the decline in critical theory, has contributed to a belief system that has naturalized the ideology of fandom. The whole of the consuming public is interpellated as fans for the purpose of marketing goods and services. As a result, the expression of being a fan or *otaku* of a particular idol or media product has become a normative means of constituting identity in contemporary Japan.

Notes

1. As Nagaike argues in Chapter 4 of this volume, the appeal of Johnny's idols for female fans is closely linked to their representation of youth (*shōnen*).
2. Nintendo Corporation, "Wii Party, Ribingu Pāti-hen" advertisement, aired 8 July 2010.
3. *Himitsu no Arashi-chan*, Tokyo Broadcasting System Television (TBS), originally aired 9 September 2010.
4. Kilburn (1998) estimates that 70 percent of commercials feature celebrities; Praet (2001) found 47.62 percent, based on a limited content analysis of 100 commercials; and Kaji (2001, 110) puts the number at 99 percent, but this is likely an exaggeration.
5. Unlike in the US and the UK, Japan's advertising agencies manage both creative production and media buying. Because media-buying power is consolidated around two large "full-service" advertising agencies, Dentsu and Hakuhodo, clients primarily pay commissions for advertisement placement in the media rather than creative. Without independent creative agencies competing for clients, the production of television ads is driven more by marketing managers than by agency creative.
6. See Suzuki (2009); Lin and Salwen (1995); Tanaka (1993); Di Benedetto et al. (1992); and Kishii (1988).
7. According to Nielsen Company (2011), 53 percent of all commercials in the US are 30 seconds long. As in Japan, commercials in the US have recently become shorter.
8. Though television advertising revenue has somewhat declined in recent years, it appears to have stabilized in 2010. However, television has not experienced anything comparable to the declines in advertising revenue for newspapers and magazines.
9. In general, the amount of television viewing tends to increase with age, and is greatest among housewives and the unemployed.
10. This figure is the average of the viewing time on weekdays and weekends. According to Nielsen Company (2011), the average US viewer watches four hours and 57 minutes of television every day.
11. In fact, for the commercial that surveyed the highest in terms of sexiness in a 2009 study, sexiness was one of the least positively evaluated criteria of the commercial's likability. The "sexiness" of the commercial was noted only 30 times in the survey, as opposed to 490 who noted its "performers," and 360 who noted its "music," as contributing to its "likability." See CM Sōgō Kenkyūjo (2010, 22–230).
12. See Sengupta and Dahl (2008); Dahl *et al.* (2009); and LaTour and Henthorne (2003).
13. In measuring the likability of a particular commercial in marketing surveys, such criteria as "performer," "humor," "sexiness," "catch copy," "music," "story," and "cuteness," among others, are evaluated.
14. Ezaki Glico, "Giant Cone, Amaesasete-ne-hen" advertisement, aired 15 March 2010.
15. This paragraph's data are based on the author's own observations and analysis of more than 50 videos about the making of commercials from various corporate websites and promotional DVDs.

16. Immersed in a culture wherein educating children and household management are encouraged through state policies and social expectations, women not only identify with, but also find subjectivity (i.e., social meaning) through, their roles as mothers in Japanese society. However, to compensate for their lack of power within a patriarchal system, women acquire subjectivity through their support of male idols. Through this identification, male idols give to the woman the phallus she lacks within the male economy of power in contemporary Japan.

17. *Moe*, as an expression of pleasure, originates from the representation of the body in anime and manga. For a discussion of the meaning of *moe*, see Galbraith (2009).

18. For example, "CM no Arashi," entry posted 11 May 2011, *Arashi Daisuki* ♪, http://25074838.at.webry.info/201105/article_10.html (accessed 7 June 2011); and "Au no CM de Iyasareru," entry posted 16 April 2011, *Minna, Arashi de Iin ja nai-ka?* http://ameblo.jp/arsstsc/entry-10863245372.html (accessed 26 April 2011).

19. For example, "Arashi-san no Shin-CM: Nintendo 3DS," entry posted 8 January 2011, *Arashi to tomo ni, Shufu no Hitorigoto*, http://blogs.yahoo.co.jp/tomoimada8/34850208.html (accessed 20 January 2011).

20. Japan Airlines Company, "Arashi, JAL de Natsu-tabi" advertisement, aired 11 June 2011. This commercial uses one of Arashi's songs in the background to promote the release of their new album.

21. "CM JAL: Nanige nai Shigusa ga Tsubo-sugiru," entry posted 12 June 2011, *My Favorite Thing*, http://kazumie830.blog97.fc2.com/blog-entry-2198.html (accessed 17 June 2011).

22. "CM & Katarogu," entry posted on 13 June 2011, *Plus One*, http://plusonearashi.jugem.jp/?eid=661 (accessed 18 June 2011).

23. Like what Roland Barthes (1975) describes as the *jouissance* of reading the body, it is outside culture.

24. Typically, Japan's commercial broadcasters will request the removal of videos for copyright violation, but often not before they have been shared and viewed online by thousands of viewers.

25. The lack of video on demand alternatives for watching missed episodes of serial television accounts for the greater tendency to record dramas.

26. AKB48 topped Arashi's record for the most commercials broadcast within 24 hours on 28 February 2012, when 90 solo members' commercials for Asahi's "Wonda Coffee Morning Shot" were broadcast for the same product within 24 hours.

27. See KDDI, "Android au," http://android-au.jp/ (accessed 1 February 2011).

28. See, for example, "Android au CM Jibunteki Memo," *Arashi to Jikan to Kūkan to...*, entry posted 29 January 2011, http://dream-alive-satoshi.cocolog-nifty.com/blog/2011/01/android-au-71df.html (accessed 10 February 2011).

29. Arashi member Ninomiya Kazunari appeared in a new commercial by Nisshin OilliO Group, Ltd. that aired 4 June 2011 ("Ninomiya Kazunari x 'Shokubutsu no Chikara'-hen"). Based on data collected from "Google Insights for Search," this commercial resulted in a 1,100 percent increase in searches for the product's name. In addition, a search on Yahoo! Japan Blogs, which is but a small percentage of all blogs hosted in Japan, recorded 45 separate mentions of the name of the product on the date the commercial

was first aired. All the blog postings were from fans who were directing their readers to the commercials and other content available on the company's website.

30. Amazon Japan sales rankings were calculated based on data from the website Amaran, http://www.rankbank.net/amaran (accessed 20 July 2010).

31. P. David Marshall (2008) defines the intertextual commodity as a franchise that engages with the interactive audience or fans through its associations in other cultural forms. In Japan, the idol or celebrity operates as an intertextual commodity to link the fan audience to other products in a process of branding and the circulation of promotional discourse.

Works Cited

Barthes, Roland. 1975. *The Pleasure of the Text*, trans. Richard Miller. New York: Hill and Wang.

Broadcasting Ethics & Program Improvement Organization (BPO). 2009. " 'Digital Nētibu wa Terebi o Dō Miteiruka? Bangumi Shichō Jittai 300-nin Chōsa" Hōkokusho." http://www.bpo.gr.jp/youth/research/ (accessed 4 June 2011).

CM Sōgō Kenkyūjo. 2010. *Heisei 21-nendo CM Kōkando Hakusho*. Tokyo: Toko Kikaku Co.

CM Sōgō Kenkyūjo. 2011. " 'SoftBank 4-renpa' Shinbun Tenbō." http://www.cmdb.jp/media/newspaper/20110120_news3.html (accessed 22 July 2011).

Dahl, Darren W., Jaideep Sengupta, and Kathleen D. Vohs. 2009. "Sex in Advertising: Gender Differences and the Role of Relationship Commitment." *Journal of Consumer Research* 36, no. 2: 215–231.

Dentsu. 2011. "2010-nen Nihon no Kōkoku-hi." http://www.dentsu.co.jp/books/ad_cost/2010/index.html (accessed 27 February 2011).

Di Benedetto, C. Anthony, Mariko Tamate, and Rajan Chandran. 1992. "Developing Creative Advertising Strategy for the Japanese Marketplace." *Journal of Advertising Research* 32, no. 1: 39–48.

Economic and Social Research Institute (ESRI). 2011. *Shōhi Dōkō Chōsa* (19 April 2011). http://www.esri.cao.go.jp/jp/stat/shouhi/2011/1103shouhi.html (accessed 12 May 2011).

Galbraith, Patrick W. 2009. "Moe and the Potential of Fantasy in Post-Millennial Japan." *Electronic Journal of Contemporary Japanese Studies* 5 (October 31). http://www.japanesestudies.org.uk/articles/2009/Galbraith.html (accessed 2 April 2010).

Gray, Jonathan. 2010. *Show Sold Separately: Promos, Spoilers, and Other Media Paratexts*. New York: New York University Press.

Grazia. 2011. "Kibun wa Eien no 14-sai! Watashitachi ga Jyanīzu Saiai-na Riyū." 1 March.

Hara Hiroyuki. 2006. *Baburu Bunka-ron: Posuto-sengo to shite no 1980-nendai*. Tokyo: Keio Gijuku Daigaku Shuppankai.

Hirai Tomohisa. 2009. "Netto Yūzā wa Terebi o Dō Mitekita-no-ka?" In *Popyurā TV*, edited by Hirai Tomohisa et al., 11–77. Tokyo: Fūjinsha.

Jenkins, Henry. 2008. *Convergence Culture: Where Old and New Media Collide*. New York: New York University Press.

Kaji Yūsuke. 2001. *Kōkoku no Meisō*. Tokyo: Senden Kaigi.

92 *Systems*

Kawashima, Nobuko. 2006. "Advertising Agencies, Media and Consumer Market: The Changing Quality of TV Advertising in Japan." *Media, Culture & Society* 28, no. 3: 393–410.

Kilburn, David. 1998. "Star Power." *Adweek*, 12 January.

Kishii, Tamotsu. 1988. "Message vs. Mood: A Look at Some of the Differences Between Japanese and Western Television Commercials." *Dentsu Japan Marketing/Advertising 1987* 27: 51–57.

Langer, John. 2006. "Television's 'Personality System.'" In *The Celebrity Culture Reader*, edited by P. David Marshall, 181–195. London: Routledge.

LaTour, Michael S. and Tony L. Henthorne. 2003. "Nudity and Sexual Appeals: Understanding the Arousal Process and Advertising Response." In *Sex in Advertising*, edited by Tom Reichert and Jacqueline Lambiase, 91–106. Mahwah, NJ: Lawrence Erlbaum Associates.

Lin, Carolyn A. and Michael B. Salwen. 1995. "Product Information Strategies of American and Japanese Television Advertisements." *International Journal of Advertising* 14, no. 1: 55–64.

Marshall, P. David. 2008. "The New Intertextual Commodity." In *The New Media Book*, edited by Dan Harries, 69–81. London: BFI.

Matsumoto Mika. 2007. *Jani-ota: Onna no Kemono Michi*. Tokyo: Futabasha.

Mizushima Hisamitsu. 2008. *Terebijon Kuraishisu: Shichōritsu, Dejitaru-ka, Kōkyōken*. Tokyo: Serica Shobō.

NHK Hōsō Bunka Kenkyūjo. 2011. *2010-nen Kokumin Seikatsu Jikan Chōsa Hōkokusho*. http://www.nhk.or.jp/bunken/summary/yoron/lifetime/pdf/110223.pdf (accessed 1 June 2011).

Nielsen Company. 2011. "State of the Media: Trends in TV Viewing." http://blog.nielsen.com/nielsenwire/wp-content/uploads/2011/04/State-of-the-Media-2011-TV-Upfronts.pdf (accessed 10 June 2011).

Nisshin Corporation. 2011. "Ninomiya x 'Shokubutsu no Chikara.'" http://www.nisshin-oillio.com/ninomiya/ (accessed 21 June 2011).

Nomura Sōgō Kenkyūjo. 2005. "Kigyō no Kōkoku, Senden Shuhō wa, Masumedia kara Kobtesu Taiou no IT Medeia e." http://www.nri.co.jp/news/2005/050531.html (accessed 5 May 2011).

Ogino Shōzō. 2004. "'Burōdokyasuto' Hādodisuku to CM." *Mainichi Shinbun*. 4 December.

Praet, Carolus L. C. 2001. "Japanese Advertising, the World's Number One Celebrity Showcase? A Cross-Cultural Comparison of the Frequency of Celebrity Appearances in TV Advertising." In *The Proceedings of the 2001 Special Asia-Pacific Conference of the American Academy of Advertising*, edited by Marilyn S. Roberts and Robert L. King, 6–13. Gainesville, Florida.

Sankei News. 2010. "Ayase Haruka ni amaeraretai! Glico 'Giant Cone.'" 10 April. http://sankei.jp.msn.com/economy/news/110118/biz11011810440070-n1.htm (accessed 15 April 2010).

Sekine Tatsuo. 2002. *CM Tarento 'Kōkando' no Himitsu*. Tokyo: Tōyō Keizai Shinpōsha.

Sengupta, Jaideep and Darren W. Dahl. 2008. "Gender-Related Reactions to Gratuitous Sex Appeals in Advertising." *Journal of Consumer Psychology* 18, no. 1: 62–78.

Shūkan Josei. 1988. "Imēji Kyarakutā wa, Donna Kijun de Kimeru no ka?" 30 August.

Stacey, Jackie. 1991. "Feminine Fascinations: Forms of Identification in Star-Audience Relations." In *Stardom: Industry of Desire*, edited by Christine Gledhill. London: Routledge.

Stern, Daniel N. 1998. *The Interpersonal World of the Infant: A View from Psychoanalysis and Developmental Psychology.* London: Karnac Books.

Suzuki Midori. 2009. "Genjitsu o Tsukuri-dasu Sōchi, Imēji CM." In *Hyōgen to Media*, edited by Inoue Teruko, 89–103. Tokyo: Iwanami Shoten.

Takano Yoshiaki. 2009. *CM Kōkando No.1 da-kedo Mono ga Urenai Nazo.* Tokyo: Business-sha.

Tanaka, Hiroshi. 1993. "Branding in Japan." In *Brand Equity & Advertising: Advertising's Role in Building Strong Brands*, edited by David A. Aaker and Alexander L. Biel, 51–63. Hillsdale, NJ: Lawrence Erlbaum Associates, Inc.

Tanimura Tomoyasu. 2005. *CM-ka suru Nippon.* Tokyo: Wave Shuppan.

Tominaga Tomonobu. 2011. " 'Terebi CM ga Kikanai' Hontō no Riyū wa?" *Nikkei Trendy Net*, 11 February. http://trendy.nikkeibp.co.jp/article/column/20110208/1034429/ (accessed 11 February 2011).

Winnicott, D. W. 1987. "Communication between Infant and Mother, and Mother and Infant, Compared and Contrasted." In *Babies and Their Mothers*, edited by Claire Winnicott, Ray Shepard, and Madeleine Davis, 89–104. New York: Perseus Publishing.

———. 1992. "The Mother-Infant Experience of Mutuality." In *Psycho-Analytic Explorations*, edited by Claire Winnicott, Ray Shepard, and Madeleine Davis, 251–260. Cambridge: Harvard University Press.

Part II
Desire

4
Johnny's Idols as Icons: Female Desires to Fantasize and Consume Male Idol Images

Kazumi Nagaike

Introduction

Every year, on 31 December, many Japanese enthusiastically watch a nationally broadcast music program called *Kōhaku Uta Gassen* (The Red and White Song Battle). On this program, singers are divided into two teams (red for women and white for men), which compete against each other. The program is extremely popular, drawing 40.8 percent of the national viewing audience in 2009. Each year, who will be offered the honor of hosting the program is a matter of great public concern, covered extensively in tabloid newspapers and other popular media. In 2010, this honor was conferred on Arashi, a male idol group with five members. Since debuting in 1999, Arashi has become the most popular male idol group in Japan today, generating ¥14.4 billion ($180 million) in CD and DVD sales in 2009. The management company or "agency" (*jimusho*) behind Arashi is Johnny & Associates (hereafter Johnny's), a dominant force in the Japanese entertainment industry. Consider the success of SMAP, the Johnny's group most popular before Arashi:

> A study of Video Research ratings by *Dacapo* magazine in summer 2002 revealed that SMAP members totaled 117 percent of ratings points in a week (Johnny's members totaled 250.7 percent); in other words, in a typical week they are seen, on average, more than once by every viewer in Japan.
>
> (West 2007, 199)

What, then, are we to make of these Johnny's idols, who are sufficiently recognized to be invited to host a national TV event and have achieved top annual sales?

The success of Johnny's as a management company began with a four-member male idol group called The Johnnys, which debuted in 1962 and became a huge hit. Since then and right up to the present, Johnny's has produced a series of male idol groups that have been enormously popular, particularly among female fans. Potential idol candidates, called Johnny's Jr, are recruited in their early teens; they dedicate themselves to practicing singing, dancing and acting, eventually becoming back-up dancers for those idols who have already achieved success. After reaching a sufficient level of proficiency, they finally debut as professional Johnny's idols. Needless to say, only a very limited number of candidates, who have won various competitions, ever officially debut as Johnny's idols. If they do, they have the opportunity to appear on TV and radio programs, in films, magazines and other media, and to hold concerts in Japan and other Asian countries, where they attract hordes of female fans.

In this chapter, inspired by Daniel Herwitz's influential book *The Star as Icon*, I argue that the popularity of Johnny's idols results from the very nature of their iconic status. I hope to initiate a specific discourse concerning the iconic status of Johnny's idols, through an examination of published interviews, as well as books written by idols and their female fans. In what follows, I outline how Johnny's idols are produced for, and consumed by, female fans within a specific context of postmodern consumable narrativity. Both the production and reception of Johnny's idols need to be articulated in terms of specific imaginative narratives created by their female fans; these narratives are constructed through a psychological process that simultaneously combines distance (fans' sense of their idols' unattainability) with apparent accessibility. In order to clarify this process, I analyze issues such as the ideological placement of *shōnen* (boys) as unattainable objects of desire within the Japanese sociocultural context, the importance of "groupism" (i.e., the fact that Johnny's idols function as members of a group, not as individuals), and the creation by female fans of a variety of fantasy narratives concerning their favorite idols.

The meaning of "emptiness" for an idol

In *The Star as Icon,* Daniel Herwitz (2008) suggests a conceptual process of "producing" star icons, incorporating a detailed analysis of theoretical frameworks such as Walter Benjamin's aura theory and Andy Warhol's postmodern art works. Employing as examples a variety of iconic female figures, including Princess Diana, Grace Kelly, Marilyn

Monroe and Jacqueline Kennedy, Herwitz concludes that the existential status of these iconic female figures can be described as "empty;" in other words, they lack depth. However, this only enhances fans' ("believers") inclination to endlessly (re)create and consume individual narratives (or fantasies) concerning these icons. For example, Herwitz writes, "she [Princess Diana] exists mostly, perhaps exclusively for her public, through fiction" (Herwitz 2008, 16). Further, "her public wanted her to live in the aura of transcendent unity (the royal/film star), but also wanted her life to remain rocky, unresolved, melodramatic so they could hang on for the next installment (the TV/tabloid goddess)" (Herwitz 2008, 27). That star icons possess a certain kind of authenticity, and the potential to initiate endless personal narratives, depends on the transcendent emptiness—here, "transcendent emptiness" signifies the entire practical reality of these iconic figures, which the public/fans can never attain—to which fans are subconsciously attracted.

Herwitz also discusses such star icons in the context of postmodern consumer capitalism, and views fans' worship of these icons in terms of the very act of producing and consuming specific narratives concerning these icons. A Japanese cultural critic, Ōtsuka Eiji (2001), analyzes postmodern narrativity from a similar perspective, asserting that consumers are not only consuming commodities, but also narratives, and at the same time are interested in producing (arranging) their own narratives.[1] Frederic Jameson (1993), a Marxist critic, argues that postmodernism reflects a negative symbolic correlation between a surface multiplicity and the "death" of the subject. I do not completely agree with Jameson's harsh criticism of postmodern consumer capitalism. However, he should be credited for his analysis, showing that the act of consumption itself is enhanced by the superficial multiplicity of the subject, which can be described as "emptiness;" thus, because the subject is de-centered (emptied), various kinds of narratives (interpretations) concerning it can be duplicated endlessly. The female iconic figures that Herwitz discusses and Johnny's idols may appear incompatible at first glance. However, as I will discuss below, the particular narratives that are produced and consumed by female fans show clearly that Johnny's idols can plausibly be viewed as iconic figures.

Nakamori Akio is a well-known cultural critic believed to have coined the term *otaku*.[2] In the following passage, he provides his conceptual understanding of Japanese idols:

Idols are not necessarily good singers or actors. If we look at them closely, we realize that they are not extremely beautiful or attractive.

They are merely cute and popular. Idols are simply admired and loved by fans, for no specific or persuasive reason.

(Nakamori 2007, 14–15)

Matsumoto Mika, a comedian and self-identified fervent fan of Johnny's idols, stresses that the lack of realistic qualities in Johnny's idols enables her to imaginatively transform them as images:

Fans like me, who have reached a certain age, never desire to "date one of the Johnny's idols" or "marry one of them." All I want is just to "look at them!" My desire to see Johnny's idols is like people's desire to appreciate artistically marvelous paintings.

(Matsumoto 2007, 10)

Both Nakamori's and Matsumoto's epistemological analysis of idols is compatible with my reading of Johnny's idols, precisely because the emptiness of Johnny's idols is constructed to present a sense of transcendence and unattainability that tempts female fans to fantasize about them.

The emptiness of Johnny's idols also becomes its own form of aesthetic expression. Kimura Takuya, a member of SMAP, obliquely symbolizes this phenomenon. As one idol critic says: "Kimura Takuya has never created anything out and out. He is surrounded by creative artists, but he himself seems to be void, like the Japanese emperor" (Kikuchi 2009, 45). Taking SMAP as an example, Fabienne Darling-Wolf (2004, 358) points out that the purported lack of singing ability among Johnny's idols never calls their validity into question. After all, Johnny's idols are not marketed as singers or actors, but as "idols." Ninomiya Kazunari, a member of Arashi, has a promising acting career, as shown by his appearance in Clint Eastwood's film *Letters from Iwo Jima* (2006). However, he once described himself as "not an actor, but an idol" (Hōsen 2009, 77). As Nakamori notes, in order to understand the idol phenomenon, we must come to terms with the fact that the iconic status of idols does not depend on, and indeed can displace, talent, as both singers and actors. As Sakai Masatoshi, a music director, remarks, SMAP are qualified as "national idols" in Japan precisely because of their "second-class" status; even if they may be best in their category, they are not first-class artists (Sakai 2009, 11). There are cases where this does not hold, for example Ōno Satoshi, the leader of Arashi, who has a reputation for his singing ability. However, some are critical of precisely this quality in him: "If I must find something bad to say about his singing ability, it's that he's too good, beyond the level of idol singers" (Hara 2009, 96).

In accordance with Herwitz's thesis that any sense of depth prevents fans from producing easily consumable narratives about icons, complexity has nothing to do with the power of Johnny's idols to attract. One Arashi fan says: "[Arashi's songs] are filled with a sense of pure love. They never hint at troublesome ideas like complex self-consciousness or the kind of strong principles frequently expressed by people who call themselves 'artists' " (Kashima 2009, 22). This fan's comment clearly demonstrates the way that the emptiness (or absence of self-consciousness and principles) of Johnny's idols provides a certain aesthetic and imaginative satisfaction.

Perhaps the key to understanding the transcendent emptiness of Johnny's idols, from the (subconscious) point of view of female fans, is the collective definition of Johnny's idols. Johnny's idols seldom debut as soloists, and the few who have become famous as such all started as members of a group: SMAP (five members, but started with six), TOKIO (five), V6 (six), Arashi (five), KAT-TUN (five, but started with six), NEWS (six, but started with nine), Kanjani Eight (seven, but started with eight), and so on. Johnny's idols also seem to deliberately promote themselves as members of a group. As Yamashita Tomohisa, the most popular member of NEWS, says: "Yamashita Tomohisa exists because NEWS exists" (Ishizaka and Jr Kurabu 2008, 87). The media coverage of Johnny's idols also reflects the centrality of the group: "Members of Arashi are, after all, Arashi members, and they excel as a five-member group" (Morita 2009, 37).

This does not necessarily negate completely the individual characteristics of Johnny's idols. Members of the same group do indeed have different kinds and degrees of popularity among fans. Moreover, most fans claim to have a specific favorite idol. However, the unity of the group, rather than the individuality of each member, constructs the initial situation that subconsciously attracts female fans. These fans desire to produce diverse narratives about their favorite idols, which is stimulated by the idea that each idol is part of a group. This is shown by such imaginative narratives as "Idol A and Idol B came to blows in competing for a woman" (Matsumoto 2007, 84), or "Nakai [Masahiro] and Kimura [Takuya, both of SMAP] got into a fistfight once . . . . This incident was the start of a new relationship between them, in which they acknowledge and respect each other, without much need for conversation" (Sugino 2009a, 50).

A strong sense of individual identity can contribute a great deal to a star's charisma, which fans can easily grasp. However, in this form, individual identity does not provide much space for fans to freely "play" with their idols imaginatively, thereby displacing strong individual identities by creating a vast range of narratives about them. In this regard, from fans' point of view, the individual identity of each idol can be displaced in a positive way by interacting with other members of his group. An idol reveals different characteristics and kinds of attractiveness, depending on how he interacts with other group members in various situations, and this provides fans with material on which they can imaginatively elaborate.

In this regard, the group identity of Johnny's idols can be discussed as a specific form of cultural discourse, defined by Azuma Hiroki (2001), a Japanese philosopher and cultural critic, as "databased" fictionality. Azuma broadens the scope of postmodern Japanese narrativity in terms of the ongoing production of an endless "dialogue" with the specific data that characterizes each individual entity within the discourse. Following Azuma, we can read each Johnny's idol as a narrative "data point." Johnny Kitagawa, the founder of Johnny's, is believed to have once said that different types of boys need to be integrated together to constitute an idol group (Kosuga 2007, 62). For example, in a group with four members, the first should be the older-brother type, the second the honor-student type, the third the naughty-boy type, and the fourth the son-of-a-good-family type. Johnny's fans are clearly attracted to such amalgamations of databased characteristic stereotypes. For example, according to one Arashi fan:

> The characteristics of the five Arashi members are perfectly balanced. Ōno [Satoshi] is so pure and natural, but he has the appropriate bearing to be the leader of the group. Ninomiya [Kazunari] is, after all, an actor type.... Sakurai [Shō] is smart enough to deliver the remarks that "the public expects him to say." Matsumoto [Jun] is the princely type.
>
> (Ōya 2009, 12)

One of the sections of a book attributed to Arashi, *Arashigoto*, is titled "Arashi's Fantasy Theater" (*Arashi no mōsō gekijō*). It includes a series of hypothetical questions addressed to Arashi members and their answers. Some examples of these questions are: "What if you met with disaster and were left alone with Sakurai Shō on an uninhabited island?" and "What if Aiba [Masaki] coached you for your full-marathon trial run?" By reading stories that Arashi members tell about other members, fans can see the relationships between their favorites and other members. In this way, they discover new aspects of their favorite idols and are enabled to create new narratives about them. Thus, members contribute a variety of different elements to their group, while simultaneously enhancing the group's overall integrity; by integrating their differing personal characteristics into the group, each group member attains greater potential attractiveness. At the same time, the sense of belonging to the same "database" intertwines them with one another even more, continually replacing the wholeness of each individual idol with that of the group.

Fans' apparent enthusiasm for fictionalizing Johnny's idols as "data" also manifests their investment in consumptive "images." In particular, female fans' strong attachments to idols are enhanced by available consumptive "images" of specific idols (data about them), as well as by the generic concept of "Johnny's idols." This hypothesis is supported by statements made by Sakurai Shō. Recalling his training years as a Johnny's Jr, he confesses his dilemma at being recognized solely as part of a whole, rather than as an independent individual: "I asked myself if these people [the fans] really like Sakurai Shō or merely Sakurai Shō as a member of Johnny's Jr" (Arashi 2005, 26). Matsumoto Mika also ironically confesses that anyone spotlighted onstage and called a Johnny's idol attracts her, to some degree:

> I realized that I liked anyone who sang and danced, wearing a specific costume, and was spotlighted on stage in Johnny's productions. Even though I still get wildly excited by Johnny's idols, my enthusiasm for them, after all, is premised on the fact that they belong to Johnny & Associates.
>
> (Matsumoto 2007, 42–43)

Appropriately enough, this fan's statement shows that the term "Johnny's" is predicated on a specific image, and thus explicitly foregrounds the fact that Johnny's idols constitute an iconic commodity.

Johnny's idols as *shōnen*

A 1995 cosmetic advertisement features Kimura Takuya, one of the most famous Johnny's idols at the time, wearing red lipstick. The image was a sensation among viewers. As Matsumoto sums up her response: "Such beings [Johnny's idols] look like men, but actually they aren't!"

(Matsumoto 2007, 12). The transcendent aspects of Johnny's idols may lie precisely in their proximity to *shōnen* (boys), who in the Japanese sociocultural context project a sense of androgyny. "Androgyny" (*ryōsei guyū*) is the very term used by Yoshimoto Taka'aki, one of Japan's most established cultural critics, in his conceptual elaboration of Kimura's archetypal attractiveness (Yoshimoto 2002, 75). The literary critic Ogura Chikako also suggests that the absence of mature masculinity in Johnny's idols enhances associations with androgynous *shōnen* (Ogura 1990, 30). Kosuga Hiroshi, who wrote a book as a Johnny's insider, also points out that idealized images of *shōnen* appear to be central to the production of idols: "One of the premises of Johnny's idols is that their origins definitely derive from their *shōnen* quality.... All of the Johnny's idols start being promoted by Johnny Kitagawa when they are still actually *shōnen*" (Kosuga 2007, 132–133). Further, as one fan says, she loves Arashi "because, as *shōnen*, they don't possess many sexual connotations" (Kashima 2009, 22).

In the previous section, I proposed that fans of Johnny's idols are stimulated to produce diverse consumptive narratives concerning their favorite idols precisely because the genuine identity of these idols is unattainable to them. The female desire to fantasize/create idealized *shōnen* images of Johnny's idols also suggests a similar attempt to transform them into fictions/fantasies rather than accept their real (male) identities. Idealized *shōnen* images of Johnny's idols can thus also be read as a reflection of a subconscious female denial of the patriarchal, masculine male. As a consequence of this, female fans of Johnny's idols indirectly contribute to dismantling established Japanese gender formations.

A *shōnen* is neither a man nor a woman, but a *shōnen*. Although this word can never be conclusively defined in terms of established gender paradigms, it is specifically as *shōnen* that Johnny's idols ultimately appeal to many of their female fans. Psychoanalytic approaches tell us that within the Symbolic Order the *shōnen*, as a man-to-be, is endowed with some degree of authoritative power. However, the *shōnen's* identity cannot be considered on the same basis as that of a mature man, since the *shōnen* is merely "progressing" toward integration as a man within the Symbolic Order. Thus, he is not a woman, *shōjo* (girl), or man, but instead incorporates all of the constructive, positive elements of these differing gender identities. Thus, the ideology of *shōnen* concerns an idealized gender synthesis that apparently transcends the binary distinction between men and women. Female fans' appreciation of the *shōnen* qualities of their favorite idols ultimately reflects this ideology.[3]

One of the most frequent adjectives used in referring to Johnny's idols is *kawaii* (cute), as the following examples show: "Aiba-chan is *kawaii*. Looking at him, even I [a man] unintentionally utter the word *kawaii*" (Narima 2010, 121); "Arashi is the only idol group I like. Why? Because they're *kawaii*" (Kashima 2009, 22); "[On stage], in a children's costume, with his innocent facial expressions and cute choreography, Ninomiya was like a *shōnen*... [H]e was extremely *kawaii*" (Takeuchi 2009, 76). The word *kawaii* does not derive from the gender-specific terminology associated with *shōjo*, but instead transcends the limits of any binary discursive analysis of gender.[4] *Shōnen* identity does not exclusively depend on age; like *shōjo* identity, it can be recognized through inner, psychological qualities.[5] To be sure, *shōnen* ideology rests on irreconcilable androgyny, as demonstrated by the fact that the gender-ambiguous word *kawaii* can be applied even to Johnny's idols who are near (or over) the age of 30. The idea of Johnny's idols as *shōnen* is intimately tied to the development of *shōnen* epistemology within a specific Japanese sociocultural context and cannot be understood outside that context.

Members of Johnny's idols are thus able to maintain a youthful *shōnen* image, despite their actual age. What I would like to emphasize here is that the *shōnen* quality of Johnny's idols is constituted on the basis of their female fans' desire to fictionalize them as *shōnen*, rather than any efforts by producers to market them this way. In other words, one could argue that the potentially subversive influence of these fans (consumers) is based on the fact that they take the initiative, forcing producers to construct specific images of Johnny's idols that better suit their ideals. This analysis relates to Laura Miller's (2006) examination of the ways that many Japanese men beautify (some might even say feminize) themselves to better match women's idealized images of men.

Considering this ambivalent *shōnen* attractiveness, it is easy to guess that the types of scandals that both Johnny's idols and their fans most dislike are those that are sexual in nature. Certainly, an avoidance of sexual scandal is a prerequisite for Johnny's idols to maintain distance from fans and become transcendent icons. The discourse surrounding (androgynous) *shōnen* thus requires Johnny's idols to avoid overtly sexual images. Though some Johnny's idols are married, their marriages took place after they had passed the peak of their popularity. Nonetheless, news of Kimura Takuya's marriage in 2000 was sensational, not only for fans, but also for the majority of Japanese people. This was due to the fact that he announced his marriage at the zenith of SMAP's career as "national idols," confessing that his fiancée (a female idol) was pregnant. After he married and became the father of two girls, Kimura's previous attractiveness as an androgynous *shōnen* might have been expected to gradually diminish. However, it did not. Kimura remains a sort of super-idol and continues to attract female fans,[6] precisely because he seldom mentions anything about his family and he maintains his *shōnen* image. As one critic says:

> Kimura Takuya never makes any comments or behaves in a way that might hint at his married life. The other members [of SMAP] also avoid touching on the issue. In this way, they have amazingly succeeded in making their fans believe that Kimura's marriage doesn't exist.
>
> (Sugino 2009b, 57)

I would add that they succeed because fans *want* to believe that Kimura's marriage does not exist—that he is a *shōnen*. Transcendent *shōnen* images never seem to detach themselves from Kimura, as long as he refuses to verbally validate the reality of his private life with his wife and children.

For ten consecutive years, Kimura was voted "the guy we'd most like to have sex with" in the popular women's fashion magazine *anan*. In contradiction to my previous analysis of Johnny's idols as *shōnen*, this fact might appear to suggest that female fans are sexually attracted to idols. However, the phrase "the guy we'd most like to have sex with" should not be taken as a literal expression of female sexual desires. Instead, following from my earlier discussion concerning the creation and fictionalization of Johnny's idols as iconic, female fans' expression of desire for Kimura can be viewed as essentially imaginative. In this sense, *anan*'s question to its female readers, "Which celebrity you would most like to have sex with?" resembles a virtually identical question addressed to the readers of *shōjo* manga (comics for girls): "Which male (fictional) character would you most like to sleep with?"[7] In this context, female fans' "sexual" desire can be termed "pseudo-sexual" desire, precisely because Johnny's idols themselves can be characterized as "pseudo-real." As Matsumoto (as well as other fans) states, her desire for Johnny's idols is entirely different from her desire for actual male lovers (Matsumoto 2007, 36).

Pseudo-intimacy between Johnny's idols and their female fans

According to Laura Mulvey (1989), the act of creating narratives is intimately bound up with the enhancement of specific forms of desire.

Mulvey's concept of "narratives of desire" can be extended by arguing that desire for narratives is indispensable within a consumer-capitalist framework. Consumer desire is activated through the process of creating narratives, each of which increases the desire to produce more narratives. This results in continuously consuming products on which narratives are based.

As Herwitz indicates, it is not merely desirable but essential that pop icons create an imaginative space in which fans can inscribe their intimate fantasies, while these icons paradoxically preserve their sense of transcendent inaccessibility. The dynamic act of consuming this form of superficiality is necessarily integrated with consumers and fans creating individual, personal narratives about Johnny's idols, thus revealing the fragmentation of these idols as established subjects. A wide range of potential narratives concerning Johnny's idols is available to female fans, who can then become active producers of such narratives, rather than merely remaining passive consumers of them.

It can be argued that a certain personal authenticity in fans' individual narratives about Johnny's idols may correspond to the individuation of overall "grand narratives" that occurs in postmodern consumer capitalism. Such grand narratives incorporate the unified, seemingly fixed, iconic images of idols, which female fans imagine that they can grasp by observing their favorite idols' performances and how they talk and behave in public and in the media. Female fans can then scrutinize, personalize, and consume these images in the form of individual narratives. Hiroshi Aoyagi, well known for his ethnographic work on the idol industry, discusses the ways in which female fans familiarize their favorite idols by personifying them in very individualized ways:

> Idol fans and audiences enjoy creating their own epoch-making stories as they relate themselves to their idols. The mass media function here as by-standers that direct people's interest toward preferred readings of the time.
>
> (Aoyagi 2005, 129)

The production system for Johnny's idols reveals the process by which "coming of age" stories are created, stimulating female fans' desire to create similar stories of their own. In this way, the production system itself is designed to subconsciously reduce the distance between fans' favorite idols and themselves. One of the premises behind the narrativity of Johnny's idols is that the system that creates them also inspires female fans to construct their own personal stories about their favorite idols, based on simulated closeness to them. The rules for spotlighting individual Johnny's trainees were established as early as Johnny's itself. For example, Gō Hiromi became famous among female fans before he officially debuted in 1972, because he played the role of the "younger brother" in Four Leaves, the top Johnny's idol group of the period, which debuted in 1968. All the members of SMAP (which debuted in 1991) used to be back-up dancers for another idol group, Hikaru Genji (which debuted in 1987). The members of Arashi were all promoted from Johnny's Jr.

The production process for Johnny's idols may thus be viewed as a marketing strategy, in which fans who have previously been kept in suspense finally experience the professional debut of their favorite Jr. However, this highlighting of an official debut scene can also be interpreted in terms of a specific scenario that is capable of endless modification and personalization by each female fan. When NEWS was formed in 2003, the selected group members remained a secret until the very day of their debut. However, many female fans were frustrated by this, since "fans always pay attention to Johnny's Jr and expect to share the historic moment when they debut as part of a new idol group" (Ishizaka and Jr Kurabu 2008, 9). As Matsumoto writes:

> We are actually willing to spend our money on the unpremeditated 'life' stories of idols belonging to Johnny & Associates. We enjoy watching their coming of age stories – seeing them fiercely compete against hundreds of teenage rivals, defeating them and finally climbing their way up the ladder to become top idols... The most pleasurable part about being a fan of Johnny's idols is observing the process by which kids whom I felt attracted to... gradually become sophisticated adult men and stars by cultivating their talent to fulfill fans' expectations.
>
> (Matsumoto 2007, 46–47)

Here, the act of creating an imaginative personal narrative about a favorite idol provides a medium that permits a fan to have a kind of pseudo-intimacy with that idol. By participating in such pseudo-relationships with her favorite idols, Matsumoto subconsciously reinforces the effectiveness and attractiveness of Johnny's idols as icons. In this context, female fans personalize Johnny's idols, and seem to resist any fixation on grand narratives concerning these idols; they segment these narratives into a variety of individual, and essentially consumptive, accounts. It is precisely this sense of intimacy that female fans of Johnny's idols desire, and this in turn serves as a medium to enhance consumptive impulses (i.e., purchasing DVDs and magazines, attending concerts and watching films and TV programs that feature their favorite idols). In this way, they feel personally involved in the continuous creation of idol narratives.

Moreover, the fact that many female fans are possessive of their favorite idols shows that they imaginatively indulge in relationships with these idols by creating their own narratives about them. A core fan of Johnny's idols chooses one specific idol among others and declares that she is the *tantō* (person in charge) of that idol. This term belongs to a sort of fan-club lingo, which is shared by core fans of Johnny's idols. It means, basically, "I am in charge of keeping track of this idol, because I support and care about him." For example, a hypothetical dialogue between fans might go as follows: "May I ask who you're in charge of?" "I'm in charge of TOKIO's [Nagase] Tomoya." "Wow, same as me! I'm also in charge of Tomoya!" Needless to say, these fans have never been asked by anyone to be "in charge" of any of the Johnny's idols. Thus, fans keep on producing consumable narratives by fantasizing a pseudo-intimacy between themselves and "their" idols, until they finally lose interest in these idols or discover new favorites.

At gatherings for core idol fans, there are also frequently references to favorite idols as *uchi* (in-group members), a figure of speech that also reinforces their personal identification with Johnny's idols. In the Japanese sociocultural context, the term "*uchi*" originally refers to a family member (i.e., a wife might use the phrase "*uchi no hito*"—literally meaning a person in the family and figuratively her husband). For instance, a popular drama, *Kisarazu Cat's Eye* (2002), provides a specific space in which fans can construct imaginary close relationships with idols like Sakurai Shō from Arashi and Okada Jun'ichi from V6, as the following conversation between two fans indicates:

"Nice meeting you. I'm in charge of Sakurai, from Arashi. May I ask who you're in charge of?" "I'm in charge of Okada, from V6." "Wow! My '*uchi*' [meaning that Okada is affiliated to me] got so much support from Sakurai, when they were featured in the drama *Kisarazu Cat's Eye.*"

(Matsumoto 2007, 48–49)

In this conversation, these fans might seem to be talking about their husbands, boyfriends or sons (treating "their" respective Johnny's idols as "*uchi*" members). The clear internalization of Johnny's idols in these scenes demonstrates the degree to which fans can imaginatively reduce the psychological gap between themselves and "their" idols by creating individual narratives about them.

Conclusion

The above discussion gives a general idea of the influence that the iconic aspects of Johnny's idols can have on certain Japanese girls and women. The principal idea behind Johnny's idols only emerges through a consideration of such dichotomous concepts as reality/fictionality and superficiality/depth, since both of these apparently oppositional pairs are paradoxically contained in the narratives concerning Johnny's idols produced by their female fans. Johnny's idols are made transcendent, unattainable images by the very fact that their realities can never be precisely signified. Their group identities, androgynous *shōnen* status and semi-professional performance abilities never allow fans to grasp entirely accessible images of them. On the other hand, they paradoxically become accessible to their female fans through the specific imaginative space that these fans create in which they can nurture fantasies of pseudo-intimacy with "their" idols. This simultaneous presence and absence of reality in Johnny's idols serves to contextualize and recontextualize their formation as icons. As long as Johnny's continues to follow this successful formula, female fans will presumably never stop fictionalizing and consuming idols. In other words, in the era of postmodern capitalism, Johnny's idols represent consumable icons. They reflect symbolic correlations between a multiplicity of surfaces and the "death" of the (modern) subject. While individual Johnny's idols may be disposable, their simulacra are endlessly duplicated by their female fans/consumers *ad infinitum*.

Notes

1. Ōtsuka Eiji's theoretical perspective on postmodern narrativity involves an examination of the concept of *monogatari* (narrative) within consumer-capitalist society. His primary focus is on the process of producing narratives, in which a basic narrative is copied from an original story, and that narrative can then be limitlessly rearranged, retold and parodied.
2. In Japan, *otaku* has been used as a derogatory term for antisocial maniacs, who are obsessed with one particular thing, especially areas of pop-culture such as manga and anime. Please refer to Galbraith (2009) for a more detailed definition.
3. The specific desire to *shōnen*-ize Johnny's idols can be discussed in relation to popular narratives containing female fantasies of male homosexuality, which are called *shōnen ai* (boys' love) or *yaoi*. The images of *shōnen* prevalent in

this genre clearly represent a strong attachment among female readers to the idealized androgynous qualities of *shōnen*. For more on this, see Chapter 5 in this volume.

4. As indicated by several critics, including John Whittier Treat (1993, 364), Tomoko Aoyama (2005, 53) and Sharalyn Orbaugh (2002, 458), *shōjo* identity has a significant place in Japanese gender discourse, in that it apparently reflects the notion of an asexual, *kawaii* being.

5. Takahara Eiri (1999) suggests that, on the cognitive level, *shōjo* identity should not be defined in terms of a girl's or woman's specific age. He concludes that a girl or woman's involvement in the *shōjo* world should be determined by whether or not she possesses what he calls "girl consciousness" (*shōjo ishiki*).

6. Examples that show his continuous popularity include *Karei naru Ichizoku* (The Wealthy Family), which received the highest audience rating for a TV drama in 2007, and *Hero* (2007), a film that grossed ¥8.1 billion ($101 million) making it number one at the Japanese box office that year.

7. *Shōjo* manga's idealized and romantic "prince-meets-princess" storylines are primarily directed at young female readers.

Works Cited

Aoyagi, Hiroshi. 2005. *Islands of Eight Million Smiles: Idol Performance and Symbolic Production in Contemporary Japan*. Cambridge: Harvard University Asia Center.

Aoyama, Tomoko. 2005. "Transgendering *Shōjo Shōsetsu*: Girls Inter-text/sexuality." In *Genders, Transgenders and Sexualities in Japan*, edited by Mark McLelland and Romit Dasgupta, 49–64. London and New York: Routledge.

Arashi. 2005. *Arashigoto: Marugoto Arashi no Go-nen-han*. Tokyo: Shūeisha.

Azuma Hiroki. 2001. *Dōbutsu-ka suru Posutomodan: Otaku kara Mita Nihon Shakai*. Tokyo: Kōdansha.

Darling-Wolf, Fabienne. 2004. "SMAP, Sex and Masculinity: Constructing the Perfect Female Fantasy in Japanese Popular Music." *Popular Music and Society* 27, no. 3: 357–370.

Galbraith, Patrick W. 2009. *The Otaku Encyclopedia: An Insider's Guide to the Subculture of Cool Japan*. Tokyo: Kōdansha International.

Hara Marihiko. 2009. "Arashi 5X4 Point Profiling: Ōno Satoshi." In *Ongaku-shi ga Kakanai J-poppu Hihyō 62: Johnny's Chō-sedai! Arashi o Yobu Otoko-tachi*, edited by Kobayashi Daisaku, 96. Tokyo: Takarajimasha.

Herwitz, Daniel. 2008. *The Star as Icon: Celebrity in the Age of Mass Consumption*. New York: Columbia University Press.

Hōsen Kaoru. 2009. "Aji-na Hatsugen Arashi Supesharu." In *Ongaku-shi ga Kakanai J-poppu Hihyō 62: Johnny's Chō-sedai! Arashi o Yobu Otoko-tachi*, edited by Kobayashi Daisaku, 76–77. Tokyo: Takarajimasha.

Ishizaka Hiroyuki and Jr Kurabu. 2008. *NEWS Photo&Episode Hishō*. Tokyo: Āruzu Shuppan.

Jameson, Frederic. 1993. "Postmodernism, or The Cultural Logic of Late Capitalism." In *Postmodernism: A Reader*, edited by Thomas Docherty, 62–92. New York: Columbia University Press.

Kashima Yoshio. 2009. "Kurōto Josei ga Arashi ni 'Yodare Jūjū'." In *Ongaku-shi ga Kakanai J-poppu Hihyō 62: Johnny's Chō-sedai! Arashi o Yobu Otoko-tachi*, edited by Kobayashi Daisaku, 22–23. Tokyo: Takarajimasha.

Kikuchi Naruyoshi. 2009. "Zasshi Hyōshi de Tadoru SMAP Feisu & Fasshon." In *Ongaku-shi ga Kakanai J-poppu Hihyō 59: SMAP '20+1 Hōfuku Zecchō,'* edited by Ino Ryōsuke, 44–47. Tokyo: Takarajimasha.

Kosuga Hiroshi. 2007. *Geinō o Biggu Bijinesu ni Kaeta Otoko Johnny Kitagawa no Senryaku to Senjutsu*. Tokyo: Kōdansha.

Matsumoto Mika. 2007. *Jani-ota Onna Kemono Michi*. Tokyo: Futabasha.

Miller, Laura. 2006. *Beauty Up: Exploring Contemporary Japanese Body Aesthetics*. Berkeley: University of California Press.

Morita Masanori. 2009. "Arashi Saidai no Tāningu Pointo wa 2002-nen ni Atta." In *Ongaku-shi ga Kakanai J-poppu Hihyō 62: Johnny's Chō-sedai! Arashi o Yobu Otoko-tachi*, edited by Kobayashi Daisaku, 37. Tokyo: Takarajimasha.

Mulvey, Laura. 1989. *Visual and Other Pleasures*. London: Macmillan.

Nakamori Akio. 2007. *Aidoru Nippon*. Tokyo: Shinchōsha.

Narima Rei'ichi. 2010. *TV Dorama wa, Johnny's Mono dake Miro!* Tokyo: Takarajimasha.

Ogura Chikako. 1990. *Aidoru Jidai no Shinwa*. Tokyo: Asahi Shinbunsha.

Orbaugh, Sharalyn. 2002. "Shōjo." In *Encyclopedia of Contemporary Japanese Culture*, edited by Sandra Buckley, 458–459. London and New York: Routledge.

Ōtsuka Eiji. 2001. *Teihon Monogatari Shōhi Ron*. Tokyo: Kadokawa Shoten.

Ōya Nobuhiko. 2009. "We Love Arashi!" In *Ongaku-shi ga Kakanai J-poppu Hihyō 62: Johnny's Chō-sedai! Arashi o Yobu Otoko-tachi*, edited by Kobayashi Daisaku, 12–13. Tokyo: Takarajimasha.

Sakai Masatoshi. 2009. "Sakai Masatoshi ga Kataru Saigo no Kokumin-teki Aidoru SMAP." In *Ongaku-shi ga Kakanai J-poppu Hihyō 59: SMAP '20+1 Hōfuku Zecchō,'* edited by Ino Ryōsuke, 10–11. Tokyo: Takarajimasha.

Sugino Chinami. 2009a. "Chapter 1: Kessei~Ninki ni Hi ga Tsuku (1988-nen 4-gatsu~1993-nen 12-gatsu)." In *Ongaku-shi ga Kakanai J-poppu Hihyō 59: SMAP '20+1 Hōfuku Zecchō,'* edited by Ino Ryōsuke, 50–51. Tokyo: Takarajimasha.

———. 2009b. "Chapter 4: Kokumin-teki Kashu~Otona no Tame no Aidoru to shite (2000-nen 1-gatsu~Genzai)." In *Ongaku-shi ga Kakanai J-poppu Hihyō 57: SMAP '20+1 Hōfuku Zecchō,'* edited by Ino Ryōsuke, 56–57. Tokyo: Takarajimasha.

Takahara Eiri. 1999. *Shōjo Ryōiki*. Tokyo: Kokusho Kankōkai.

Takeuchi Yoshikazu. 2009. *Boku ga, Arashi o Suki ni Natta Riyū*. Tokyo: PHP Kenkyūsho.

Treat, John Whittier. 1993. "Yoshimoto Banana Writes Home: *Shōjo* Culture and the Nostalgic Subject." *The Journal of Japanese Studies* 19, no. 2: 353–387.

Yoshimoto Yoshiaki. 2002. "Shitteiru Kagiri de SMAP no Koto." *Kōkoku Hihyō* 264: 74–76.

West, Mark D. 2007. *Secrets, Sex, And Spectacle: The Rules of Scandal in Japan and the United States*. Chicago: University of Chicago Press.

5
From Boys Next Door to Boys' Love: Gender Performance in Japanese Male Idol Media

Lucy Glasspool

Male idol groups form one of the most successful contemporary Japanese popular music genres aimed at a female audience. Previous writing on the subject (Aoyagi 2000; Darling-Wolf 2003; 2004) suggests that their image and performance, which pervade many types of mainstream media, promote obedience to hegemonic social norms such as a male-dominated hierarchical system and the privileging of heterosexuality. I would like to explore this through the locus of gender: the presentation of male idols in terms of masculinity and the homosocial, in official media and in texts produced and consumed by female fans. Coming to focus on the strategic performance of male–male attraction, I will discuss the ways in which mainstream media images position idols between youth and adulthood, the nonsexual and the sexual, and how certain fans manipulate these performances to create their own texts centering on male–male relationships, especially in the form of "boys' love" *dōjinshi* (fan-drawn comics depicting romantic or sexual relationships between male characters). Finally, I will consider how far these images may set up a space for women to encounter nonhegemonic masculinities and alternatives to heteronormativity.

This chapter will focus on the idol group Arashi, managed by the ubiquitous company Johnny and Associates (hereafter Johnny's). Having celebrated their ten-year anniversary at the end of 2009, this group are at the height of their career, and may be said to be the next generation of idols succeeding the hugely popular SMAP.[1] Arashi has a large domestic fan base, which is largely female, ranging from early teens to middle age (I will return to the consideration of fan demographics and the implications they may have regarding the consumption of idol performances in a later section).

Idol performance is not limited to music-related media; their image and influence, since the 1980s, have spread to the extent that "time spent in front of the television camera rather than in the recording studio or the concert hall is the definitive attribute of an idol" (Stevens 2008, 50). This may indeed be said of Arashi, who, under the powerful umbrella of Johnny's, the management company that controls the majority of male idols in Japan, are visible in many media, including but not limited to music CDs, promotional videos, music TV performances, concert DVDs, idol magazines, women's magazines, product advertising, stage plays, variety TV shows, radio, websites, film, newscasting, and TV dramas. This kind of exposure, so far in excess of anything seen in contemporary Western pop music culture, renders it almost impossible to avoid the images being projected by such groups, images which "inform their viewers about appearances and personal qualities that are considered socially appropriate and trendy" (Aoyagi 2005, 3).

Hegemonic and "new" masculinities

What exactly is being promoted to female audiences as "socially appropriate" in terms of gender (i.e., the performance of masculinity that "should" be desirable to them)? Can images of male idols be considered to uphold a hegemonic masculinity that attempts to define the boundaries of legitimate female desire?[2]

Hegemonic masculinity is "the currently most honored way of being a man," requiring "all other men to position themselves in relation to it" (Connell and Messerschmidt 2005, 832). Not necessarily describing the practice of masculinity that the majority of men enact, it is nevertheless normative, the standard by which other forms of masculinity, and certainly femininity, are legitimized or subordinated. Japanese hegemonic masculinity has, since the 1950s, centered on the "salaryman," a figure that embodies "the notion of the Japanese male as the archetypal ... husband/father and producer/provider" (Dasgupta 2003, 119). Two of the crucial features underpinning this particular discourse are heterosexuality and adulthood, both of which are ideally attained through marriage (Hidaka 2010, 84), which also serves to delineate the space in which the hegemonic ideal of femininity is set:

the heterosexual breadwinners work hard and faithfully for their companies, supporting the economic development of Japan and the well-being of their families, whereas their wives do all the housekeeping and bear and raise children for the convenience of patriarchal and industrial capitalism.

(Hidaka 2010, 3)

This discourse strives to fix the roles of gender and sexuality, delegitimizing configurations of masculinity that may not adhere to the central pillars of the company and the (heterosexual) family.

Although male idols generally look nothing like the "white shirt, dark business suit... neat hairstyle" image of the salaryman (Dasgupta 2003, 123), their performance, in some respects, supports this dominant masculinity, and in doing so continues to promote the acceptability, even desirability, of that discourse. Johnny's idols are part of a traditional company structure based on a hierarchical senior/junior (*senpai/kōhai*) system, in which junior groups provide backup dancers for established acts and senior idols interview their juniors on TV music and variety shows. The maintenance and promotion of this particularly Japanese system of group work and seniority can be seen in the premise of the variety show *Arashi ni Shiyagare*, in which Arashi members learn various "skills" from an "older brother guest" (*aniki gesuto*), often an actor, sports star, or older Johnny's member. This not only highlights the importance of a hierarchical social organization to the upkeep of this particular type of masculinity, but also marks the field of worthwhile knowledge as one occupied by men.

The idealization of adult masculinity is also visible in print images, particularly as groups pass their mid-20s, when they may be permitted to put on suits and appear in media not aimed primarily at teenagers or idol fans. One example is shown in the January 2010 issue of the interview magazine *Cut*, in which Arashi appear alongside interviews with "real" (i.e., instrument-playing) musicians and Hollywood actors like Christian Bale. Photographed in black and white, wearing uniform black suits and serious expressions next to a cover heading proclaiming them "Men of the Year 2009," this image positions the group in the context of adult celebrities rather than teen pop stars, while the text, in the form of an award, proclaims that this adult incarnation is a positive one.

The idea of heterosexuality as a facet of desirable masculinity is also upheld in many aspects of male idol media; indeed, at first glance it appears to be the ideal, and as such is reflected in a large part of official performance. This image is almost always of heterosexuality in very vague terms; it does not often extend as far as the specifically *sexual*, since one of the main Johnny's tenets is that idols should seem romantically unattached, in order to remain attractive to their female audience, many of whom may use them as "a convenient romantic attachment, which need not be feared, can be idealized, and can be symbolically available at will" (Karniol 2001, 62). Male idols should appear, if not chaste, then at least not sexually active with a specific woman. The maintenance of a well-behaved public image is strictly policed by the management company: idols, especially those still in their teens and early 20s, must appear nonspecifically heterosexual, in the form of articles and interviews about future girlfriends or wives, and song lyrics relating to generalized, unnamed lovers. This vagueness is supported by the presentation of the performers' bodies in specialist idol magazines like *Duet*—almost always fully clothed, demurely donning pajamas if the setting for the photos is a bed; on the rare occasions that they are depicted shirtless, it is usually "with some 'utilitarian' function written into the scene" (Bordo 1999, 28), such as sport or dance, where the body is presented as a healthy tool for action rather than as an object of purely sexual desire.

There are exceptions to this nonsexualized performance; again, this tends to occur when both idols and target audience are older, and involves the performance of a more active heterosexuality in terms of asserting desire and acknowledging that the female audience may use the idol as the focus of their own desires (Darling-Wolf 2004). This may be seen in some images of second-oldest Arashi member Sakurai Shō, who is rather unusual in that he has a degree in economics from the prestigious Keiō University and a side job as a newscaster (most Johnny's idols do not graduate from high school). These achievements return us to the adult salaryman model of masculinity, neither of them being related to typical idol activities, but belonging rather to the still male-dominated professional domain. With an attractive, decoratively muscled body,[3] Sakurai was put on display in the January 2010 issue of women's magazine *anan* under the heading "The Beautiful Body," alongside articles on sex and drawings of naked heterosexual couples. Unlike idol magazines, which often involve long question and answer sections as well as pictures, Sakurai's photo-shoot is eight pages long with a mere one-third of a page of text: pictured almost naked on a bed, gazing appealingly at the camera, he exists purely as an example of sexually desirable masculinity for the visual pleasure of the reader, the object of an almost entirely female gaze.

The display of the male body as an erotic object, however, problematizes hegemonic salaryman masculinity, insofar as it may upset the historical process of "the dominance of men and the subordination of women," which has been a product of its formation (Connell and Messerschmidt 2005, 844), at least in terms of who is the bearer and who the object of sexual desire. Darling-Wolf argues that in a society where "male sexual pleasure has typically taken precedence ... these representations may offer subversive and potentially liberating avenues for women to explore sexual identities" (Darling-Wolf 2003, 77). Susan Bordo also finds positive potential for women in the increase of images of men intended to cater to female pleasure:

> women have been the beneficiaries of what might be described as a triumph of pure consumerism ... over ... the taboos against male vanity, male 'femininity,' and the erotic display of the male body that have gone along with it.
>
> (Bordo 1999, 179)

This may be beneficial to female consumers as an alternative to the pervasive images of eroticized women in contemporary Japanese media, but it does not do much to support the ideal of salaryman masculinity, which—through 50 years of reiteration—has formed a system of male dominance and female subordination.

The above example shows one way in which "the masculinity that derives from the power of the company and the unquestioned normality of heterosexual marriage ... entails vulnerability" (Hidaka 2010, 2)—the acknowledgement of female desire and the possibility of the male body as a sexual object. As Connell and Messerschmidt (2005, 835) explain, "challenges to hegemony are common." In the context of contemporary Japan, these challenges have become more frequent since the collapse of the bubble economy in the 1990s, and have included alternative constructions of masculinity that attempt to redraw the fixed gender boundaries and heterosexual norms of the dominant salaryman discourse.

A number of these alternative masculinities are highly visible in images of male idols, and may even be considered the dominant performances of the genre. There are three elements in these performances which appear to diverge from the traditional configuration of masculinity: (1) emotional sensitivity and domesticity, which were previously considered the domain of women; (2) youth; and (3) the performance of male–male relationships that tread a fine line between the homosocial and what could be considered homosexual.

Many media images of Arashi portray an ideal of sensitive, somewhat domestic manhood, which Darling-Wolf sees as stemming from the "new man" (*shinjinrui*) culture of the 1990s (Darling-Wolf 2004,

361): men who can cry, cook, take care of children. Arashi are certainly not shy about crying in public, in films and dramas, and at suitably moving achievements or charity events. Idols are also shown in staged domestic situations, such as the appearance of members Ōno Satoshi and Ninomiya Kazunari in women's magazine *Non-No* in February 2009, wearing aprons and apparently enjoying cooking while discussing the food their mothers make, food they would cook for a girl, and food they enjoy together as a group. The article also contains details of their clothing, combining fashion, domesticity, and discussion of relationships.

The "new man" concept has, in recent years, been somewhat eclipsed in Japanese media by another masculinity that moves even further from the hegemonic model: the "herbivore man" (*sōshokukei danshi*). Young men given this label, like the "new man," are said to be interested in fashion and domesticity, with many of the same interests as their female friends. However, they differ from this model for being criticized in some media as uninterested in sexual relationships. This criticism tends to come mostly from female writers. Sakuragi Piroko, an author of handbooks on various aspects of female sexual assertiveness, vilifies "herbivores" in a book entitled *Carnivorous Girls' Love Study: How do they devour herbivorous boys?* She complains: "men who have absolutely no sexual desire are on the increase," and that "nobody wants 'herbivorous men.' Rather, they hate them" (Sakuragi 2009, 1–2). In order to ensure that this attitude does not extend to idols, whose livelihood rather depends on being attractive to women, the representation of sensitive masculinity in idol media is carefully balanced with a display of interest in the opposite sex, which is reputedly lacking in the "herbivore man," through public discussion of their ideal girlfriend or future wife (Darling-Wolf 2003, 79). Thus male idols retain their status of desirability.

The performance of youth may also be considered central in idol images, and is a construction of masculinity that differs from both the sensitive "new man" and the hegemonic salaryman figure. Indeed, thanks to the specific construction of the hegemonic adult man, "children and unmarried men are ... outside the category of the fully human" (Lunsing 2001, 14), incidentally rendering the nonspecific heterosexuality and "singleness" reiterated by idols rather problematic in terms of upholding such a construction. The depiction of youth may seem unsurprising, given that the majority of idols begin work in their mid-to-late teens, but even Arashi—the eldest of whom is now in his early

30s—perform a type of "boyishness" far more often than they do the mature adult male.

In terms of appearance, male idols are considered by many to fall into the category of *kawaii* (cute), "a term more often applied to babies, girls, certain types of women, and baby animals than men" (Yano 1997, 339), but which is nevertheless an image strongly linked to contemporary female consumption (Kinsella 1995, 220). Idols smile "with bared (though often crooked) teeth and clear, sparkling eyes" (Aoyagi 2000, 312) to display marketable cuteness. This a fair description of the covers of idol magazines like *Duet* or *Popolo*, in which the pictures are often digitally enhanced to make lips pinker and eyes sparkle with stars. Invariably slender, stylishly dressed against brightly colored backgrounds, the overwhelming impression is of nonthreatening cuteness, a visual mode that women are inundated and familiarized with on a daily basis, from Hello Kitty to the *shōjo* manga (girls' comics) that have been a staple of female consumption since the 1950s. The link to this type of manga has been considered by Darling-Wolf (2004) and Kimberly S. Gregson (2005), who compare the cuteness of male idols with the *bishōnen* or "beautiful boy" image so often found in girls' comics. The attraction of this young and pretty type, particularly for adolescents, may be that it provides a "safer" form of masculinity: Rachel Karniol points out that what are considered feminine characteristics, such as "being cute and lovable" (Karniol 2001, 63), may be preferable in young girls' fantasy partners, as "viewing these males as feminine makes them safer objects of love" (Karniol 2001, 72).

This emphasis on idol appearance as boyish, rather than the more adult "manly," may also have a positive function for the female audience. Bordo highlights the contrast between the position of the boy, who is permitted a certain amount of fluidity or passivity in relationships, and the adult man, who must be active, in control. As she points out, "boys are permitted to be seductive, playful, to flirt with being 'taken.' *Men* must still be in command" (Bordo 1999, 193). This brings the idea of power relations into play, in a society where "sex is … seen as an activity taking place between an active and a passive person, characterized by an imbalance of power" (Lunsing 2001, 321). Hegemonic constructions of male domination and female subordination have traditionally placed women in the passive role, but the figure of the boy opens up the possibility of a woman, or even another man, assuming sexual control of a male body. This returns us once again to girls' manga and its boys' love subgenre, where the figure of the *bishōnen* is under the control of female authors and audiences, encouraging readers to "experiment with nonhegemonic gender and sexual practices" (Welker 2006, 855).

These "sensitive" and "youthful" masculinities, then, differ in many respects from the hegemonic salaryman model, and offer the potential for female audiences to consider alternative modes of desire and the possibility of shifting sexual power relations. However, hegemonic masculinity is used to being challenged, and so it "appropriates from other masculinities whatever appears to be pragmatically useful for continued domination" (Connell and Messerschmidt 2005, 844). The performance of alternative masculinities, therefore, cannot be considered unquestionably positive; the images deployed are not empty or passive but "exert considerable power over us—over our psyches, our desires, our self-image" (Bordo 1999, 186). Images of cute, youthful idols that evoke the *bishōnen* of *shōjo* manga are presented as desirable, legitimately masculine figures with which to play out more fluid sexual and gender roles. Yet this figure conforms to a widespread *kawaii* cultural ideal that is already inextricably linked with consumer culture, making it less a new vision of malleable masculinity than a marketable tool giving the illusion of free play. In this way, subordinate models of gender that pose a challenge to the dominant system of adult masculinity are partly drawn into that system and made to do its work. I will now consider this in terms of the strategic use of male–male attraction in idol media.

Sexual ambivalence as a strategy of consumerism

Despite the apparent emphasis on heterosexuality, sexual ambivalence is present in idol performance, as "fan service" (deliberate performance for the purpose of fans' pleasure) and as a buffer against scandal. Fan service (*fan sābisu*) in idol media often takes the form of the emphasized performance of homosociality, whose relationship with homo*sexuality* is described as being rendered "radically discontinuous" by the heterosexual imperatives of a patriarchal society (Sedgwick 1985, 5). The homosocial itself is very much entwined with hegemonic masculinity, promoting "clear distinctions between women and men through segregation in social situations" (Bird 1996, 121). In the performance of idols, however, a space is maintained where fans may interpret the homosocial as homosexual if they wish, creating a continuous spectrum between the two. Most idols play with this homosocial/homosexual continuum to some extent through what is termed "member-*ai*"—the affectionate display of friendship between members, and "skinship" (*sukinshippu*) or the expression of closeness through physical touch. These techniques are helpfully open to interpretation either as the close bonds of male friendship or as homoerotic attraction, and are easily refuted as pure playfulness should anyone object to the latter. When "practiced out in the open and in the manner of a joke, homosocial bodily contact defies immediate labeling as too intimate and therefore as homoerotic" (Kaplan 2005, 584), but at the same time does not deny the possibility of becoming erotic through the interpretive gaze of the audience. Just as the *kawaii* aspect of male idols has been linked with the *bishōnen* of *shōjo* manga, so fan service of this type may stem in part from an awareness of the popularity of boys' love or *yaoi* manga. This subgenre of *shōjo* manga emerged in the 1970s as *dōjinshi* featuring male characters from established anime and manga, as female readers and authors began to tire of male-dominated heteronormativity, with stories of love between boys becoming more and more popular (Aoyama 1988, 188) and then spreading into other media fandoms, including those of male idols.

Within the section of Arashi fandom that does choose to interpret homosocial performance in this way, there are fans of many specific member "pairings." Indeed, the mainstream media do not discourage this. Members of a group are often split into pairs for TV shows or articles in magazines: the June 2011 issue of *TV Guide* included a special Arashi section featuring a "Favorite Combi Ranking," where readers voted for their favorite pairs. The winners of this particular contest were Ōno Satoshi and Ninomiya Kazunari, the best-known pair within Arashi, who for a number of years performed comedy skits as a subunit in the middle of concerts, under the stage name "Ōmiya SK" (an amalgamation of their surnames). This term is now used both in mainstream media, when Ōno and Ninomiya work together, and by fans who give their relationship a sexual interpretation and use it as a description of their romantic pairing. Ōmiya certainly make it easy for fans to interpret homoeroticism in their relationship: spontaneous and choreographed instances of member-*ai* and skinship exist in their performances, ranging from hugging to absent touching to casual groping, from kissing on stage to unashamed declarations of love and discussion of their "romance" in magazine and TV interviews. This can be explained away as friendship by those fans who prefer their idols strictly heterosexual, and by comments such as Ōno's casual "it's just a habit" when asked to explain why he was so frequently groped by the aggressively tactile Ninomiya.[4]

Nevertheless, the pair on occasion push this to the edge of ambiguity, as shown in a series of messages in the monthly idol magazine *Wink Up*.

Each month there is a section where idols leave very short messages to one another, usually regarding recent events or one another's projects. Ōmiya's exchange began in 2007 with:

11.2007 Ninomiya: '...We didn't go out for dinner!'
12.2007 Ōno: 'I'd rather eat you than dinner.'

This flirtation continued in the same vein for several months, sparking much speculation and fan discussion online and concluding in 2008 with:

06.2008 Ōno: '...When I'm spacing out, I naturally think about you. I guess I'm no good without you. I love you, Kazu!'
07.2008 Ninomiya: 'I'm so happy about those feelings...'
08.2008 Ōno: 'That hot kiss we shared at Fukuoka Dome, I thought, of course, these are your lips. No other lips can compare to yours.'

This performance of homoeroticism is playful, but so frequently reiterated that it has become naturalized within Arashi fandom to the point where it is no longer seen as unusual. The public performance of their relationship blurs the "disruption" in the homosocial/homosexual continuum, leaving fans able to attach their own preferred meanings. On Japan's online message board *2-channeru*, opinions range from "they're just close as friends" or "Ninomiya just likes being spoiled by his seniors, Ōno just likes skinship" to "they probably have a sexual relationship" or "all of Arashi seem homo."[5] The possibility of homosexuality is partially normalized and certainly attracts less attention than the rumor of an idol engaging in a *heterosexual* relationship.

This leads to the second function of the performance of same-sex attraction: preventing scandal. In the idol world, strict unwritten rules state that heterosexuality must remain vague. Idols may discuss anonymous ex-girlfriends, or speculate on their ideal future partner, but should not be publicly seen to have one. Even the rumor of a female lover can be fodder for scandal, where the "breach...of a law or a norm results in significant social disapproval or debate" (West 2006, 6). These scandals involving sexuality are "not of legal rules, but of powerful social norms" (West 2006, 241). In the idol world, these consist of the female audience's expectation of an idol's theoretical romantic availability, which allows for no display of overt sexual behavior. In Japan, as Mark D. West (2006, 198–208) argues, a breach is dealt with by temporary or permanent expulsion from the public sphere.

Companies like Johnny's police their own idols and exact punishment themselves, such as sending a misbehaving idol abroad. Yet the precarious image of idols is also threatened when the company itself is implicated in scandal, whether financial (Ugaya 2005, 221) or sexual, as when the head of the company was faced with rumors of sexual misconduct with young idols in his charge (Stevens 2008, 76). While scandal on the part of the company rather than individual idols may have altered the way in which Johnny's is viewed, the company is powerful and well enough connected to have weathered the scandals with no appreciable drop in popularity.[6]

These techniques for coping with scandal both involve a kind of silencing. However, there is another way of dealing with the threat of scandal involving women: a swift redressing of the balance, something to swing attention away from the display of specific heterosexuality. In Arashi's case, this has taken the form of pushing the possibility of same-sex attraction to the fore, and once again involved the Ōmiya pair. In August 2007 rumors appeared in the tabloid *Nikkan Sports* that Ninomiya was involved with one of his female drama co-stars. This was unsubstantiated and swiftly denied by Johnny's, and—as if to make doubly sure—on a subsequent broadcast of the TV show *Music Station* interviewers brought up the subject of Ōmiya's relationship, which was discussed at length.[7] This being a topic that Ōmiya tend to initiate themselves, Ninomiya later complained on his blog that the show's producers and the company had instructed them before recording that they were to talk specifically about this subject. Fan commentary on message boards made it clear that the broadcast was regarded as a ploy to throw attention off his supposed relationship with a woman. In this instance, then, the performance of same-sex attraction may be a calculated tactic to swing perceived sexuality back to a nonspecific middle point. This tactic, of course, could also operate in reverse if required.

So, although the idealized image of idols is one of generalized heterosexuality, the performance of same-sex attraction can serve as a buffer to prevent performers falling from boyish, youthful romantic sensibility into direct, adult heterosexuality. The ambiguity between homosocial and homosexual performance is also carefully calculated, allowing those female fans who are attracted to images of male–male sexuality to use idol media as a space for fantasy play, while other fans are able to maintain their own fantasies of idols as heterosexual romantic partners.

Fan manipulation of idol performance

The previous sections have examined the ways in which idols perform potentially non-hegemonic roles of gender and sexuality for the
pleasure of female fans. But what are these pleasures? How do fans negotiate the consumption of the controlled images in mainstream media,
which, given the tendency of hegemony to annex subordinate models of gender and sexuality to maintain its own dominance, may "do
little to challenge the status quo" (Darling-Wolf, 2003, 86), and production and consumption of their own fan texts? After all, idol fans
"may well be objects of manipulation, but they are also manipula-
tors of consumption" (Yano 1997, 337), and do not merely passively
consume the gender ideals presented to them in official media. This
section will look at how fans use the idol characteristics of youth and
homosociality/homoeroticism in the creation of boys' love *dōjinshi*.

Male pop idols are widely considered to provide "a 'safe' target of
romantic love" (Karniol 2001, 63) for teenage girls, a romantic fantasy
which has none of the complications of real-life relationships and "saves
the adolescents from disillusion" (Raviv *et al.* 1996, 633). It is true that
many Japanese idol fans do fit this category; but there are also fans in
their 30s, 40s and upward (the 'Favorite Combi Ranking' article mentioned earlier included the comments of women from age 11 to 55),
who may find quite different pleasures in idol performance. It is married adult women, after all, who are the most immediately affected by
the prescriptive gender ideals of salaryman masculinity; idol fandom, in
this context, may serve as a different kind of fantasy space in which such
women temporarily privilege their own romantic and sexual desires.
The online community "Arashi Housewife Club" (*Arashi Shufu no Kai*),
which has close to 900 members, supports this concept in its front-page
introduction:

All you housewives with a loving family but who have fallen for these
five cute people. Escape from reality for a little while, and let's talk
lots about cute Arashi![8]

Again, the emphasis on cuteness may be indicative of dissatisfaction
with the figure of the hegemonic salaryman model with which the role
of the Japanese wife is inextricably linked, or it may be nostalgia for
"memories of their own younger days" (Aoyagi 2005, 81) when they had
not yet taken on the responsibilities of adult life. Alternatively, Christine
Yano (1997, 339) posits that, instead of the ideal romantic partner, the

male star may provide a fantasy ideal of a son, who, "unlike real sons who may leave home . . . is always there via broadcast media." There are many types of pleasure involved in idol fandom, and the scope of this chapter cannot cover them all, but it is crucial to bear in mind the multiplicity of female desire and the many uses to which a specific genre may be put.

There is another type of fan who makes romantic or erotic use of idol performance. However, the fantasies they envision do not directly involve a connection between themselves and the idol, but instead focus on the relationships between idols to the exclusion of heterosexuality, providing another link between male idols and boys' love manga through the production and consumption of homoerotic, and sometimes explicitly pornographic, *dōjinshi*. These unofficially produced comics and novels, and the websites supporting them, have no direct commercial benefit for the management companies. *Dōjinshi* are distributed through conventions or the artists' own websites, and a high value is put on private dissemination. Most artists print requests that buyers do not resell *dōjinshi* through online auctions (a futile request, as they are readily available on auction sites and at second-hand manga stores) or otherwise draw attention to them, as they involve depictions of "real" people in alternative sexual configurations. Many websites contain elaborate passwords that the visitor must guess before being allowed access, usually from clues about the idol that only a dedicated fan would know. This self-regulation maintains the idea of a private space in which being a fan is a prerequisite for entry, an area in which fans have control over what is considered legitimate desire.

The desires involved in women creating narratives of male–male sexuality have been comprehensively theorized in the large body of writing on boys' love manga and the emerging work on *fujoshi* (literally, "rotten girl"), a term for some boys' love fans much discussed in popular Japanese media (Takahashi 2005, 25) and mentioned in direct connection with Johnny's fans by Mori Naoko (2010, 73–74). Some scholars focus on the two main sexual roles of boys' love characters, the *seme* ("top") and *uke* ("bottom"),[9] and the idea that some readers may identify feminine characteristics in the *uke*, reading romantic or sex scenes as pseudo-heterosexual (Penley 1992) and placing themselves in a sexual scenario in which the *uke*, or the partner being penetrated, invariably receives great sexual pleasure (Wood 2006). Others consider the *uke* body to be subversive in that it crosses between genders, creating a new kind of body that is not tied to the hegemonic dominant-male/subordinate-female binary (McLelland 2000; Welker 2006) and providing a space for women to explore alternatives to dominant ideals without the threat of a controlling male gaze (Buckley 1993). For other readers there may be a vicarious pleasure in the illicitness of a homosexual relationship, or even in being an "unseen" third-party voyeur who takes pleasure in a sexual situation without fear of consequences (Mori 2010)—sex removed from the purpose of procreation, without the considerations of marriage or motherhood (Aoyama 1988). Or it may simply be visual pleasure in the aesthetics of two beautiful boys (Lunsing 2001, 288).

In the case of idol *dōjinshi*, any number of these possibilities may apply to each fan. In addition, given that these are texts based on "real" people whom female fans may actively desire, *dōjinshi* give fans the opportunity to indulge in visual depictions of their favorite idols in sexual situations, without the threat of a female character to damage the fantasy of the idol being a potential partner for the fan. It is more acceptable to imagine one's chosen idol with another idol of equal attractiveness, one who is already familiar to the reader, than as already "taken" by a woman. As one fan explains of Ōmiya on *2-channeru*, "I'd rather see them as homos than getting caught by some strange woman."[10]

Many Arashi *dōjinshi* are explicitly pornographic, featuring every imaginable pairing. According to Jane Juffer, not only the content of pornography made by and for females but the very act of making it has the potential to challenge hegemonic constructions of sexual roles: "the ability of women to literally enter into the means of production of erotica" can be considered a "material transgression" (Juffer 1998, 233) into a domain that is overwhelmingly male-controlled. The creation, dissemination and consumption of images of men for female pleasure reverses the dominant patterns of heterosexual porn, in which images of women are manipulated for male pleasure (Mori 2010, 232). It is unlikely that most boys' love *dōjinshi* are made with the aim of directly challenging heteronormative pornography, but they do prioritize women's sexual pleasure and provide them with reasonably inexpensive material with which to achieve it, without having to engage with the mainstream porn industry.

The emphasis on cuteness in official media and among fans makes it seem slightly surprising, at first, that these same fans are so eager to put their idols into hardcore sexual situations. However, if we return to the link between cuteness and youth as an alternative to hegemonic models of masculinity, we may consider the connection between cuteness and the image of the "boy" (in Bordo's writing) to suggest sexual fluidity, a potential for male passivity (and female control) that hegemonic adult masculinity forbids. The aesthetics of boys' love manga employed by many artists encourage the image of youth, "rendering the distinction between adolescent and adult murky at best" (Wood 2006, 408).

The flexibility in sexual roles found in the figure of the boy can be seen in idol *dōjinshi*, especially if taken as a genre, where different artists see particular idols in both *seme* and *uke* roles (though it is true that most authors, once they have picked a dynamic for their favorite pairing, tend to stick to it, thus limiting the possibility for fans to read the text as a challenge to static sex roles). In the popular Ōmiya fandom there are many *dōjinshi*, such as artist Heat Bug's, in which group leader Ōno, who is small and generally regarded as rather yielding and easy-going in personality, takes the *uke* role. Yet there are just as many by other artists in which Ninomiya, who tends to initiate skinship and be more dominant in official media, but who is equally small, takes that role while Ōno plays the *seme*. Fans may prefer one pattern over the other, but it does not appear to cause much contention. Since the members of Arashi all fit the *kawaii* model to some degree, it is fairly easy for artists to reverse roles. The author Mamedeppo has Ōno and Ninomiya switch roles in her *dōjinshi*, while another, N. G. Trap, makes a point of writing down her interpretation of their "mental" and "physical" roles. She sees the mental role as "Ninomiya x Ōno" (i.e., Ninomiya *seme* and Ōno *uke*), while their physical roles are labeled "reversible." The reversibility of the Ōmiya pairing does allow a certain amount of fluidity and blurring of sexual roles, although this may be simply due to the fact that they are almost identical in size, while roles in many boys' love *dōjinshi* are determined by the height of the characters. So, while it cannot be definitively stated that articulations of sexual roles in idol *dōjinshi* are unfixed and thus subversive of hegemonic norms, these romantic and pornographic texts provide a space for fans' personal fantasies and experimentation with alternative sexual and gender ideals that is not policed by mainstream media or management companies. Fans can, if they wish, frame the petite, quiet Ōno as a sexually aggressive *seme*, or muscular and "mature" Sakurai as a willing *uke*. Writers and consumers of fan comics, in their reading of sexuality in idol relationships that are set up as homosocial, question the "obligatory" heterosexuality that "is built into male-dominated kinship systems" (Sedgwick 1985, 3).

Conclusion

Can the images of alternative masculinities, such as the sensitive man and the boy, and the performance of homoeroticism in idol media, destabilize hegemonic, heteronormative masculinity in any way? Or, do they simply reinforce it?

Official idol media contain many images of "new" masculinities, which superficially suggest possibilities for more flexible sexual and gender roles, and place great importance on catering to female desire, something that is largely unaddressed in the dominant model of adult salaryman masculinity. This can also be seen in the performance of same-sex attraction specifically geared toward the pleasure of fans. Yet these "alternatives" to the hegemonic norm, instead of being subversive beyond the highlighting of female desire, can be co-opted and manipulated for consumerism and the maintenance of that same hegemonic masculinity, which embraces useful aspects of subordinate masculinities and sexualities when under threat, in order to ensure the continuation of male dominance.

In the areas where fans interact with idol performances in creative ways, producing and consuming boys' love *dōjinshi*, there may be more room for uncontrolled exploration of nonhegemonic gender and sex roles. Fans provide themselves with a private space in which women are able to experiment with new constructions of sex and gender ideals that help define their own legitimate desires and sexualities, and in terms of personal meaning these activities may be very fulfilling, both sexually and otherwise. The very act of creating and disseminating pornography for women generates a kind of independence, the ability for female fans to satisfy their sexual desires without recourse to the commercial, male-biased world of mainstream pornography. However, fan creation is unlikely to have a disruptive impact on powerful management companies and the ideals they present in their idols. Boys' love *dōjinshi* readers will keep being fans, keep consuming official media for a glimpse of their favorite idol or pair. What they do in their very private fan groups may do little to improve female standing as delineated by hegemonic masculinity, other than ensuring the power of female consumption and the continued insistence on female desire.

Notes

1. This has been previously discussed by Fabienne Darling-Wolf (2003; 2004) and Carolyn Stevens (2008).
2. I use a definition of gender drawn from Judith Butler's theorization that gendered practices are not determined by the binarisms of masculine/feminine or male/female, but that they rather serve to constitute these categories (Butler 1993, 4–5).
3. Although, in line with Stevens' argument that idols should be fallible and not extraordinary enough to be beyond the reach of their audiences (Stevens

2008), he has a "flaw" in the form of steeply sloping shoulders (*nadegata*) that are often made fun of by the other members.

4. *Hanamaru Café*, Tokyo Broadcasting System Television (TBS), originally aired 4 February 2007.

5. Data from *2-channeru* come from search results of posts in May 2007 using http://unkar.org.

6. Stevens (2008, 76) suggests the possibility of corporate influence being used to minimize coverage in the press by coercing major media outlets.

7. *Music Station*, TV Asahi, originally aired 31 August 2007.

8. "Arashi Shufu no Kai." http://group.ameba.jp/group/wKteF9zHJox0 (accessed 5 August 2011).

9. The terms *seme* and *uke* are used in manga and anime, especially in the genre of boys' love, to refer to male same-sex relationships. The *seme* is the dominant or penetrative partner, while the *uke* is considered to be the submissive or receptive partner in anal sex.

10. Data from *2-channeru* come from search results of posts in May 2007 using http://unkar.org.

Works Cited

Aoyagi, Hiroshi. 2000. "Pop Idols and the Asian Identity." In *Japan Pop! Inside the World of Japanese Popular Culture*, edited by Timothy Craig, 309–326. London: M.E. Sharpe, Inc.

———. 2005. *Islands of Eight Million Smiles: Idol Performances and Symbolic Production in Contemporary Japan*. Cambridge: Harvard University Asian Center.

Aoyama, Tomoko. 1988. "Male Homosexuality as Treated by Japanese Women Writers." In *The Japanese Trajectory: Modernization and Beyond*, edited by Gavan McCormack and Yoshio Sugimoto, 186–204. Cambridge: Cambridge University Press.

Bird, Sharon R. 1996. "Welcome to the Men's Club: Homosociality and the Maintenance of Hegemonic Masculinity." *Gender and Society* 10, no. 2: 120–132.

Bordo, Susan. 1999. *The Male Body: A New Look at Men in Public and in Private*. New York: Farrar, Strauss and Giroux.

Buckley, Susan. 1993. "'Penguin in Bondage': A Graphic Tale of Japanese Comic Books." In *Technoculture*, edited by Constance Penley and Andrew Ross, 163–196. Minneapolis: University of Minneapolis Press.

Butler, Judith. 1993. *Bodies That Matter: On the Discursive Limits of 'Sex.'* New York: Routledge.

Connell, R.W. and James W. Messerschmidt. 2005. "Hegemonic Masculinity: Rethinking the Concept." *Gender and Society* 19, no. 6: 829–859.

Darling-Wolf, Fabienne. 2003. "Male Bonding and Female Pleasure: Refining Masculinity in Japanese Popular Cultural Texts." *Popular Communication* 1, no. 2: 73–88.

———. 2004. "SMAP, Sex, and Masculinity: Constructing the Perfect Female Fantasy in Japanese Popular Music." *Popular Music and Society* 27, no. 3: 357–370.

Dasgupta, Romit. 2003. "Creating Corporate Warriors: The 'Salaryman' and Masculinity in Japan." In *Asian Masculinities: The Meaning and Practice of Manhood in China and Japan*, edited by Kam Louie and Morris Low, 118–134. Oxon: RoutledgeCurzon.

Gregson, Kimberly S. 2005. "Lead Character Like Me? Girl Fans of Shoujo Anime and Their Web Sites." In *Girl Wide Web: Girls, the Internet, and the Negotiation of Identity*, edited by Sharon R. Mazzarella, 121-140. New York: Peter Lang Publishing, Inc.

Hidaka, Tomoko. 2010. *Salaryman Masculinity: Continuity and Change in Hegemonic Masculinity in Japan*. Leiden: Brill.

Juffer, Jane. 1998. *At Home With Pornography: Women, Sex, and Everyday Life*. New York: New York University Press.

Kaplan, Danny. 2005. "Public Intimacy: Dynamics of Seduction in Male Homosocial Interactions." *Symbolic Interaction* 28, no. 4: 571–595.

Karniol, Rachel. 2001. "Adolescent Females' Idolization of Male Media Stars as a Transition Into Sexuality." *Sex Roles* 44, no. 1/2: 61–77.

Kinsella, Sharon. 1995. "Cuties in Japan." In *Women Media and Consumption in Japan*, edited by Brian Moeran and Lise Skov, 220–254. Surrey: Curzon Press.

Lunsing, Wim. 2001. *Beyond Common Sense: Sexuality and Gender in Contemporary Japan*. London: Kegan Paul Limited.

McLelland, Mark. 2000. *Male Homosexuality in Modern Japan: Cultural Myths and Social Realities*. Oxon: RoutledgeCurzon.

Mori Naoko. 2010. *Onna wa Poruno o Yomu: Josei no Seiyoku to Feminizumu*. Tokyo: Seikyūsha.

Penley, Constance. 1992. "Feminism, Psychoanalysis, and the Study of Popular Culture." In *Cultural Studies*, edited by Lawrence Grossberg, Cary Nelson, and Paula A. Treichler, 479–500. New York: Routledge.

Raviv, Amiram, Daniel Bar-Ta, Alona Raviv, and Asaf Ben-Horin. 1996. "Adolescent Idolization of Pop Singers: Causes, Expression, and Reliance." *Journal of Youth and Adolescence* 25, no. 5: 631–649.

Sakuragi Piroko. 2009. *Nikushokukei Joshi no Renaigaku: Kanojotachi wa Ika-ni Sōshokukei Danshi o Kuimakuru no ka*. Tokyo: Tokuma Shoten.

Sedgwick, Eve Kosofsky. 1985. *Between Men: English Literature and Male Homosocial Desire*. New York: Columbia University Press.

Stevens, Carolyn S. 2008. *Japanese Popular Music: Culture, Authenticity, and Power*. New York: Routledge.

Takahashi Sumire. 2005. " 'Yaoika' Suru Shisen, Sono Senryaku ni Mukete: 'DEATH NOTE' Dōjin Manga o Rei ni." *Joseigaku Nenpō* 26: 20–40.

Ugaya Hiromachi. 2005. *J-Poppu to wa Nani Ka? Kyodaika Suru Ongaku Sangyō*. Tokyo: Iwanami Shinsho.

Welker, James. 2006. "Beautiful, Borrowed, Bent: 'Boys' Love' as Girls' Love in *Shōjo* Manga." *Signs: Journal of Women in Culture and Society* 31, no. 3: 841–870.

West, Mark D. 2006. *Secrets, Sex, and Spectacle: The Rules of Scandal in Japan and the United States*. Chicago: University of Chicago Press.

Wood, Andrea. " 'Straight' Women, Queer Texts: Boy-Love Manga and the Rise of a Global Counterpublic." *Women's Studies Quarterly* 34, no. 1/2: 394–414.

Yano, Christine. 1997. "Charisma's Realm: Fandom in Japan." *Ethnology* 36, no. 4: 335–349.

6

The *Homo* Cultures of Iconic Personality in Japan: Mishima Yukio and Misora Hibari

Jonathan D. Mackintosh

In his entry "Who is a Gay Icon?" the *Tenoru Gay Times* blogmaster notes, "There is a word, *gei aikon* (gay icon). It probably comes from America. Although I've heard it ... I'm unfamiliar with it" (Maruyama 2008). The blogmaster's uncertainty highlights two ambiguities characterizing male gay culture in Japan. While it is evident that some celebrities—for example, pop singer Matsuda Seiko—hold special appeal for gay men, it isn't wholly clear why their "charisma" is such that they attract the "worship" specifically of these men.[1] What is it about being gay that these so-called icons articulate?

Furthermore, is the imported concept of the "gay icon" even meaningful? Indeed, it is a 1970s neologism emerging as a project of that decade's Anglo-American Movement for Gay Liberation: visible and representative of gay value, the admirable qualities and special accomplishments of highly visible celebrated individuals were deployed to act as a rallying point in the political resistance of gay people against their oppression (Dyer 2009, 12–14, 16). In contrast to this movement, which was "pivotal in making homosexual identity" (Rosenfeld 2003, 3), Japanese projects to effect similar change were limited, giving voice to some but hardly providing an axiomatic political model of identity for the vast majority of men-loving-men or the wider Japanese population (cf., McLelland 2000, 222–240).

Nonetheless, it is overly pessimistic to write off the concept of "gay icon" as irrelevant to Japan. As this chapter will demonstrate, what I shall refer to as the "*homo* cultures of iconic personality" are of historical and cultural analytical use. In their definition, they describe a defining moment in the early 1970s for the history of male homosexuality, or, as it was known in the culture of men-loving-men in Japanese at that time, *homo*. Between 1971 and 1975, Japan's first commercial and nationally distributed magazines by and for *homo* appeared,[2] and in the pages of *Barazoku* (founded 1971), *Adonis Boy* (1972), *Adon* (1974), and to a lesser extent *Sabu* (1974), aspiration was often palpable. In entering into the Japanese mediascape, these magazines sought to mobilize *homo* identity and effect community consciousness, and, most far-reaching, advocated a political space to affirm the legitimacy and equality of *homo* in the Japanese public sphere. Despite the momentary high profile of *homo*, modern *jōshiki* (heterosexual normality)[3] remained steadfast, *homo* activity returned to being largely invisible, and *homo*-phobic society went unchanged (Minami 1991, 130). The *homo* cultures of iconic personality are not the only factors that explain the nonemergence of a unified voice in the 1970s moment. But, in the diversity of priority and aspiration that these cultures reflected, we can begin to understand why, in the early 1970s, the *homo* history of Japan evolved largely in contradistinction to that of the Anglo-American West—despite the fact that both histories emerged out of a global synchronicity of capitalist modernity.

Specifically, the celebration in the *homo* magazines of two contemporary personalities illustrates divergent *homo* historical trajectories that give insight into the ambiguities characterizing the male homosexual experience in Japan. These are author and ultra-nationalist Mishima Yukio (1925–1971) and singer–actress Misora Hibari (1937–1989). On the one hand, a textually visualizing and evocatively imagined visual culture of Mishima emerged that seemed particularly suited to this new medium. In all the *homo* magazines, this culture was shaped to give witness to *homo* genius, and, in one conception, the Mishima-fired imagination envisaged a *homo* sexual revolution. Yet, as will be seen, the actual author's eccentric nationalist politics seemed to belie the culture–sex link, and the iconic appeal of the Mishima-*cum-homo* configuration to a liberationist political cause was awkward. In the case of "Hibari-*chan*," as her fans knew her—the suffix "*chan*" is a term of endearment—no special attempts were made in the *homo* magazines to see her effect a new public-sphere visibility. Rather, it seems to have been that spectacular voice which inspired; less self-consciously intellectual and forcefully discursive compared with Mishima, the audio culture of Misora's iconic personality was mnemonically powerful in its largely unarticulated sensibility, enabling men to position themselves in Japanese—hence, globalized—postwar history: it was a highly, if privately, affective act, an apparently a-political "performative utterance"

(Certeau 1984, 19) of personal identification within the world that, in a politically potent gesture, pooh-poohed *jōshiki*. A note about the primary sources cited in this chapter. A close textual analysis of all writings appearing in the first year of production of the magazines includes articles, fiction, and images as well as hundreds of personal ads[4] and letters from readers. More recent fan-based material supplements the analysis of Misora and is explained below.

Mishima Yukio

The idiosyncratic author might initially seem an unsurprising candidate to herald the entrance of *homo* into the Japanese mediascape (Appadurai 1996, 35) and public sphere. His graphic depiction of Tokyo's *homo* haunts in *Kinjiki* (Forbidden Colors), for instance, made for compelling *homo* reading. His extra-literary activities, including nude modeling and bodybuilding, confirmed a narcissistic appreciation of the male and often his own form. Rumoured flirtations with men fueled *homo* media gossip: membership of a secret Roppongi man-on-man sex appreciation club (Fujita 1972, 74), trysts with *Sabu* founder Mishima Gō, and the list goes on. Handsome and stylish, he was seen to mingle with Japan's cultural *illuminati*: Nobel recipient Kawabata Yasunari and acclaimed director Ichikawa Kon, to name a few (Nosaka 1970, 3–42, 87). Here was something of a Renaissance man, a contemporary if dead man-loving-man whose literature and life generated a highly evocative and visceral visual culture in text and image that, in the eyes of some, elevated *homo* to vindicate publicly their existence and worth.

For some, it was Mishima's literature that held out a model for sexual revolution. To *Adon* contributor Ueno Tetsu (1974, 46–47, 49), *Kinjiki* protagonist Yūichi stands out as a "representative" model of "first-rank character" for "homosexual independence." Regular contributor and Marcuse-inspired Nōkami Teruki (1972a, 25) takes a more politicized stance, arguing that the author's *Kinjiki* portrayal of Tokyo's public-toilet male–male-sex scene subverted a sexually repressive bourgeois morality to epitomize a universal, carefree, and undiscriminating love. Cultural critic and Mishima apologist Okuno Takeo (1970, 80–81) similarly argues that Mishima epitomized a "profound relationship between literature and action," according to which beauty—including *nanshoku* (male homosexuality)—must correspond with life. Based on this equation, it was a logical step for Nōkami (1972b, 19) to argue for the "normalization" of *nanshoku* as a matter of daily life in postwar Japan.[5]

Mishima's concern over beauty was self-consciously articulated as a visually eroticized spectacle of masculinity: in still photo, Mishima himself was depicted as a near-nude St Sebastian or in battle mode, chest bared, sword cocked, that ferocious glare crowned by the *shichishō hōkoku*[6] headband; in moving image, taking the lead in his 1966 film *Yūkoku* (Patriotism), in which he dramatizes his future suicide, or a supporting role as a statue that receives a 'gay kiss' in Fukasaku Kinji's 1968 *Kurotokage* (Black Lizard) (Stringer 2000, 121–122). In this visual culture featuring Mishima, a wider intertextual imagination includes film adaptation, as in the five remakes of *Shiosai* (Sound of the Waves), of which Moritani Shirō's 1971 image of naked youth was said to be "especially refreshing" (*Barazoku* 1972c, 66). Mishima's prose could itself be cinematically evocative. Consider the following description of protagonist Yūichi from *Kinjiki*:

> The gently sloping chest...the slightly tapering, chastely mature trunk, the long easy sinewy legs. When one took these and added them to the matchless, pure, youthful, statuesque shoulders, the eyebrows like narrow blades, the melancholy eyes, the truly boyish lips, the white, orderly, correct teeth, and the beautiful head they composed, the potential lovely harmony between what one saw and could not see.
>
> (Mishima 1971, 97)

The movement of the male *homo* gaze that this passage describes might be likened to a film camera. Cutting up the body into objectified parts, the cruising *homo* eye/camera appraises an initially headless body, tracking from torso downwards, and back up again to study each part of the face, finally ending in a full-shot contemplation of the whole package that is simultaneously an anticipatory sizing up of that which is hidden. All of this is to suggest that visuality as constructed through an intertextual "progression of texts and discourses...over years" (De Angelis 2001, 71) was central to the *homo* visual culture of Mishima's iconic personality.

This visual fantasy seems to have been as inspirational as it was evocative. In the following personal ad entitled "Bingo," the cinematic quality of Mishima's prose is directly referenced, providing the ad author with a potent means to describe himself and his desired other:

> **Bingo** 23 year-old, single, engineer. An avid reader of Mishima's literature. I'm like Yūichi, the hero of *Kinjiki*, and have even been scouted

by film producers... Please write if you are up to the same age as me, and are confident in your looks, which are like mine....

(*Barazoku* 1972b, 92, ad 123)

The spectacle of manly beauty that animates the imagination of a bodily self was taken up by others to be deployed as a potent tactic that might assert a public presence of *homo* cultural and social value. For example, in his critique of the 1972 nude-photo collection entitled *Otoko* (Man) by Mishima-peer Yatō Tamotsu, Nōkami rails: "it is difficult... to tolerate the current climate of Japan in which a photo collection of naked males can only automatically be thought of as homosexual" (1974, 54). In response, he calls for a "pluralization of value" that emerges from an aesthetic and universal appreciation of "the intense charms of the youth of Japan" and "the beauty of the male flesh" that is none other than a "*homo* cultural legacy" (1974, 54).

While Nōkami's adulation of Mishima took the form of intellectualized encomia, others paid tribute in uniquely creative ways, for example, works created in homage. Wakabayashi Takaichirō's (1971–1973) serialized novel *Eikyoku* (Profane Melody) is a "latter day tale of 'Forbidden Colors'" featuring the offspring of *Kinjiki*'s protagonist Yūichi. Mamiya Hiroshi's 1971 novel *Warui Yume* (Bad Dream) similarly draws on *Kinjiki* in its depiction of a character who, in reference to the novel's Yūichi-manipulating antagonist Shunsuke, sadistically deforms his young charge's penis. To this list we must add Inoue Kenji's photo-tribute *Makoto: Seppuku Nūdo* (Sincerity: Suicide Nude), the very first high-gloss photographs to appear in *Sabu* that portray a *fundoshi* (loincloth)-clad young man disembowelling himself with a samurai sword (1974, 7–10).

While the respect paid by the creators of these works may have been sincere, the value of their contributions to the Mishima legacy seems ambivalent. Their lurid portrayals—the obviously fake blood in Inoue's photos, for example—cheapen the authenticity of the originals they seek to *re*-present, while the boundary between male beauty and pornographic excess is blurred, so that Mishima's erotic aesthetic is clichéd: a sado-masochistic *eros-to-thanatos* masturbation-fantasy of sexy suicide. Yet, it is precisely this creative energy that is central to the generation of the *homo* cultures of iconic personality. In this fandom, Mishima becomes truly potent: his consumption ignites fans' imaginations and re-signifies sex, gender, bodies in the case of Inoue, and the nation for Nōkami; a Mishima-inspired *homo* sensibility is detectable.

Which brings us to the appeal Mishima had for *homo* more generally. In the personal ads, only Bingo above cites Mishima directly, though more references are found in other reader contributions. In his letter to *Adon*, 45-year-old Murasaki Teruhiko describes how he keeps safe the treasured reply to his fan letter that he received from the author (1974, 121). In fact, Murasaki exemplifies a particular kind of manliness that was frequently explored in the new *homo* media, one that drew from Mishima's aesthetic politics. In his fondness for uniform—living in the policeman's dorm for single officers was "just paradise!" he recalls (1974, 120)—Murasaki paints a highly embodied image of *takumashii* (brawn) whose bodily materialization animates a traditionalistic idiom of love (see note 5). Speaking of his lover Z, he writes, "He is attracted to uniform and loincloth because his deceased father was a Maritime Safety officer. When just we two are together, he calls me 'papa'" (1974, 121).

This erotically charged, militaristic image of male camaraderie corresponds with Mishima's ethno-nationalist aesthetics, whose most radical articulation was the author's ritual suicide. Although nihilistic, it was, as Iida observes, a "symbolic sacrifice made in order to revitalize...the Japanese cultural ethos," a spiritual—and very manly—aesthetics that, for Mishima, had once defined the soul of Japan, but that had withered under the nation's feminization in the Allied Occupation (1945–1952), its subsequent modernization-*cum*-Westernization, and the emperor's humanization (Igarashi 2000, 20–35; Iida 2002, 148–149). The point was not lost on apologists like Nōkami, who understood that Mishima's act of "discovering death" was the "discovery of the meaning of life," which is also to say the reinjection of manly beauty into Japan's postwar history (1972a, 22). Although it is impossible to ascertain how widely inspirational Mishima's more extreme romantic gestures to escape modernity were, it does appear that beauty, manliness, love, and Japan together helped articulate one idiom of *homo* desire, as the following personal ad suggests of a young Osaka man. Invoking the prewar *Roman-ha* (Romantic School) movement that initially exposed Mishima to ethnic nationalism and romanticism (Doak 1996), it reads:

Roman-ha I'm 20 and a university student who continues to pursue a movement to protect Japanese culture and traditions as passed down through literature and martial arts. I'm waiting for a *bishōnen* [beautiful youth] who is able to uphold sincerity together with me, giving his life to this cause.

(*Adon* 1974, 125, ad 125)

Given the extremes of Mishima's ultra-nationalist expression, one won-
ders to what extent "everybody's favourite homofascist" (Vincent 2000)
was suited to representing the aspirations of some *homo* for public-
sphere visibility, equality, and political rights. His literature and life
extolled the virtues of closeted sexual desire, the pleasures of Tokyo's
homo culture furtively pursued if highly enjoyed. Mishima's brand of
manly beauty was also just one of many idioms in an increasingly seg-
mented and sometimes-conflicting *homo* gaze. In another iconic *homo*
culture of what might be framed as European occidental beauty, for
example, Alain Delon, the "Ice-cold Angel" of Melville's 1967 *nouvelle
vague* classic *Le Samouraï*,[7] features alongside Dirk Bogarde and Peter
O'Toole; together, they describe a vulnerable and complicated manliness
which 1960s and 1970s *auteur*-inspired film culture increasingly privileged in its male representations (Miller 2010, 112–113). Their citation
is telling, since this contemporary, bourgeoisified, and cosmopolitan
male–male spatial mapping of desire within the global mediascape
sees the West ambiguously objectified, at once appreciated for its projected cultural authenticity and objectified as an erotically consumed
postcolonial "other." Mishima's recidivist nationalism was, by contrast,
camply serious, and it could make the place of a navel-gazing Japan in
the contemporary global imaginary exotic and/or awkward.

That Mishima was a figure of great notoriety is beyond doubt. His
genius, born of his homosexuality (Nakano 1972, 4–8), situated him
at the centre of an iconic culture whose traditionalistic aesthetics resonated with the erotically nostalgic desires of *some* Japanese men for
manly men. Nōkami notwithstanding, the liberationist aspirations of
the *homo* project seemed incidental, if not ill-related, to the ultra-
patriotic expressions that configured the consumption of the Mishima
visual culture—this, even as male–male eroticism was nonetheless central to its manly aesthetics. Indeed, although his suicide was regarded
as a "pageant of a death of passion," in the opinion of *homo* activist
and *Adon* founder Minami Teishirō, the spectacle of manliness that
Mishima's vision described was of negligible contribution to the opening of the public sphere for *homo*: "1970...the gay novelist died. Not
one thing changed" (Minami 1991, 128–129).

Misora Hibari

It was reported in the *homo* magazine *Adon*, "Amongst the men who like
Misora Hibari [1937–1989], there are lots of *homo*" (Guriin Kurabu 1974,
95). As this snippet overheard in a *homo* sauna suggests, this female

paragon of *enka*[8] vocal artistry held special appeal for *homo*. Three decades later, the popularity of Japan's "Eternal Songstress" (Hibari Production Group 2003) was said to have dwindled little for *homo*—now known as gay—who, in their 60s and above, first encountered her when they were in their 20s and 30s in the 1960s.[9]

Actually, in contrast to Mishima, references to Misora are few in the *homo*-magazine sampling. This scarcity renders a close analysis of the contemporary *homo* magazines difficult. To supplement primary texts, this chapter turns to later Japanese gay-fan writings. While it is recognized that the obscuring role of memory which "privileg[es] the present... as a condition of constructing the past" (Harootunian 2000, 13) limits the applicability of these writings to historical inference, they nevertheless provide insight into the *homo* appreciation—an unarticulated sensibility perhaps—of Misora's pre-1970s. I also draw upon studies of the pre-Gay-Liberation culture of iconic personality in the Euro-American West. This comparative perspective facilitates a theorization of the global synchronicity of capitalist modernity.

Let's turn to two personal ads that appeared in the *homo* magazines:

O I awaken through '*Hibari no nakigoe*' [bird-song of Misora/a skylark].[10] I am a laid back sort of guy who lives alone, 30 yo, 164 cm, 70 kg. Please send me a letter if you are in your teens or 20s...

(*Barazoku* 1972a, 36, ad 76)

Hibari I'd like a fun relationship with somebody in their 50s, 60s. I'm 27-years-old, 160 cm, and single. I'm an ordinary public official whose hobbies include *fundoshi*, drinking *sake* [alcohol/rice wine], and tea ceremony...

(*Barazoku* 1972a, 53, ad 313)

These self-portraits hint at how the *homo* cultural sensibility of Misora's iconic personality enabled some to articulate who they are. In the story of "O," an image is presented of a man average in height if stout in stature, alone in Tokyo's vast sub-urban conurbation. The reference to "*Hibari no nakigoe*" evokes the singer's musical talents. Take, for example, the song "Ringo Oiwake" (Apple Blossom Song): an arpeggiated Vaughan-Williams-*Lark-Ascending*-like introduction on flute gives way to the gently rocking rhythm of a horse-drawn cart, to which Misora sings in trademark fashion from low to falsetto-high, and, in the climax, a mellifluous vocal *fushi-mawashi* (trill) mimics the flute which mimicked a bird. In its passages that celebrate blossoming youth and laments its passing through parting and death, "Ringo Oiwake" above all sings of uncertainty. It was released in May 1952 against a backdrop of monumental historical change: although the implementation of the San Francisco Peace Treaty just one month prior brought the Allied Occupation to its formal close, Japanese freedom was far from being associated with economic prosperity. This song, which is synonymous with Misora's voice—"no singer has managed yet to sing it like her" wrote one gay fan (*2-channeru* 2004, entry 41)[11]— cues a memory of the early postwar era in which melancholic doubt and defiant resilience were all personified by this singer (Tansman 1996, 111).

Yet, the revival of Japan which saw the country become the world's second-largest economy in 1968 was an epic tale of comeback, one that was charted in the evolution of Misora's media personae: from the innocent orphan she played in the 1949 film *Kanashiki Kuchibue* (Mournful Whistle) to the samurai figure of her 1965 performance of "Yawara" (The Gentle Way) on NHK's (Japan Broadcasting Corporation) new year *Kōhaku Uta Gassen* (Red and White Song Battle) gala, she gives voice to the hardships endured and pains suffered that accompanied poverty, reconstruction, and prosperity. By 1965, the theme of endurance, focus, and eventual triumph that "Yawara" described were now more a matter of nostalgia than contemporary experience. But, in the remembrances of everyday struggle it evoked, "*Hibari no nakigoe*" was also a popular-cultural audio fragment echoing in Japan's collective postwar memory, the voice of a "working-class singer" (Tansman 1996, 121) made good. Less a socioeconomic description than a signifying function that recalls victimhood of ordinary people, the "working-class" image endowed Misora with the "authority of common feeling possessed by all the nameless" (Tansman 1996, 107). Her very unordinary vocal gifts ensured that this "authority" was potently iconic in the original sacred sense. That is, in embodying the ordinary people, she was endurance and the power to overcome incarnate, and, in this transcendence, she held out the prospect of gaining "intimate access to the authentic self" (Gledhill 1991, xvii; Dyer 2009, 13). The "authentic self" is precisely what "Hibari" in his personal ad seems to wish to show. For him, authenticity is found in his own highlighted ordinariness: an unexceptional job in the bureaucracy; an unencumbered manliness baring nearly all in a single strip of cloth; the simple pleasures of drink, sipping *sake* and the simplicity of the Japanese art of tea. Through Misora, "Hibari" reveals a true self and is endowed with that highly affirming of qualities, ordinariness.[12]

Despite appeals like those that "Hibari" made to "Japanese-ness," the *enka* music which Misora helped to distinguish is, according to Yano, the "song of Japan" by design. Highly contrived and commercial in its mass production, *enka* may have had roots in indigenous popular forms, but its postwar incarnation is a relatively recent invention whose largely Western instrumentation and harmonic forms are overlooked (Yano 2003, 78–79). The hybridity that Yano hints at is fully explored by Mōri Yoshitaka (2009), who directs our attention to Kōga Masao, the composer behind such Misora hits as "Yawara." Kōga's composition incorporates a variety of *already* hybridized influences ranging from America and Europe to continental Asia, all of which are distilled through the composer's boyhood experiences in colonial Korea. "Kōga melody" may now be understood as synonymous with "the heart and soul of Japan" (Mōri 2009, 220), but his *enka* exemplifies that "Japanese postwar popular music was hybridized from the very beginning of its history," or, as Mōri theorizes, "hybridity as origin" (2009, 222–223).

"Hybridity as origin" goes beyond conceiving of modernity as a simplistic equation of global–local transnational cultural flows, according to which the local is merely an adaptation, a "glocalizing" Japanization (Iwabuchi 2002, 46–47) of some imported authentic source. Rather, modernity is generated through the "synchronous interpenetration and interconnection" (Iwabuchi 2002, 119) of material and cultural experience in the everyday of the capitalist world: the epistemological reference points which this experience assembles are shared in the perception of macro-historical events and trajectories, and hence the understanding of one's specific place in the world.

The *homo* cultural sensibility of Misora's iconic personality emerges out of an articulation of a particular mid-twentieth-century experience in ways synchronous with figures like Judy Garland in the US and others elsewhere. For example, they respond to war and economic privation in similarly sentimental, if cynical, ways: to Garland's "We're-Off-to-See-the-Wizard" ditty that saw her Toto-toting Dorothy and her motley mates skip fatefully off to meet a snake-oil-prescribing charlatan all in spectacular Technicolor (Evans 2009), there is Misora's ironic "O-Matsuri Mambo" (Festival Mambo). Its Latin rhythms mix with lyrics so fast as to rival the Victorian patter of any modern Major-General, all to describe how a local festival in old-town Tokyo raucously thumps onwards despite the burning and thieving of the houses of festivity-inebriated festival-goers. Reflecting on the punch-line pun of the final verse—"cry all they might, it's all twenty-twenty hindsight!"[13]—one gay fan observes that "there is something pretty profound within the songs of Hibari" (*2-channeru* 2004, entry 22). According to this critique, fulfill-ment is not found in social spectacles, no matter how enticing they might be. Rather, and this describes the mid-twentieth-century con-cern over individual authenticity to which both Garland and Misora appealed in these examples, it comes only in the very homely wisdom born of self-reflection.

Known through cinema, record, radio, and television, Misora and Garland were fashioned within an "epistemology of melodrama" whose "gestural, visual, and musical excess" stylized ethical conflict and the pathos of life (Gledhill 1987, 30–31). Just as the song "Kanashii Sake" (1967) expressed the suffering of women, in the understanding of one gay fan who quotes a television interview with Misora—"my family, my brothers, too many painful things" (*2-channeru* 2004, entry 23)—so too did Garland's 1954 torch song "The Man That Got Away." In both cases, sentimentality scripts the public disclosure of private emotion, and in this melodrama, where Misora and Garland are seen and heard to suf-fer at the hands of men, personal tragedy is a broader social one. They are sympathetic role models in a postwar era that contradictorily offered women a leading role in the Japanese and Euro-American "romance of democracy" (Eley 1996, 84), and then failed to see the patriarchal order transformed. This history of gender inequality cast in a narrative of lost love relates specifically to the experience of women, but it resonated too with *homo*, if one self-proclaimed *okama* (*homo*, "poof"), who affects an effeminate drawl, is indicative. According to him, Misora's 1972 "Aru Onna no Uta" (Song of A Woman), which laments lost love and suf-fering at the hands of a man, "is popular with *okama* . . . I like it too" (*2-channeru* 2004, entry 529).

Suffering brings us to another way that the mid-postwar experience was articulated. As personae constructed out of studios' desire to put forward images of propriety to hide the actual individuals' own tur-bulent lives, an image of the indefatigability of the ordinary puffed out the melodramatic myth further, so that, as one gay fan asserted of Misora, "she completely inhabited the heroes in the lyrics . . . she created her own world of song" (*2-channeru* 2004, entry 61). To this end, the Misora of "Yawara" was perseverance itself in the face of her brother's mafia associations, and, in the words of one sympathetic fan, his "*baka musuko*" (foolish son) who fell into her care (Tansman 1996, 128; *2-channeru* 2004, entry 35); Garland kept on smiling through her cocktail of drugs mixed with inappropriate men (Dyer 1987, 150–152); while France's Edith Piaf never regretted in spite of her accidents and addictions. These melodramatic tales are morality plays that affirm the centrality of the individual to modernity. With Japan's emperor system now largely defunct and the West on both sides of the Atlantic on a secularizing path, there was no appeal to be made to transcendent moral value. "Personality," therefore, as Gledhill argues, "becomes the source of overriding imperatives... The moral is personal" (1987, 30–31).

In Habermas's interpretation, this moral elevation of personality degraded the public sphere into the "privatized consciousness of the consuming public," and "sentimentality toward persons and corresponding cynicism toward institutions which with social psychological inevitability result naturally" (1992, 171–172). It's an apt description of Misora's fan adulation, but perhaps Habermas's saturnine appraisal misses something. Indeed, there was potency in the empathy audiences felt when she and other songstresses "resist[ed] the corruption of commercialization" (Tansman 1996, 128), not to mention the increasing bureaucratic rationalization of the individual in the latter half of the twentieth century (Hogan 1987, 3; Turner 1996, 12–3, 49–50); this even at their own personal risk of losing all, in the case of Misora when NHK snubbed her, and Garland when MGM dumped her.

All of these examples suggest that the *homo* cultural sensibility of Misora's iconic personality was generated through an intersection of competing social–cultural discourses and the self-narration of one's place in the world. As a product of state-*cum*-corporate entertainment interests, Misora was mass-produced on an industrial scale and mass-mediated at electronic speed to feed a rationalized bourgeois market. In this sense, it is appropriate to understand the singer in terms of "kitsch genius" (Tansman 1996, 125). Yet Tansman is also right when he observes that her "audacious artificiality" was "also deeply sincere" (1996, 103). First and foremost, the cultural sensibility of Misora's iconic personality must be understood as a highly affective personal identification that gives emotional meaning to one's place in history. Writing of Garland's iconic status, Dyer writes: "[she] works in an emotional register of great intensity which seems to bespeak equally suffering and survival, vulnerability and strength, theatricality and authenticity, passion and irony" (1987, 155). So, too, does Misora.

Aside from a more general identification, why did *homo* specifically identify with her? One could point to her melodramatic excess through which "distortions and contradictions of bourgeois—or petit bourgeois—ideology" (Gledhill 1987, 7) are revealed to lend critical, some might say camp and queer, value (Cleto 1999, 28). Certainly, in those postwar decades when homosexuality had to be hidden, Misora, Garland, and others gave a nod and a wink to transgressive desire through their gender-play. To Garland's campy androgynous tramp in *Easter Parade*'s "We're a Couple of Swells" (1948) (Dyer 1987, 176) and Marlene Dietrich's tuxedoed woman-to-woman kiss in *Morocco* (1930) (Weiss 1991, 284–287), we must add Misora's 1965 "Yawara" performance. She is not dressed as any samurai warrior, though the image buttressed the association of Japan's salaryman with *kigyō senshi* (corporate warriors) (Plath 1964, 35; Ueno 1995, 216). Rather, she plays a *wakashū* (male warrior retainer), replete with erotically resplendent *maegami* (forelocks) (Pflugfelder 1999, 32). A straightforward reading might argue that this performance revives her role in the 1958 hit film *Hanagasa Wakashū* (Young Man in a Flower-Garlanded Hat), which it certainly does. But this is to overlook a number of ambiguities. The *wakashū* is the youthful counterpart to an older lover in the premodern *nanshoku* male–male-erotic coupling (Pflugfelder 1999, 29–44). Although the *yaoi* manga (male-homoerotic comic-book) genre for young women was still yet to appear (Kinsella 2000, 115–117), its stylizations were already foreshadowed in the all-female Takarazuka stage troupe, popular in particular, it is said, with *homo* (Guriin Kurabu 1974, 95). To raucous applause and cheers reminiscent of Takarazuka audiences, Misora acknowledges with a wave one fan who squeals out *"Hibari-chan, kakko ii zo!"* (You're cool/handsome Hibari-*chan*!).

The queer implications are clear. Izumo Marō's study of Misora's "drag king" persona observes a playful "spirit of transcending woman/man/gender/class" (2002, 64; cf., Kyūshū Danji *n.d.*). Some fans go so far as to suggest that Misora was herself homosexual.[14] Regardless of these rumors' veracity, it seems that, for some, personal identification was configured in terms specifically of *homo* performativity, identity, and/or desire. Like Mishima, Misora possibly inspires a common cultural value or "sensibility" (Babuscio 1999, 118): which is not to say a movement for *homo* liberation, since, as this analysis observes, the *homo* cultural sensibility of Misora's iconic personality and the *homo* magazines' aspirations are incidental to each other. Unlike Mishima, whose iconic culture was generated by men like Nōkami to represent an essential *homo* quality and quantify its worth, thereby conflating a private desire with a public discourse, Misora's cultural sensibility loosely wove together a diversity of largely unconnected individualized expressions authored by fans. Little attempt was made by the *homo* magazines to manage or augment this expression.

In this sense, the *homo* cultural sensibility of Misora's iconic personality charts a very different historical *homo* trajectory from that which Mishima initially seemed to suggest and that Garland across the Pacific came preeminently to represent as the ultimate icon of Gay Liberation. In de-emphasizing any effective representational function that Misora's cultural sensibility may have played, an important prospect is opened, one that interrogates an automatic positioning of *homo* within the subaltern. Certainly, the suffering and struggle, which Misora spoke to, may have been experienced by some fans as the *homo*-phobic oppressions of *jōshiki*. But, they might equally have highlighted these same fans' concern to understand their suffering and struggle in terms of postwar narratives of national reconstruction and economic achievement. The cultural sensibility of Misora's iconic personality enables those who generate it to find a place in history as *homo* men and/or as men who may be *homo*.

Conclusion

Despite the initial promise the new *homo* media seemed to offer, "epochal change" (Minami 1991, 130) that would open the public sphere to *homo* did not transpire. While it is tempting to regard this lack of change simply in terms of divergence from Western gay history, which was hegemonically configured through Gay Liberation, the *homo* cultures of iconic personality paradoxically suggest how we might approach this moment alternatively. Accordingly, a model of global cultural flow configured along a West-to-rest directionality is inappropriate. So, too, is the reverse position, which asserts that the "local destabilizes the homogenizing tendencies of global gay formations" (Grewal and Kaplan 2001, 671): it inadequately explains the *homo* cultures of iconic personality in the absence of a transnational-Gay-Movement dynamic. Yet, it is neither coincidental nor accidental that Garland's name appears interchangeable with Misora's. Both are global phenomena, cultures of iconic personality that were epistemologically possible and perhaps culturally probable in their capitalist mediascapes. Although they took increasingly different practical forms, especially from the 1970s onwards, they emerged synchronously out of a twentieth-century globally shared modern condition whose discourse of sexuality—in its characterization of homosexuality as abnormal—never so fully foreclosed the possibility of its own destabilization. Despite the impetus of the modern state to mould its citizenry through bureaucratic rationalization, popular culture was a site where individuals might open a space shaped by their own desires and experiences. In the case of Mishima for some and in America for many others, men strategically mobilized culture to make *homo* identity essential: the private became public and political. That the culture of Mishima's iconic personality was intellectually contradictory in part explains why it failed to command a universally recognized representative position for *homo*. With Misora's cultural sensibility—and Garland's, too, before and for many even after the 1970s, for that matter—the focus was maintained on a private self to be shaped through the highly affective inspiration of a public persona. Tendentiously *homo* in orientation, the spaces of individual exploration it opened were ambiguous and did not necessarily reduce men-loving-men to an essential identity.

All of this is to say that Mishima and Misora are generated as aspects of Japanese modernity emerging through a global epistemology of intersecting historical trajectories, or as Manalansan IV observes, "the local and national are inflected and implicated in manifold ways with each other and with the international/transnational on the level of the everyday" (2003, 224).

The appearance of the everyday at this juncture is useful because it recognizes the historically contextualized place of individuals negotiating identity and desire. In this maneuvering, in which mass-produced cultural products and mass-mediated meaning are perpetually if momentarily reshaped by individuals, the everyday becomes a perspective highlighting potent contradiction as opposed to a powerful politics of conflict: the expressions of *homo* desire are publicly private, globally Japanese, and resistant in their complicity with the dominant order. As Certeau observes, the "everyday practices of consumers" are "tactical" and " 'clever' tricks of the 'weak' within the order established by the 'strong,' an art of putting one over on the adversary on his own turf" (1984, 40). It is this artful "trickery" (Certeau 1984, 26) that enabled *homo* fans to generate Mishima and Misora as cultures of iconic personality, privately and sometimes publicly political in significance, shared possibly in sensibility, and meaningful to the articulation of one's desires and history in global Japan.

Notes

1. "Gei ni totte Saigo no Karisuma Kashu, Matsuda Seiko," entry posted 28 May 2005, *carpediem mementmori.* http://blogs.yahoo.co.jp/carpediem_ mementmori/3721903.html (accessed 31 December 2010).
2. For example, *Barazoku* was greeted with *homo*-phobic vitriol in Japan's tabloid press, where it was denounced typically as perverse and depraved (Mackintosh 2010, 3, 29).
3. Literally, "common sense." See Lunsing (2001), whose exploration of *jōshiki* describes patriarchal heteronormativity.

4. The introduction of a nationwide personal ads system in the magazines through which men sought relationships with other men was an innovation of defining importance. The expansive detail many men provided about themselves is notable (Mackintosh 2010, 135–148).
5. The term *nanshoku* is seen in the *homo* magazines often to reference premodern Japanese male–male eroticism. *Nanshoku* typically aestheticizes male–male relationships according to an age-structured hierarchy in which maturity signifies paternal care and youth equates loyalty with physical beauty. For fans like Nōkami and Okuno, Mishima's ultra-nationalist ideology was conflated with *nanshoku*.
6. Warrior slogan extolling self-sacrifice, literally "devote your seven lives to the service of the nation."
7. See, for example, Hamahara (1971, 51–53).
8. *Enka* is a genre of "Japanese melancholic ballads" (cf., Yano 1994, 75; Mōri 2009, 221).
9. "Gei ni totte Saigo no Karisuma Kashu, Matsuda Seiko," entry posted 28 May 2005, *carpediem mementmori*. http://blogs.yahoo.co.jp/carpediem_mementmori/3721903.html (accessed 31 December 2010).
10. Hibari also means "skylark" in Japanese.
11. This quote comes from a gay discussion board on the topic "Gays Speaking About Misora Hibari" on the popular Internet forum *2channel* between 27 January and 4 May 2004. Because its 588 entries are mostly anonymous, identities and motivations are indeterminate.
12. In the *homo*-magazine personal ads, 8 percent of men who listed nonphysical qualities expressly desired 'ordinary' in a potential partner.
13. The idiomatic expression *ato no matsuri* means "with the benefit of hindsight."
14. See, for example, Paghat the Ratgirl (2005).

Works Cited

2-channeru. 2004. " 'O-Jō' Gei ga Kataru Misora Hibari 'Barihī'.' " *Kakō Burogu Sōko: 2-channeru no Kakō Burogu 1*. http://mimizun.com/2chlog/gay/love2.2ch.net/gay/pool/1075173421.html (accessed 9 February 2011).
3M. 1974. "Watashi no Shōnenki." *Adon* 5 (October): 132–134.
Adon. 1974. "Adon Puraza." July.
Appadurai, Arjun. 1996. *Modernity at Large: Cultural Dimensions of Globalization*. Minneapolis: University of Minnesota Press.
Babuscio, Jack. 1999. "The Cinema of Camp (*aka* Camp and the Gay Sensibility)." In *Camp: Queer Aesthetics and the Performing Subject*, edited by Fabio Cleto, 117–135. Edinburgh: Edinburgh University Press.
Barazoku. 1972a. "Barazoku Tsūshin." September.
———. 1972b. "Barazoku Tsūshin." January.
———. 1972c. "Hadaka no Seishun o Egaita Sawayaka-na Futatsu no Hōga kara." January 3.
Certeau, Michel de. 1984. *The Practice of the Everyday*. Trans. Steven Rendall. Berkeley: University of California Press.

Cleto, Fabio. 1999. "Introduction: Queering the Camp." In *Camp: Queer Aesthetics and the Performing Subject*, edited by Fabio Cleto, 1–42. Edinburgh: Edinburgh University Press.

De Angelis, Michael. 2001. *Gay Fandom and Crossover Stardom: James Dean, Mel Gibson, and Keanu Reeves*. Durham and London: Duke University Press.

Doak, Kevin M. 1996. "Ethnic Nationalism and Romanticism in Early Twentieth-Century Japan." *Journal of Japanese Studies* 22, no. 1: 77–103.

Dyer, Richard. 1987. *Heavenly Bodies: Film Stars and Society*. Basingstoke and London: Macmillan Educational Ltd.

———. 2009. *Gay Icons*. London: National Portrait Gallery.

Eley, Geoff. 1996. "Legacies of Antifascism: Constructing Democracy in Postwar Europe." *New German Critique* 67 (Winter): 73–100.

Evans, Stephen. 2009. *Over the Rainbow with Yip Harburg*. BBC Radio 4. 6 October.

Fujita Ryū. 1972. "Maboroshi no Hanabi: Homo Poruno no Shashinka o Itamu." *Barazoku* 3 (January): 72–74.

Gledhill, Christine. 1987. "The Melodramatic Field: An Investigation." In *Home is Where the Heart is: Studies in Melodrama and Women's Film*, edited by Christine Gledhill, 5–39. London: British Film Institute.

———. 1991. "Introduction." In *Stardom: Industry of Desire*, edited by Christine Gledhill, xiii–xx. London: Routledge.

Grewal, Inderpal and Caren Kaplan. 2001. "Global Identities: Theorizing Transnational Studies of Sexuality." *GLQ* 7, no. 4: 663–679.

Guriin Kurabu. 1974. "Saakuru Mura." *Adon* 2 (July): 95.

Habermas, Jürgen. 1992. *The Structural Transformation of the Public Sphere*. Trans. Thomas Burger and Frederick Lawrence. Cambridge: Polity Press.

Hamahara Midorigo. 1971. "Eiga no Naka ni Arawareta Otoko-dōshi no Ai no Katachi." *Barazoku* 1 (September): 51–54.

Harootunian, Harry. 2000. *History's Disquiet: Modernity, Cultural Practice, and the Question of Everyday Life*. New York: Columbia University Press.

Hibari Production Group. 2003. *Misora Hibari Kōshiki Uebusaito*. http://www. misorahibari.com/ (accessed 31 December 2010).

Hogan, Michael J. 1987. *The Marshall Plan: America, Britain, and the Reconstruction of Western Europe, 1947–1952*. Cambridge: Cambridge University Press.

Igarashi, Yoshikuni. 2000. *Bodies of Memory: Narratives of War in Postwar Japanese Culture, 1945–1970*. Princeton: Princeton University Press.

Iida, Yumiko. 2002. *Rethinking Identity in Modern Japan: Nationalism as Aesthetics*. London and New York: Routledge.

Inoue Kenji. 1974. "Makoto: Seppuku Nūdo." *Sabu* 1 (November): 7–10.

Iwabuchi Kōichi. 2002. *Recentering Globalization: Popular Culture and Japanese Transnationalism*. Durham: Duke University Press.

Izumo Marō. 2002. *Chanbara Kuiin*. Tokyo: Pandora.

Kinsella, Sharon. 2000. *Adult Manga: Culture and Power in Contemporary Japanese Society*. Richmond, Surrey: Curzon Press.

Kyūshū Danji. *n.d.* "Chanbara Kuiin, Izumo Marō (Pandora)." *Kyūshū Shūdōin*. http://www.myagent.ne.jp/~redcat/matsu/syudo/n_s_2.html (accessed 9 February 2011).

Lunsing, Wim. 2001. *Beyond Common Sense: Negotiating Constructions of Sexuality and Gender in Japan*. London: Kegan Paul International.

Mackintosh, Jonathan D. 2010. *Homosexuality and Manliness in Postwar Japan*. London and New York: Routledge.

Mamiya Hiroshi. 1971. "Warui Yume." *Barazoku* 4 (March): 61–66.

Manalansan IV, Martin F. 2003. "In the Shadows of Stonewall: Examining Gay Transnational Politics and the Diasporic Dilemma." In *Theorizing Diaspora: A Reader*, edited by Jana Evans Braziel and Anita Mannur, 207–227. Oxford: Blackwell Publishing.

Maruyama Tenoru. 2008. "Gei Aikon, Dare ni Suru?" *Tenoru Gay Taimuzu*. http://tapten.at.webry.info/200801/article_8.html (accessed 31 December 2010).

McLelland, Mark J. 2000. *Male Homosexuality in Modern Japan: Cultural Myths and Social Realities*. Richmond: Curzon Press.

Miller, Jacqui. 2010. "The French New Wave and the New Hollywood: Le Samourai and its American Legacy." *Film and Media Studies* 3: 109–120.

Minami Teishirō. 1991. "Sengo Nihon no Gei Mūbumento." *Impakushon* 71, 124–133. Tokyo: Impakuto Shuppankai.

Mishima Yukio. 1971. *Forbidden Colors*. Trans. Alfred H. Marks. London: Penguin Books.

Mōri Yoshitaka. 2009. "Reconsidering Cultural Hybridities: Transnational Exchanges of Popular Music in between Korea and Japan." In *Cultural Studies and Cultural Industries in Northeast Asia: What a Difference a Region Makes*, edited by Chris Berry, Nicola Liscutin and Jonathan D. Mackintosh, 213–230. Hong Kong: Hong Kong University Press.

Murasaki Teruhiko. 1974. "Homo Sodachi." *Adon* 3 (August): 120–121.

Nakano Hisao. 1972. "Dōsei no Moto ni Umareta Mishima Yukio nado no Geijutsuka-tachi." *Barazoku* 3 (January): 4–8.

Nōkami Teruki. 1972a. "Essei Romanchika." *Barazoku* 5 (May): 20–25.

———. 1972b. "Homo Chūdoku Kanja no Shuki." *Barazoku* 7 (September): 16–22.

———. 1974. "Harutachi Kaeru Yorokobi—Yatō Tamotsu-cho Shashinshū—Otoko Shō." *Adon* 1 (May): 52–55.

Nosaka Akiyuki. 1970. "Mishima Yukio Tokusen Gurafu Shū." *Shūkan Gendai— Zōkan: Mishima Yukio Kinkyū Tokushū-gō* (December 12): 3–42.

Okuno Takeo. 1970. "Mishima Yukio Nyūmon." *Shūkan Gendai—Zōkan: Mishima Yukio Kinkyū Tokushū-gō* (December 12): 77–81.

Paghat the Ratgirl. 2005. "Hibari-san's Gender-Bending Chambara." *Kurotokagi Gumi*. http://www.weirdwildrealm.com/f-hibari.html (accessed 9 February 2011).

Pflugfelder, Gregory M. 1999. *Cartographies of Desire: Male-Male Sexuality in Japanese Discourse, 1600–1950*. Berkeley: University of California Press.

Plath, David. 1964. *The After Hours: Modern Japan and the Search for Enjoyment*. Berkeley: University of California Press.

Rosenfeld, Dana. 2003. *The Changing of the Guard: Lesbian and Gay Elders, Identity, and Social Change*. Philadelphia: Temple University Press.

Stringer, Julian. 2000. "Two Japanese Variants of the Absolute Transvestite Film." *Journal of Homosexuality* 39, no. 3: 111–126.

Tansman, Alan M. 1996. "Mournful Tears and *Sake*: The Postwar Myth of Misora Hibari." In *Contemporary Japan and Popular Culture*, edited by John Whittier Treat, 103–133. Richmond: Curzon Press.

Turner, Bryan S. 1996. *The Body and Society: Explorations in Social Theory*. London: Sage Publications Ltd.

Ueno Chizuko. 1995. "Introduction." *Danseigaku*. Vol. *bekkan* of *Nihon no Feminizumu*, edited by Inoue Teruko, Ueno Chizuko and Egawa Yumiko, 216. Tokyo: Iwanami Shoten.

Ueno Tetsu. 1974. "Mishima Yukio-cho: Kinjiki, Hiyaku ni okeru Dōseiaisha no Jishusei." *Adon* 3 (August): 46–49.

Vincent, James Keith. 2000. "Writing Sexuality: Heteronormativity, Homophobia and the Homosocial Subject in Modern Japan." PhD diss., Columbia University.

Weiss, Andrea. 1991. "A Queer Feeling When I Look at You: Hollywood Stars and Lesbian Spectatorship in the 1930s." In *Stardom: Industry of Desire*, edited by Christine Gledhill, 283–299. London: Routledge.

Yano, Christine R. 1994. "Longing for *Furusato*: The Shaping of Nostalgia in Japanese Popular *Enka* Music." *Proceedings of the Fifth Annual PhD Kenkyūkai Conference on Japanese Studies*. Tokyo: International House of Japan: 75–95.

———. 2003. "The Burning of Men: Masculinities and the Nation in Japanese Popular Song." In *Men and Masculinities in Contemporary Japan: Dislocating the Salaryman Doxa*, edited by James E. Roberson and Nobue Suzuki, 77–90. London and New York: RoutledgeCurzon.

Wakabayashi Taka'ichirō. 1971–1973. "Eikyoku." *Barazoku* 2–10 (November– March).

Part III
Difference

7
Idol as Accidental Activist: Agnes Chan, Feminism, and Motherhood in Japan

Alexandra Hambleton

On a clear February day in Tokyo in 1987, Hong Kong-born idol and media personality Agnes Chan was preparing to return to work after the birth of her first child. Having received permission from her manager to bring her three-month-old son with her, Chan headed to the Tokyo television studio where she would be making her first media appearance in several months, unaware that she was about to spark the "Agnes Controversy," a contentious debate about the role of women, work, and motherhood in Japan.

A common misconception about Japanese popular culture is that, prior to the Korean wave of the early 2000s and subsequent popularity of K-pop, it was generated almost entirely within Japan, featuring Japanese stars for Japanese consumers. Instead, from as early as the 1960s and 1970s, a number of non-Japanese idols, performers, and personalities have experienced success in the Japanese popular culture market. This chapter examines the career of one such idol, 1970s singer and idol Agnes Chan. Chan's career has spanned four decades and undergone numerous challenges, controversies, and transgressions as she progressed from cute ingénue idol to mother, harbinger of social change, and, more recently, UN spokesperson and university professor. Chan is an unusual idol in that she defied convention to continue her education and career after marriage and motherhood, was partially responsible for launching the career of well-known Japanese feminist scholar Ueno Chizuko, and sparked extraordinary media debate on the role of women and mothers in the workplace in Japan.

Examining Chan's early image in the 1970s, the 1987 "Agnes Controversy" that threatened her career, and the ways in which she reinvented herself, this paper will seek to understand Chan's unusual career path and her impact on the feminist movement in Japan. Foreign idols are often placed in a precarious position, required to use their foreignness as a way to differentiate themselves while at the same time ensuring that they remain nonthreatening to fans who seek to identify with them. This is particularly true for women, who are burdened with the expectation that they will represent, protect, and pass on traditional values and culture, while at the same time offering themselves up for public consumption. Agnes Chan's career has spanned four decades. The way in which she has been portrayed by the Japanese mass media, the scandals she has been involved in, and her ability to maintain a presence in the Japanese popular cultural landscape provide a window through which to examine issues of the role of women and the contemporary history of feminist scholarship and debate in Japan.

Early career, Asian ingénue

Agnes Chan was born in Hong Kong in 1955. She learned to play the guitar and was discovered at the age of 15 when she performed on a music television program, after which she was chosen to record a cover of Joni Mitchell's "Circle Game" for an upcoming album. The song was released as a single in 1971, topped the charts, and made Chan a star. Chan's opportunity to work in Japan came as a result of her sister, who had been studying music in Japan, introducing her to singer/songwriter Hirao Masaaki. Chan recorded her first single in Japanese in 1972, "Hinageshi no Hana" (Poppy Flower), and went on to win the Japan Record Award for Best New Artist in 1973. While experiencing continued success in her singing career, Chan did not neglect her education, and graduated from the American School in Japan the same year, before progressing to higher education at Sophia University. Chan may have found fame somewhat quickly as a pop idol in Japan, with her cute style and imperfect but sweet-spoken Japanese, yet it was a variety of factors that combined to lead to her success in the Japanese market, as well as giving her career a deeper significance in the long term. First was Chan's image. Chan's choice of dress, hairstyle, and movement was very similar to that of her Japanese peers and was one of pure innocence. Wearing little makeup, with long straight black hair and often dressed in white or pastel-colored dresses, Chan embodied the innocence expected of an adolescent idol in Japan at a time when the idol genre was just beginning to take off. Chan was, however, able to differentiate herself when necessary. Many fan sites today comment that it was her innocence and cuteness, combined with her habit of performing in mini-skirts, that appealed to fans as the perfect mix of sweet idol with just a hint of sex appeal. Aoyagi (2005) examines the role of women in Japanese society through the lens of young female idols singers, arguing that idols embody images of adolescent femaleness. Until the early 1990s, idols were required to be "cute" (*kawaiko-chan*), with fans adoring them for their cuteness and sweetness, evoking a sense that they should be protected by those who idolize them. He further explains that idols' images are composed of singing, dancing, and speaking in a way that is not only "cute" but also "meek" and "adorable." Agnes Chan embodied all of these traits, with her hairstyle and makeup, child-like Japanese and cute, meek media personality, but added her own touch by wearing minis at a time when longer skirts were in fashion.

Chan is said to have expressed distaste at the direction in which her Japanese management was taking her career. As she had begun her career as a folk singer, Chan was uncomfortable with the way in which she was expected to adhere to the conventions and extra media appearances that come with the label of "idol" in Japan. Despite her initial discomfort, however, at the insistence of her management and the media, Agnes Chan became a true idol. Scandals erupted around her choice of clothing, haircuts, and even her decision to change the side on which she parted her hair. Similarly, her on-air persona contributed much to her image as an idol. In early television appearances, Chan's high voice, broken yet childishly cute use of the Japanese language, and particular "Asianness" are highlighted. In many of her television appearances Chan appears as an awkward teenager negotiating a very adult world, even in appearances in which she is only required to sing in front of an audience rather than speak or be interviewed. It is this very awkwardness that endeared her to her fans, who—despite her foreignness and "difference"—could identify with the persona on display. Chan played the ingénue well, giggling awkwardly in response to interviewers' questions and smiling cutely for the camera. When on stage, her image, speech, movements, and gestures were very similar to those of her Japanese idol peers such as Sawada Junko and Asada Miyoko, young female singers who could arguably be described as the very first generation of Japanese idols. Chan's image was one of a young, non-Japanese girl adhering to idol culture convention, while adding her own touch. Where Chan differed markedly from her peers, however, was the way in which she was described by the Japanese media.

Despite the similarities she shared with other Japanese-born idols of her generation, Chan was often described by the Japanese media as possessing a personality and values that harked back to an earlier, simpler time. In an interview featured in the *Asahi Shinbun* on 24 October 1983, Chan compares her experiences in Japan and overseas. She explains that the softer, less confrontational style of working in Japan suits her better, and that she feels an affinity with Japan. The article concludes that Chan has an "Asian heart" (*tōyōjin no kokoro*), a phrase that was used often in the media to refer to Chan. At a time when the image and role of women in Japanese society were in transition, this heavily loaded description at once placed a burden on Chan to provide an image of a nostalgic escape to her fans—escape to a simpler time that, it was imagined, could still be found in Japan's neighboring (and, by implication, less developed) countries. In reference to the contemporary popularity of Asian popular culture in Japan, Skov and Moeran (1995, 8) refer to "the consumption of tradition." However, the implication of such feelings is that Japanese audience cannot connect with the rest of Asia on a level plain and cannot "engage in a dialogue with Asia," but instead simply consume for the purpose of "recuperation and refreshment" (Iwabuchi *et al.* 2004, 153). Chan's popularity in Japan and her treatment by the Japanese media could be described as part of the "first wave" of such nostalgia, at a time when Japan was undergoing great economic development and social change, at the supposed expense of traditional values and innocence from a time gone by. In addition to the burden of her "Asian heart," the media referred to Chan as "the fairy from Hong Kong" (*Honkon kara no yōsei*), in reference not only to her long hair and sweet, cute look, but also her soft, charming voice and almost magically innocent public personality. Darling-Wolf (2004, 331) mentions that "the Japanese popular cultural scene is quite segregated along gender lines," but that there has been very little research into how consumers might negotiate representations of gender. Both Felski (1995) and Yuval-Davis (1997) explain how women are commonly used as signifiers of tradition. Freedman (2001, 85) describes women as "the key actors in the transmission of the community's values . . . and active participants in national struggles." Such ideas inform the image of foreign women in the Japanese popular cultural landscape and became particularly prescient in the case of Chan and her career after marriage.

After spending two years studying at Sophia University, the then 20-year-old Chan took a break from her singing career to study at the University of Toronto in Canada, before returning to Japan to resume her career in 1978. In the early 1980s she also returned to participating in various charity events and volunteer activities, something Chan had been involved in from a young age, including a visit to Ethiopia as

part of Nippon Television Network's "24-Hour Television" annual charity broadcast. Upon returning to Japan, Chan had difficulty with her
management and struggled to return to the level of popularity she had
experienced before her time abroad. However, under the guidance of a
new manager, Kaneko Tsutomu, Chan's career began to evolve from idol
to that of a multitalented *tarento* (celebrity performer), taking advantage
of her intellect, overseas experience, and education. Chan wrote essays,
books, hosted television programs, continued with her philanthropic
efforts around the world, and even lectured at universities in Japan.
She had begun the process of evolution and transgression, necessary for
survival in the idol industry where short careers and fast turnarounds
are common. This evolution into a self-sufficient adult personality, far
removed from her idol beginning, was given extra momentum by the
scandal that erupted as a result of a seemingly innocent act in 1987
upon the birth of her first child. This scandal had a greater impact on the
career of Agnes Chan and on Japanese society than anyone could have
possibly imagined. Marshall (1997) argues that celebrities cannot maintain the same public image and hope to remain in the public eye for
long. Instead, they are required to go through a process of what Marshall
terms "transgression," in which their image is transformed through their
participation in "extratextual" activities and risky career choices that
differ greatly from their previous image. Agnes Chan had been making conscious efforts to evolve in her career ever since returning from
college in Canada, with limited results. Appearing on regular television
programs and releasing albums gave her some success, but failed to raise
her media profile to previous levels. Ultimately, it was the inadvertent
transgression in the form of the "Agnes Controversy" that propelled her
back into the spotlight, ensured career longevity, and cemented Chan's
place in the Japanese popular culture landscape.

The "Agnes controversy": transgression and progression

Until very recently, idols in Japan who decided to marry or have a family
were expected to retire graciously from public life. Popular idols such as
Yamaguchi Momoe, Mori Masako, and Sakurada Junko all gave up their
careers upon deciding to marry, and it has even been speculated that
many female idols chose marriage or motherhood as a way of escap-
ing the increasing pressure placed on them by their management to
maintain successful careers, as they would never be expected to continue working upon marriage. While in recent years many 1980s idols,
including Mori, have been staging comebacks, it was incredibly rare for

an idol to remain in the spotlight after marriage, making Agnes Chan's decision to continue working after her marriage to Kaneko Tsutomu very unusual. She was even more unusual in deciding to continue her education and to return to work after the birth of her first son—a sight the Japanese media were particularly unaccustomed to in the case of idols. It was these decisions that had the biggest impact on how she was perceived in the media as she transitioned from innocent ingénue to adult woman.

At the end of 1986, Chan's first child was born in Canada; and in 1987 she and her family returned to Japan, where she returned to work. At the time she was making regular appearances on over ten different television programs, and had been asked by her management and production companies to return to work as soon as possible. Chan was even told that she could bring her son if this aided her return. What followed was a scandal that no one could have predicted. Chan was criticized for bringing her son to work, and debate raged in the media about the role of women in the workplace, motherhood, and childrearing. "Agnes" was even selected as one of the most influential words of 1988. The controversy sparked widespread debate on the role of working mothers, with conservatives criticizing Chan for continuing to work after the birth of her child, various commentators supporting Chan's position and calling for understanding, and some feminists even criticizing Chan for purporting to speak for all women, when she was so clearly financially well off and therefore unable to understand the struggles of "ordinary" women. As Strober and Chan (2001, xii) explain, "a group of writers banded together to condemn Agnes's position, accusing her of trying to mess up society with ideas of the privileged class. Feminist scholars, in turn, tried to pull the controversy back to the core question of women's position in society." The controversy sparked newspaper and magazine articles, and even inspired the Group for the Enjoyment of the Agnes Controversy (Agunesu Ronsō o Tanoshimu Kai) to put together the 1988 book *Agunesu Ronsō o Yomu* (Reading the Agnes Controversy), which documents news reports about the controversy. Offering a different perspective, the book *Otoko ga Sabaku Agunesu Ronsō* (Men Dispute the Agnes Controversy) was published in 1989 and gave a detailed explanation of the scandal, as well as the protagonists and positions involved. Well-known Japanese feminist academics and writers analyzed the scandal from the perspective of journalistic ethics, patriarchal society, and theories of motherhood and childrearing, in opposition to social commentators who discussed workers' rights and responsibilities and the role of women in the workplace. The controversy became a struggle between people who preferred women to stay in their traditional role and those who wanted more choices for women in contemporary Japanese society. The issue grew to become both emotionally and politically explosive, and Strober and Chan describe it as opening "a well-covered, but festering, sore in modern Japanese society" (2001, xii).

The sore may not have been as well covered as Strober and Chan believed. Just a few years earlier, similar debate had raged about the role of women in Japanese society, instigated by the UN Decade for Women and international pressure to enact the Equal Employment Opportunity Law in 1985. For centuries, gender politics and policy and been informed by the ideology of "good wife, wise mother" (*ryōsai kenbo*) (Hirao 2001, 192). The importance of educating women to be good wives and wise mothers was first promoted by government officials in the 1890s to emphasize that the role of women was not participation in the public sphere, but to take care of the home, their husbands, and their children. Women were expected to dedicate their lives to supporting their families and bringing up children who were viewed as essential to a future powerful Japan. In the postwar period, although the concept of "good wife, wise mother" may no longer have been openly championed by the government, many policies focusing on workplace law, childcare, and families were to some extent influenced by such values.

Mackie (2003, 181) outlines the employment laws as they stood before the implementation of the 1985 Equal Employment Opportunity Law (Danjo Koyō Kikai Kintō Hō). In the immediate postwar period, the Labor Standards Law of 1947 dictated the rights of workers, with particular provisions for female workers. All women were entitled to menstruation leave (thought necessary due to the postwar shortage of materials essential for the production of sanitary products), and pregnant women were entitled to maternity and nursing leave. One unusual provision, however, was that all women, whether mothers or not, were treated under the law as "potential mothers." As Mackie explains, "This is revealed by the fact that the legislation does not distinguish between women who do and do not have children. All women are protected from shift work or late-night work on the grounds that they potentially have responsibility for childcare. The health of young women is protected for future childbearing." These laws were categorized as "protection of motherhood" (*bosei hogo*), a revealing phrase which indicates exactly what was expected of women, whether they were mothers, workers, or both. By the 1980s, Japan was increasingly under international pressure to reform its laws in relation to equal opportunity for men and women.

This external pressure came as a result of the United Nations' International Decade for Women and the expectation that Japan would become a signatory to the Convention on the Elimination of All Forms of Discrimination against Women (CEDAW), an act which would require, among other things, an overhaul of workplace equality law.

The enactment of the law, however, "resulted in significant failure to meet the expectations of most women's organizations" (Ueno 2009, 121) and instead further categorized the labor force into career track (*sōgōshoku*), non-career track (*ippanshoku*), part-time and casual workers. As expected, the majority of non-career track workers were women, a situation that has continued to this day. The law focuses on "equality of opportunity" (Mackie 2003, 184) with the expectation that, if they wish to participate in the workforce with the same opportunities as men, women must also make the same "efforts" as their male counterparts—in other words, dedicate themselves to their jobs to the detriment of their private and family lives. The law, however, completely overlooks the reality that women remain responsible for the majority of childcare and housekeeping. There may have been great optimism about the potential for change during the UN Decade for Women, but this began to dissipate as the Equal Employment Opportunity Act (EEOA) laws came into effect and women began to realize, as Mackie explains, that "reform of institutions would be meaningless without reform of the attitudes and ideologies which informed the practices of these institutions" (2003, 193). In fact, attitudes and ideologies have altered little in the subsequent decades. As Ueno (2009, 118) explains, "Since the 1980s the situation surrounding women has become even more ambivalent."

The "Agnes Controversy" came three years after the introduction of the EEOA and, upon close inspection, very closely resembles the debates undertaken in the early 1980s. Feminist scholars argued that if women were to take a greater role in the public sphere then corporations, workplaces, and men also would have to change. Commentators instead argued that women had to "earn" their place in the workplace, demonstrating that they could compete with their male colleagues on the current terms and playing field. Social commentators such as Hayashi Mariko took a position similar to the EEOA, arguing that, if women wished to be taken seriously in the workplace, they must put in the same effort and responsibility as their male counterparts. Hayashi argued that Chan had done a disservice to working women everywhere, showing them to be less dedicated than men and thereby harming all women's chances for hiring and promotion. Discussing the introduction of the EEOA, Tokuhiro (2009, 37) argues that the debate was informed by the Japanese concept of *bosei* (motherhood). The "Agnes Controversy" was framed within these very terms, with the responsibility of the mother positioned against greater social responsibilities. The debate was also informed by the idea that idols and celebrities are expected to keep their personal lives out of the spotlight. As mentioned above, it was common for singers and idols to retire upon marriage, and Chan was unusual in continuing to make public appearances after her marriage and the birth of her son. Most telling was a comment from singer Awaya Noriko, who remarked on Fuji Television's morning program *Ohayo Nice Day* on 20 March 1988 that "celebrities are in the business of selling dreams, so bringing a child to work is a bad idea as it means that show business will become as dull and wearying as domestic life." After spending so many years of working within the strict framework of Japanese show business and idol convention, Chan had dared to show the reality behind the dreams show business sells. She was no longer just a product for consumption, no longer an idol to be protected, and no longer innocent. Instead, she had done the unthinkable for an idol, put her domestic life on display—an act that threatened to destroy the dreams of her fans all over Japan.

Despite the opportunity that the controversy provided to discuss the issues women were facing in the light of the legal and social changes that had taken place in the 1980s, the media preferred to focus on the scandal itself, turning it into a sensational battle between two opposing camps of women. Tokuhiro (2009, 40) explains that "the media's negative and distorted reporting of women's liberation in the early 1970s, has served to strengthen the negative image of feminism (*feminizumu*) even today." The "Agnes Controversy" proved no different as the media focused on heated arguments rather than the substantive issues at the heart of the debate. In the end, the debate's potential for further understanding and meaningful change was lost.

For her own part, Chan defended her behavior and even gave testimony at a 1988 Diet hearing into women, work, and childrearing, stressing that hers was a dilemma that many working mothers confronted. "This is the biggest problem women are concerned with right now. There must be many mothers who face the same worries as me" (*Yomiuri Shinbun* 1988). Chan also expressed her surprise at the widespread reaction to her decision to take her son to work, and garnered applause from female Diet members when she stated that the women's movement (*josei undō*) should also be considered a men's movement (*dansei undō*), as male-dominated society has little understanding of what it means to be a woman raising a child in Japan.

Was Agnes Chan so heavily criticized in the media because she was a foreigner, because she was a woman, or because she was an idol? Most likely a combination of many factors led to her decision to bring her son to work becoming the scandal that it did. Ueno (2009, 119) explains that it is an accepted custom in Hong Kong for women to bring their children to work, so from her own cultural perspective Chan was taking the role of the traditional "Asian mother" and doing what she thought was best for her child. In Japan, however, her behavior was "in line with the postmodern orientation," one in which shorter working hours and flexible workplaces are sought. From Ueno's perspective, Chan was caught between her own desire to care for her son in the best way she knew how and the expectations of a culture with which she was not completely familiar, one which had entirely different expectations of what it meant to be a good and responsible mother. The time Chan spent in Canada at university meant that she was exposed to not one, not two, but three different cultural perspectives from which to conceptualize her role as a worker and mother, and it may have been her overseas education which had the greatest impact on what she chose to do next. Earlier media focus on Chan's "Asian heart" and image as a sweet, innocent girl from another time meant that her behavior was perceived as more shocking than it might have been from a star who had not been burdened with the same expectations. Rather than her implicit role as the bearer of traditional Asian values, Chan instead became an accidental revolutionary. Although she had progressed to be somewhat of a career woman as she evolved from idol to media personality, Chan appeared to have, in one moment, thrown away the memory of the innocent idol and instead begun to stand for something entirely different—a working mother. Traditionally, idols have been expected to leave the limelight upon marriage and motherhood. While it could be argued that all female idol singers are career women, this reality starkly contrasts with the public image they are expected to create. In Chan's case, it was nostalgia for a lost past and an image that in reality was the opposite of her career aspirations as an academic. Chan's attempt to combine both meant that she created a disconnect in long-established patterns of media discourse surrounding women in Japan. This process, however, gave Chan the opportunity to extend her career far beyond the length of that of a typical idol. Chan's inadvertent "transgression" in the form of the "Agnes Controversy," as well as her later graduate school education and philanthropic pursuits, has contributed greatly to her longevity in the fickle Japanese media market.

Launching careers: the "Agnes Controversy" and feminism in Japan

Ultimately, the "Agnes Controversy" proved to be a debate between two groups taking starkly different positions that closely resembled the major discourses of a few years earlier, as Japan debated the introduction of the EEOA in 1985. It also provided a platform for debate between feminist scholars and social commentators in Japan, and brought several feminist scholars into the public eye for the first time. Mackie (2003, 163) explains that "most teachers of women's studies are on the fringes of the academy, reflecting the already marginal place of women in tertiary institutions." Despite the UN Decade for Women and the debate it generated within Japan, feminist scholars remained marginalized. The "Agnes Controversy" provided a platform for a number of scholars to raise their media profiles, the most famous of whom, Ueno Chizuko, has a firm media presence even today.

The controversy also launched a new stage of Chan's career. Upon reading about the "Agnes Controversy" in the American publication *Time Magazine*, Stanford University academic Myra H. Strober invited Chan to study under her supervision. Chan, who was awarded a PhD in 1994, has since gone on to lecture at several universities and take up posts as an assistant professor at several Japanese universities. In recent years it is not Chan's songs that she is most known for, but her work as an activist, working as an ambassador for UNICEF Japan as well as participating in events ranging widely from cancer awareness forums to discussions on the education opportunities available to non-Japanese in Japan. Her public image has evolved even further from the innocent pop idol, to a career woman who is now rarely criticized but instead lauded for her philanthropic work.

Conclusion

Agnes Chan's career has suffered many ups and downs and is remarkable in its longevity. The reasons for this longevity, particularly in the face of the extraordinary scandal surrounding the "Agnes Controversy," are Chan's ability to evolve as a performer and branch into other areas of both the media and academia. Her charity work has also allowed her to shift focus from the "Agnes Controversy" to the issues about which she is most passionate: education and the rights of children. Essential to ensure career longevity in the notoriously fickle Japanese media, Chan managed to undergo what Marshall (1997, 105) refers to as the process of "transgression," in which the star's "extratextual life" or personal life becomes the focus of media discourse. Rather than reinventing variations of her former image, Chan the idol underwent transgression and evolution, as an increased focus on her personal life (albeit unexpected and unwanted) allowed her to transcend her image as an innocent idol, and become a television personality and respected activist and academic in her own right. While Marshall refers to transgression in the case of American film stars, I believe it constitutes an important tool for understanding the career of Agnes Chan. When Chan, by bringing her son to work, violated the media understanding that an idol must have no personal life and must dedicate herself entirely to her craft, she was severely criticized by the Japanese media. Only by undergoing the process of transgression and becoming a scholar and activist has Chan remained in the public eye. The Agnes Chan who was initially burdened with the expectation of representing an innocence lost inadvertently became a champion for working women throughout Japan and a target of criticism for conservatives. Chan's evolution as a star ensured that her career has survived to this day.

It has been more than two decades since the "Agnes Controversy," and yet little has changed in terms of women's equal participation in the workplace in Japan. Though Japanese women participate in the labor force at a similar rate to women in Western industrial nations, they are disadvantaged in economic terms (Brinton 1993, 3). Women continue to constitute the majority of the part time and non-career track workforce, receive less pay for the same work, and, as a result of government policies restricting access to childcare, are still often required to choose between having a family and having a career. The EEOA and "Agnes Controversy" may have brought the issue of working women into the spotlight, but long-term change failed to eventuate. The idol world, however, has seen some change in recent years, with a number of 1980s idols making comebacks as their children enter adulthood. Similarly, current idols are finding that they are no longer required to leave the public eye upon marrying or becoming pregnant; instead, a new genre of idol, the *mamadoru* (mama idols), has developed. Within this niche market idols are able to use their role as mothers to garner new fans and create new career opportunities. Whether or not this shift in popular culture indicates future change in other arenas of Japanese society, however, is yet to be seen, although it may provide some hope for those who believe that celebrities have the ability to launch social trends and movements.

Works Cited

Agunesu ronsō o Tanoshimu Kai. 1988. *Agunesu Ronsō o Yomu*. Tokyo: JICC Shuppankyoku.
Asahi Shinbun. 1983. "Tōyōjin no Kokoro." 24 October.
Aoyagi, Hiroshi. 2005. *Islands of Eight Million Smiles: Idol Performance and Symbolic Production in Contemporary Japan*. Cambridge: Harvard University Press.
Brinton, Mary C. 1993. *Women and the Economic Miracle: Gender and Work in Postwar Japan*. Berkeley: University of California Press.
Darling-Wolf, Fabienne. 2004. "Sites of Attractiveness: Japanese Women and Westernized Representations of Feminine Beauty." *Critical Studies in Media Communication* 21, no. 4: 325–345.
Felski, Rita. 1995. *The Gender of Modernity*. Cambridge: Harvard University Press.
Freedman, Jane. 2001. *Feminism*. Buckingham: Open University Press.
Hirao, Keiko. 2001. "Mothers as the Best Teachers: Japanese Motherhood and Early Childhood Education." In *Women's Working Lives in East Asia*, edited by Mary C. Brinton, 180–203. Stanford: Stanford University Press.
Iwabuchi, Kōichi, Stephen Muecke and Mandy Thomas, eds. 2004. *Rogue Flows: Trans-Asian Cultural Traffic*. Hong Kong: Hong Kong University Press.
Mackie, Vera C. 2003. *Feminism in Modern Japan: Citizenship, Embodiment, and Sexuality*. Cambridge: Cambridge University Press.
Marshall, P. David. 1997. *Celebrity and Power: Fame and Contemporary Culture*. Minneapolis: University of Minnesota Press.
Skov, Lisa and Brian Moeran. 1995. *Women, Media and Consumption in Japan*. Honolulu: University of Hawai'i Press.
Strober, Myra H. and Agnes Miling Kaneko Chan. 2001. *The Road Winds Uphill All the Way, Gender, Work, and Family in the United States and Japan*. Cambridge: MIT Press.
Tokuhiro, Yoko. 2009. *Marriage in Contemporary Japan*. New York: Routledge.
Ueno, Chizuko. 2009. *The Modern Family in Japan: Its Rise and Fall*. Melbourne: Trans Pacific Press.
Yomiuri Shinbun. 1988. "San'in de 'Netsuben' Agunesu Sankōnin Kosodate to Kashu Ryōritu, Josei Shokuba Kankyō no Kaizen." 19 February.
Yuval-Davis, Nina. 1997. *Gender and Nation*. London: Sage.

8
Emotions, Desires, and Fantasies: What Idolizing Means for Yon-sama Fans in Japan

Ho Swee Lin

Introduction

Korean idol Bae Yong Joon seems to have lived up to the nickname "Yon-sama" coined by his fans in Japan.[1] He was the first among many Korean idols to offer his condolences and financial aid, amounting to one billion won ($900,000), days after a massive earthquake and tsunami struck northeast Japan on 11 March 2011.[2] Many of his fans were moved by the gesture, especially those living in Fukushima prefecture, directly affected by the disasters. It was not the first time the idol had shown his generosity; he also donated 300 million won to victims in Japan following an earthquake in Niigata in 2004. In April 2010, the idol was reported to have visited the Intensive Care Unit for premature infants at the Yokohama Children's Medical Center, which was named after him following a donation of an undisclosed amount. Similar facilities at seven other hospitals have also received money from the idol (Moon and Yoon 2011). In March 2010, the idol reportedly went to four hospitals in South Korea's Gangwondo area to visit a total of 30 Japanese fans, who sustained minor injuries when some props fell down during the launch of the animated version of *Winter Sonata* (2002), the TV drama that made Bae famous. To his fans, many of whom are Japanese women between the ages of 30 and 70, these gestures reinforce his image as the epitome of benevolence, thoughtfulness, and kindness— qualities that are consistent with his onscreen image as a gentle, caring, self-sacrificing, devoted, and loving person.

This perhaps explains why his fan following in Japan has yet to show any sign of abating, even though nearly a decade has elapsed since the Korean television drama *Winter Sonata*[3] was first broadcast by

Japan's national broadcaster, Nippon Hōsō Kyōkai (NHK), in April 2003. On 3 April 2004, for example, some 5,000 fans swarmed Narita International Airport to greet the idol, and 50,000 attended his first "fan meeting" at Tokyo Dome later that week. On 30 May 2008, more than 6,000 fans greeted him at the Kansai International Airport, and 35,000 at Osaka Hall the following evening for the promotion of the drama *The Legend*.[4] On 27 September 2009, more than 3,000 fans gathered yet again at Narita International Airport, with 50,000 packing the Tokyo Dome once more later that week for the official launch of the animated version of *Winter Sonata*. These were just several of his visits to Japan. Each time he arrives, thousands flock to airports to wait in line the night before, and even queue overnight for tickets to attend his fan events, which are always completely sold out. Apart from official gatherings, Japanese fans also invest a considerable amount of time and money in organizing and participating in fan activities, monitoring the idol's itineraries, traveling to various drama production sites in South Korea and Japan, and consuming a plethora of items splashed with his smiling countenance.[5] His popularity, and that of *Winter Sonata*, later generated a surge of interest in all things Korean—television dramas, movies, popular music, idols, Korean language, food and culture, and travel to the country—a phenomenon known as *hanryū*, or the "Korean Wave." Bae even earned the title of "cultural ambassador," conferred on him by the South Korean government.

Many Korean idols have had a similar reception, though Yon-sama is unquestionably one of the most popular Korean idols in Japan today, if not the most popular. Yet, one might ask why this is the case, when South Korea's three major broadcasting stations churn out 30 new dramas every three months and an endless stream of new faces, both male and female. Bae is hardly the most sought-after idol in his home country. What indeed could have lured, and still continues to lure, thousands of Japanese women to airports and tens of thousands to fan events, where they scream the idol's name, and even unashamedly shout *"Saranghaeyo!"* ("I love you" in Korean) in public?

The Korean Wave in Japan has drawn a considerable amount of academic attention in recent years. Some studies point to the co-hosting of the 2002 FIFA World Cup by Japan and South Korea as a "crucial turning point" in boosting the transnational flows of cultural goods between the two countries (Kim 2005; Mōri 2008). Several attribute the low costs of Korean television dramas in comparison to those produced in Japan, Taiwan, and Hong Kong as having contributed to the increase of program sales, which enhanced the presence and popularity of Korean television dramas across Asia (Kim 2005; Chua 2008). Some suggest that the "proximity" of Korean culture to other Asian cultures allows the spread of popular culture (Iwabuchi 2008; Shim 2008). Iwabuchi Kōichi (2008, 249) attributes the interest to the "personal-oriented desire" of Japanese women to learn about the " 'real' Korea." Mōri Yoshitaka (2008, 133), on the other hand, explains idolizing as a means of alleviating the void in the lives of many middle-aged and older women in Japan, whose children have grown up and who are hence transferring their "mothering needs" to Yon-sama and other idols. Christine R. Yano (2004, 56) offers a similar interpretation in an earlier work, regarding the fan activities surrounding a young male Japanese singer: idolizing is a compensatory intimacy for women who "abnegate" maternal roles and wifely duties.

There is indeed no shortage of literature on the Korean Wave. While studies have explained how Korean idols provide many Japanese women with a sense of purpose and help them restore their subjectivities, few have explored the more personal aspects of idolizing, investigated the desires and fantasies of Japanese fans, or examined what young male idols mean to women. Many Yon-sama fans who are housewives do have more free time today than when their children were younger, but, if temporary diversion is what they seek, why have they not chosen other leisure activities, such as Hawaiian dance, as many have done in the past? Why have they chosen instead to become ardent fans of a Korean idol? Why *Yon-sama*, and not other Korean idols, or American, Chinese, or Japanese idols? Surely these women's public displays of affection when encountering their idol express also their desire for intimacy and emotional gratification, and not just the desire for relief from domesticity (or to extend domestic roles).

This chapter extends existing studies by peering beneath the instrumentality of idolizing to examine what it means to many Japanese women at the individual level. Drawing on ethnographic data and interviews with 36 Yon-sama fans,[6] this study analyzes women's discourses on the reclamation of female desire and redefinition of femininity in a society that has ignored their emotional needs by assuming that middle-aged women—especially those who are mothers—are de-sexualized and de-eroticized beings. The sample size is too small to generalize about the experiences of all Japanese fans of Korean idols, or even of all Yon-sama fans, and it is also not the aim of this study to do so. However, this study can offer a better understanding of idolizing in terms of the role of the imagination and emotions in self-making and identity production.

Arjun Appadurai (1996, 3) remarks that the imagination is a "constitutive feature of modern subjectivity," as it can provoke—through consumption, for example—"resistance, irony, selectivity, and in general, agency." While he adds that "where there is consumption there is pleasure, and where there is pleasure there is agency" (Ibid., 7), Appadurai does not explain that, where there is agency at work, the imagination can also be transformative. As Kim Hyun Mee (2004, 43) has argued in her study of Korean women's desiring and idolizing of Korean soccer players, female fans are not only replacing the conventional practice of women being the object of male desire with the "female gaze" as a "new collective experience of pleasure by women as the viewers of men's bodies" in the public arena, but they are also realigning their subordinate position relative to that of men in society. However, these fans are also doing more than shedding the image of women as passive viewers of the popular game of soccer in public. As some participate in fan activities, others move on to follow matches played by teams from other countries. They acquire new vocabularies to talk about the game, thus becoming as conversant as male fans, and also changing men's perceptions of women.

This study thus expands on Appadurai's views by interpreting idolizing by Yon-sama fans as processes of "resistance" and "selectivity" that are transformative, and also extends Kim's arguments by analyzing the transformative aspect of idolizing that helps alter women's "structural positioning" in society in order to gain greater control of their lives and achieve a more meaningful sense of self. This chapter contends that idolizing offers more than the instrumental value of pleasure or stress-relief, but that it can also be a process of renewal, rejuvenation and re-sexualization of the gendered self. At the same time, it is important that women's needs and desires are understood in terms of the sociohistorical conditions that have shaped those needs and desires, particularly the social construction of gender in Japan. In what follows, I examine the discourses of Yon-sama fans to illustrate that "nostalgia" (*natsukashisa*) is a way of reconstructing the self and regaining the capacity to experience and express emotions. I argue that the ability to re-engage emotions is deeply personal, reflecting a woman's erotic desire for a "lover" and not a mother's desire for a "son." Further, women's imagination and fantasy are "realizable," albeit through imagination, consumption, and commercially staged activities.

Why Korean idols? Why Yon-sama?

Yon-sama was little known to most Japanese when he first appeared on television screens in Japan in 2004, but *Winter Sonata* was by no means the first drama from South Korea to be broadcast in Japan. Several had entered Japan after South Korea began lifting bans on the importation of Japanese popular culture in 1998, which helped improve diplomatic relations between the two countries. Cultural exchange continued to improve following the 2002 FIFA World Cup, and after Kusanagi Tsuyoshi, a member of the popular Japanese male idol group SMAP, promoted Korean culture and travels to South Korea on his television shows (Mōri 2008, 129). Given that Japan was for many years dominated by local and American popular culture, Korean television dramas offered a fresh alternative, especially to a particular segment of the population: middle-aged and older women.

This does not mean, however, that Korean dramas targeted these women specifically. Many production companies and broadcasters in South Korea were as surprised as their Japanese counterparts by the sudden surge in popularity of Korean dramas. For many middle-aged Japanese women, Korean male idols diverge markedly from American and Asian offerings. American stars are said to be popular because of their outstanding physical and personal attributes (Herd 1984, 77–78), but these are considered to be unappealing, because actors such as Tom Cruise, Ben Affleck, Brad Pitt, and George Clooney are too clever, self-centered and intimidating (larger than life). They are often cast as superheroes on missions to save America (or the world) from catastrophic natural disasters or acts of terrorism, and seek to redress injustices and restore order to humanity. Given that Chinese and Hong Kong television dramas have never been shown in Japan, the only names widely known are martial artists such as Jet Li, Bruce Lee, Jackie Chan, and Chow Yuen Fatt—hardly idols. As for popular Japanese male idols such as Kimura Takuya and Oguri Shun, many middle-aged women consider them to be "too skinny," "too weak," "too feminine," "too masculine," or "arrogant."

Many Korean idols also play characters that are heroic and violent, though those who do are less likely to rank among the most popular in Japan. The few who do also exude what my informants describe as "human qualities," that is, they are often portrayed as devoted lovers, protective husbands, filial sons, responsible fathers, loyal friends, caring citizens, and even benevolent strangers. More importantly, these idols are also seen as having "feminine" qualities (thus balancing out "masculine" qualities), such as the ability to express a wide range of human emotions. Given that Korean television dramas are mostly about complex human relationships, misunderstandings, and tragedies, it is not uncommon to see male idols cry when they are sad, smile when they are happy, yell when they are mad, beg forgiveness when they have wronged others, forgive others despite their pain, and at times die to protect loved ones. Unlike many American stars, who are portrayed as alpha males who express love with ravaging kisses and sexual desire, Korean idols do so with patience, self-sacrifice, gentleness, and bashfulness, content to simply hold the hand of the woman they love. Many middle-aged Japanese women do not find heavy petting and explicit sex scenes repulsive, but they prefer subtle expressions and sexual references, which have the effect of fanning their erotic desires by encouraging imagination and intensifying fantasies.

Yon-sama is certainly perceived as possessing all these attributes and qualities, both onscreen and offscreen. In dramas such as *Winter Sonata* and *The Legend*, as well as movies such as *April Snow* (2005),[7] the idol is cast as a tormented but devoted lover, an angry but forgiving husband, a frustrated but filial son, or a jealous but responsible brother. Most of all, what differentiates Bae from many other Korean idols and earned him the nickname Yon-sama is that he is always garbed immaculately and stylishly in white and light pastel-colored clothes. He behaves gently and patiently, moves in a dignified manner, speaks politely and humbly, and smiles incessantly when he is not crying. In *Winter Sonata*, for example, the idol plays the character Kang Jun-Sang, who falls in love with Jung Yu-Jin when he returns to his mother's hometown to uncover the identity of his biological father. He is involved in a car accident, which causes him to suffer temporary memory loss and his classmates to presume that he is dead. Ten years later, still suffering from amnesia, Jun-Sang returns to South Korea under the name Lee Ming-Young, and falls in love again with the same woman. Despite regaining his memory, following yet another accident, Jun-Sang's plan to marry Yu-Jin is frustrated, this time by his mother's lie that the lovers are half-siblings. When the truth is finally brought to light, Jun-Sang is diagnosed with an incurable eye condition, which prompts him to return to the US and give his blessing to his half-brother, who also loves Yu-Jin. With the many breathtaking scenes of snowfall and repetition of romantic ballads throughout the entire 20 episodes, *Winter Sonata* has all the ingredients of melodrama at its best.

Lost and found: the nostalgic regaining of the self

Iwabuchi Kōichi (2008, 245–246) attributes the "unprecedented" reception of *Winter Sonata* in Japan to its focus on the intensity of young people's romances, problems, and relationships, and interprets this as inducing a sense of "nostalgic longing" among many fans for the "lost social vigor" that existed before Japan's bubble economy declined in the early 1990s. Many Yon-sama fans I interviewed also lamented the weakening of familial bonds and communal ties when they described their initial reactions to *Winter Sonata* and the character of Jun-Sang as "nostalgic" (*natsukashii*). However, they were also referring to a different kind of "loss," of having forgotten the ability to feel and to express emotions. Yet, in regaining the capacity to engage one's emotions, many fans also recover the ability to fantasize and imagine, and hence reclaim the gendered self.

Fifty-nine-year-old Kawabata Keiko finds the countless close-up shots of Yon-sama crying "moving," "liberating," and "comforting," because most grown men in Japan—especially her husband—hardly express their emotions, let alone cry. While she feels reassured to know that men, like women, are emotional beings with the capacity to feel and respond, she is confronted by the realization that she, too, has been disconnected from her emotions. She sees in Bae the possibility of reconnecting with those emotions and reclaiming a lost portion of herself. The Tokyo housewife says her husband stopped being expressive, affectionate, and communicative after the birth of their first child, and they only talked about their children's health and education, the household budget, and other domestic matters. But, since he worked hard to send their three children to university and even purchased a house for the family in a prestigious urban neighborhood, Kawabata felt her feelings of neglect and loneliness were trivial and petty. She bottled them up. Those pent-up feelings finally found an outlet in 2005, after several co-workers at a local supermarket (where she still works as a part-time cashier) told her about *Winter Sonata*. While watching it, Kawabata sobbed for the first time in years, and felt "liberated" as a result. She rediscovered her "old self," not only by re-engaging her emotions, but also by having friends of her own in other Yon-sama fans, thus expanding her social circle beyond the wives of her husband's friends and mothers of her children's classmates. Kawabata laments the breakdown in communication with her husband, but also feels rejuvenated by having friends who are unconnected to the family or local community. With them, she is able to relax, play, and enjoy herself as she used to as a young and carefree woman. She explains:

Men are supposed to be strong and not cry, while women are emotional and cry all the time. However, I had forced myself to be strong for so many years that I became more like a man. I stopped feeling, and I also stopped crying, until I saw *Yon-sama* cry. I know men seldom cry in real life, and what I see in dramas is only acting, but seeing him cry and crying along with him made me feel like myself again.

For housewife Toyonaga Ayaka, feelings of nostalgia are about realigning some of the asymmetries in her life, and reaffirming her sense of place and status in Japanese society. The 56-year-old native of Fukuoka married the man she loved 30 years ago, and later quit her job to perform her expected roles as a supportive wife, a devoted mother, and a dutiful daughter-in-law. As the wife of a lawyer, who is the only son of a respectable dentist, Toyonaga was the envy of her peers. Hers was the white-collar worker/full-time housewife (*sarariiman/sengyō shufu*) family model that was the ideal in Japan at the time. However, the situation began to reverse as several of her friends sought part-time and full-time employment to supplement the household income after the collapse of Japan's bubble economy in the early 1990s. Toyonaga, a University of Tokyo graduate, remained a housewife. Though she is today proud of her daughters for having successful careers, Toyonaga also envies them— and many young women in Japan—for being able to pursue both family and career without being socially criticized as much as women of her generation. In an effort to assert herself, she took lessons in French and Italian cooking, and even enrolled in a part-time course to earn a Master's degree in European history and politics. The demands of caring for her elderly parents-in-law later forced her to abandon the latter. Unlike her husband, who is today free to pursue various leisure activities, Toyonaga's domestic chores increased after his retirement, leaving her with the financial means, but not the time, to pursue any leisure or educational activity. She eventually regained her self-esteem and sense of self-worth after participating in activities with other Yon-sama fans, with whom Toyonaga is still learning Korean, experimenting with Korean cooking, and reading about Korean history and culture. As she says:

> I felt lost and inferior for many years, but now I feel confident and fulfilled. It doesn't matter if people think that women like me are merely bored housewives with nothing better to do, or that we are silly, emotional people who are desperate for love and romance. Now that I have my own friends and my own activities, I feel good about myself.

These women's discourses clearly indicate their dissatisfaction with how the sociohistorical construction of gender in Japan has made them wives, mothers, and caretakers, and denied them as individuals and as women. They also reflect how changes in the social and economic environment in Japan in the past three decades have led women to feel unappreciated and undervalued. Given also that marriage in Japan has always been intimately tied to childbirth and childrearing, and not the conjugal union of a man and a woman based on love, these women's frustration and discontentment were exacerbated by the popular media in Japan, which have persistently associated women's proper place in Japanese society with domesticity and ignored the needs of middle-aged and older women as *women*. As 53-year-old housewife Mori Chikako from Aomori prefecture explains:

> Many people still think that women at my age who are mothers are too concerned about the welfare of their children and the household, and that what gives us pleasure is eating and shopping. They don't perceive us as women, or as human beings with feelings, desires and fantasies.

Indeed, until the early 2000s, the proliferation of things "cute" and "cool" in Japan catered mostly to the needs of a younger market, interpreting older women as consumers of food, household goods, and luxurious fashion labels (Aoyagi 2000; Miller 2006). It was not until *Winter Sonata* and other contemporary Korean dramas arrived in Japan that many commercial enterprises finally awakened to the fact that this category of women also had desires and fantasies—a huge, untapped, and potentially lucrative market. For many Yon-sama fans, becoming consumers of Korean popular culture enables them to realign the biases that exist in conventional perceptions of femininity against those who are middle-aged, housewives, and mothers. As they move out of the home to become active consumers of contemporary popular culture and users of modern communication technologies, such as the Internet and mobile telephones, they also reposition themselves as visible participants in the public sphere. Idols thus provide these women with, to use Hiroshi Aoyagi's (2000, 323) words, "a point of reference" to make sense of their place in a changing social and economic environment by enabling them to "enter modernity" (Felsky 1995, 18–19).

Not a "son" but a "lover:" becoming "young" and a "woman" again

At the same time, these women's passage to modernity through idolizing also involves a re-sexualization of the self. This is achieved through desiring, imagining, and immersing themselves in fantasy, not by having an actual, physical, sexual relationship. Even then, this helps many Yon-sama fans re-feminize themselves, as they reverse conventional perceptions of middle-aged women as de-eroticized and de-sexualized entities. Many women, for example, talk about experiencing palpitations of the heart and sudden rushes of ecstatic sensation when they watch and rewatch *Winter Sonata*, and each time they see Yon-sama in dramas, on merchandise, and in person. As they recover the capacity to feel and express their emotions, they also regain erotic desires and feel like "real women" again. Admitting this, however, requires a considerable amount of courage, which prompted many to initially explain to me that they wished they had a son or son-in-law with the same qualities and attributes as Yon-sama. Following years of fieldwork, after establishing a greater degree of trust and familiarity, many women admitted that their desires were never those of a mother for a son, but of a woman for a man. Yon-sama is like a "lover," not a "son."

Nomura Toyoko was an ardent fan of the idol when I first met her in Tokyo in 2006. The 57-year-old housewife from Sendai, who works part-time in a local department store as a sales assistant, insisted that Yon-sama was merely the ideal a mother has for a son or son-in-law. When I met Nomura for the fourth time, in Seoul in 2009, during her trip to South Korea to attend the launch of the animated version of *Winter Sonata*, her discourse had shifted to love, desire, and fantasy. She explained that embarrassment had prevented her from admitting this openly to me in the past, since a woman at her age is generally regarded as devoid of erotic desire, uninterested in fantasy, and even unconcerned with seeking sexual gratification. In reality, for her, idolizing Yon-sama has always been about love, desire, and fantasy—all of which help her feel like a "real woman" again:

> What a waste it would be to imagine him only as a son! That would also make me a pervert [*hentai*]! No, I definitely like him as a man. He is a young and charming man who makes my knees wobble, and my heart pound madly, like a woman in love.

Toyota Mayumi also sees the idol as an object of her fantasy, and is particularly drawn to his "feminine" image and features. He is to her a "beautiful man" (*binan*), who gives her a warm, tingling feeling whenever she imagines herself as the heroine in a drama or movie and the object of the idol's affection and devotion. Fantasizing also helps her forget about the lack of intimacy in her marriage. Toyota and her husband have not held hands for years, and her marriage has been sexless for more than 20 years. The 49-year-old housewife tried reading romance novels, as she did when she was young, but her daily routine was so exhausting that Toyota often fell asleep soon after she started reading. She then turned to watching Japanese dramas, but found the themes uninteresting, the actors unattractive, and the performances flaccid. Watching Korean dramas and fantasizing about Yon-sama is more enjoyable, and makes her feel like "a young woman again":

> Why would I want to imagine him as a son when I can fantasize about him as a lover? I don't feel ashamed or guilty anymore, as I used to. It is normal for humans to desire love and fantasize, right? After all, I am not committing real adultery.

Many women feel that idolizing is "safe" (*anzen*). Not only does the sheer number of Yon-sama fans assure them of normalcy, but fantasizing also poses little or no threat to family life. For Ikeda Etsuko, a marketing manager from Tokyo, idolizing Yon-sama is safe because it does not have the complications of a real relationship, and also gives her a sense of control in her life. The 43-year-old divorced single mother says that it is difficult for middle-aged women to find a male partner because most Japanese men prefer younger women. She is also tired of dating men, mostly divorcees and widowers, who either disappeared upon realizing she is a divorced single mother or were too eager to get married. Ikeda is not prepared to remarry, as that would mean more domestic duties and a life bound to a specific gender performance. Having Yon-sama as a "lover" (*koibito*) is thus safe, as she can preserve her current independent lifestyle and enjoy a carefree "relationship." As she explains:

> Who needs a real man when Yon-sama is so perfect? Of course, it would be nice to have a real boyfriend who loves me, and with whom I can have sex, but real relationships can be so complicated! I would rather be safe with an imaginary boyfriend.

Ikeda's is a rational choice shaped by the conditions in which some middle-aged women, especially those who are divorced single mothers, are caught.

Not all stories involve giving up on satisfaction in married life or dating. For accountant Sugiyama Tomoko from Tokyo, the positive impact of Yon-sama in her life led to improvements in her marriage. Her husband—who used to be shoddily attired, brash, and crude—one day began purchasing toiletries and stylish clothes in colors that Yon-sama is often seen wearing. This was perhaps because he had noticed that Sugiyama had become more conscious about the clothes that she wore and the makeup she used. While there is little that he can do to make his muscular body feel less like a "tree trunk" whenever he hugs her, or prevent his wife from imagining that she is hugging Yon-sama's seemingly soft body, Sugiyama takes comfort in seeing her husband become more soft-spoken, attentive, and considerate. As she says:

He can never be like Yon-sama no matter how hard he tries [laughs]. And I also don't want him to be like Yon-sama. But I'm happy to know that I'm not the only one in the family who fantasizes about Yon-sama!

Up close and intimate: enmeshing fantasy and reality

Idolizing may be mostly about imagination and fantasy, with some Yon-sama fans deriving real benefits, but these women's fantasies are not entirely unrealizable. Yon-sama is neither an unreachable celebrity nor, as one informant put it, a "distant star in the sky." There is one other aspect of idolizing that is critical to fanning desire for, exciting imagination of, fueling fantasies about and extending interest in Yon-sama: fan meetings. Despite being strategically staged, commercial events to sustain loyalty, fan meetings present the idol as a "real" figure with whom his fans in Japan can be intimate. They bring to life all of his perceived qualities and attributes, as the idol performs beyond the necessary routines of an actor.

A typical Yon-sama fan meeting—like those of many other Korean idols—lasts three to four hours, during which time the idol talks to his fans, takes questions, tells jokes, plays games with the audience, reads aloud, sings, dances, cooks, and even strolls through the aisles and shakes hands. Throughout the event, fans scream the idol's name, narrowing the distance by excitedly yelling "Yong Joon-*shi!*"[8] and *"Oppa!"*[9] as though he were a lover. Such euphoria usually begins as soon as the idol steps on the stage, bows, and greets his fans politely with his trademarked phrase, "Good afternoon, my dear family" (*kazoku no minna-sama, konnichiwa*). It lasts until the end, when he blows a flying kiss to the audience and bids farewell with one magic word in Japanese that all his fans long to hear: *"aishiteiru"* (I love you). By then, most fans are in tears, as his departure leaves a huge void in their lives, which many fill by consuming Yon-sama merchandise and keeping busy with a variety of fan activities until they "meet" again.

Anne Allison (2006, 19) remarks that "friendship" can be made with and through products of popular culture, which incite desires and blur the boundary between fantasy and reality. Fan meetings are an example of this, inciting and intensifying fans' desires, and blurring the boundary between the fantasy and reality of intimacy with the idol. However unreal this sense of intimacy may be, it gives meaning to the time, money, and emotions that these women invest in being Yon-sama fans. Many women feel the same way as Takahashi Sayaka, a 46-year-old sales assistant from Tokyo, who views fan meetings as moments when she can feel "close" to her idol, as they are "together at the same place and at the same time." Others are like Matsumoto Mioko, a 59-year-old widow from Osaka, who likens a fan meeting to going on a date with her "boyfriend" (*kareshi*), which helps relieve the loneliness and emptiness consoled by Yon-sama photographs, posters, bags, handkerchiefs, towels, cups, umbrellas, cushion covers, and even life-sized inflatable dolls. Fan meetings also confirm that she has made the right decision in switching from idolizing stars of the Japanese, all-female Takarazuka Revue to idolizing Yon-sama.[10] Compared with Takarazuka stars (who are women impersonating men), Yon-sama is a "real man." Yon-sama also offers intimacy in ways that Takarazuka stars cannot, as their fan meetings are governed by strict rules that prohibit fans from interacting directly with, let alone touching, the idols:

> I still like a few Takarazuka stars, but they are so aloof, whereas he [Yon-sama] makes me feel close. I know his company makes money from these fan meetings, but they also make me happy. After all, he also gives back to Japan. This means that he cares. He really deserves to be called Yon-sama.

Conclusion

My informants' experiences show that idolizing is closely bound up with and dominated by consumer capitalism, but also that women willingly participate in the process as individuals. While idolizing certainly offers pleasure as a form of relief from the toils of domesticity for some women, it also provides an important means of better understanding and articulating their conditions, which in turn enables them to develop new ways to resist, challenge, and even transform their identity as women. Their desires and fantasies are certainly those of women, not mothers. While their pursuits are contained within the bounds of heterosexuality and reinforce conventional associations of female desire with emotional needs and perceptions of women as having a greater capacity than men for romance and passion (Radway 1984), idolizing Yon-sama also opens up new possibilities for women to regain self-esteem and reposition themselves in a society that has neglected, ignored, and forgotten them. It does not matter whether the idol truly possesses all the attributes and qualities that these women imagine him as having. What is important is that the idol reflects, to borrow Aoyagi's (2000, 325) words, "the concerns and dreams" of his fans. As long as these women want to believe in and imagine Yon-sama, idolizing will continue to be fulfilling, meaningful, rejuvenating, and self-affirming.

Acknowledgements

I am grateful to many for this research, especially Kim Hyun Mee, David Slater, Anne Allison, Ueno Chizuko, and also many of my informants who have made it possible for me to participate in many fan events. I am also indebted to the Korea Foundation for granting me a Postdoctoral Research Fellowship to make research in South Korea possible, and to the Institute of Social and Cultural Anthropology for the Bagby Scholarship for my fieldwork in Japan.

Notes

1. Bae Yong Joon, born on 29 August 1972 in Seoul, began acting in the early 1990s, but became popular only after *Winter Sonata* was aired by the Korean Broadcasting System in 2002. Since the Japanese language does not accommodate a word ending in two consonants, or the consonant "g," part of the idol's name "Yong" is thus written and pronounced as "Yon." The suffix *"-sama"* is usually attached to a person's name as an honorific form of address. While the nickname Yon-sama is used by Japanese fans as an honorific way of addressing the idol, many also jokingly say they are referring to him as a deity, which suggests respect, admiration, elevation, and distance.
2. A statement appeared on the website of the idol's official fan club for Japan on 13 April 2011. For more information, see http://www.yongjoon. jp (accessed 14 April 2011).
3. The drama, known in South Korea as *Kyeoul yeonga* (literally, "winter love song"), was renamed *Fuyu no Sonata* (Winter Sonata) by NHK prior to its first broadcast in Japan in 2004. *Winter Sonata* was one of four dramas directed by Yoon Suk-Ho known as *The Four Seasons*, all of which are tragic love stories. For more information, see http://www.yoonscolor.com.
4. This drama, known in Korean as *Tae wang sa sing gi* (The Legend of the Great King of Four Gods), was aired by South Korea's Munhwa Broadcasting Corporation in 2007, and features the idol as a mythical figure who is devoted to only one woman and chooses death in order to be united with her.

5. The idol's official website for Japanese fans offers a wide range of merchandise for sale, with items ranging from ¥3,000 to 30,000 ($38–375). These include rings, pendants, wallets, stuffed toys, watches, posters, photographs, books, calendars, and DVDs. See http://www.yongjoon.jp/goods.asp (accessed 2 April 2011).

6. The fieldwork was conducted over a 50-month period in Japan and South Korea, during which I also conducted participant observation of many fan activities. All my 36 informants are female: 18 are married, nine divorced, six unmarried, and three widowed. Half of those who are married are full-time housewives, while six hold part-time jobs and three are in full-time employment. Eight of the women who are divorced are single mothers in full-time employment, while one is retired. Of the six unmarried women, four have professional careers—marketing manager, accountant, business consultant, designer, pharmacist, and sales manager—while two are teachers.

7. This movie is the Korean remake of the 1999 Hollywood movie *Random Hearts*, which features Harrison Ford and Kristin Scott. Unlike the character played by Harrison Ford, the Korean idol is cast less as an angry husband and more as a forgiving and caring husband, who still looks after his injured wife despite knowing about her infidelity.

8. The suffix "*-shi*" is added to a person's first name in South Korea as an informal and intimate form of address among friends.

9. *Oppa* (which literally means "elder brother" in Korean) is used only by women to address an older male, who may be a sibling, husband, boyfriend, friend, or acquaintance.

10. The Takarazuka Revue, which was established in 1913 near Osaka, still produces an all-female cast of singers and dancers today. Their performances are like a mixture of Broadway and The Rockettes. See Robertson (1998).

Works Cited

Allison, Anne. 2006. *Millennial Monsters: Japanese Toys and the Global Imagination*. Berkeley: University of California Press.

Aoyagi, Hiroshi. 2000. "Pop Idols and the Asian Identity." In *Japan Pop!: Inside the World of Japanese Popular Culture*, edited by Timothy J. Craig, 309–326. New York: M.E. Sharpe.

Appadurai, Arjun. 1996. *Modernity at Large: Cultural Dimensions of Globalization*. Minneapolis and London: University of Minnesota Press.

Chua, Beng Huat. 2008. "Structure of Identification and Distancing in Watching East Asian Television Drama." In *East Asian Pop Culture: Analysing the Korean Wave*, edited by Chua Beng Huat and Koichi Iwabuchi, 73–90. Hong Kong: Hong Kong University Press.

Felsky, Rita. 1995. *The Gender of Modernity*. Cambridge: Harvard University Press.

Herd, Judith Ann. 1984. "Trends and Taste in Japanese Popular Music: A Case Study of the 1982 Yamaha World Popular Music Festival." *Popular Music* 4: 77–96.

Iwabuchi, Kōichi. 2008. "When the Korean Wave Meets Resident Koreans in Japan: Intersections of the Transnational, the Postcolonial and the Multicultural." In *East Asian Pop Culture: Analysing the Korean Wave*, edited by Chua Beng Huat and Koichi Iwabuchi, 243–264. Hong Kong: Hong Kong University Press.

Kim, Hyun Mee. 2004. "Feminization of the 2002 World Cup and Women's Fandom." *Inter-Asia Cultural Studies* 5, no. 1: 42–51.

———. 2005. "Korean TV Dramas in Taiwan: With An Emphasis On the Localization Process." *Korea Journal* 45, no. 4: 183–205.

Miller, Laura. 2006. *Beauty Up: Exploring Contemporary Japanese Body Aesthetics.* Berkeley: University of California Press.

Moon, So-young and Oh Yoon. 2011. "Celebrities Offer Condolences, Aid to Japan." *Joong Ang Daily*, 16 March. http://joongangdaily.joins.com/article/view.asp?aid=2933478 (accessed 18 April 2011).

Mōri, Yoshitaka. 2008. "Winter Sonata and Cultural Practices of Active Fans in Japan: Considering Middle-Aged Women as Active Agents." In *East Asian Pop Culture: Analysing the Korean Wave*, edited by Chua Beng Huat and Koichi Iwabuchi, 127–142. Hong Kong: Hong Kong University Press.

Radway, Janice A. 1984. *Reading the Romance: Women, Patriarchy, and Popular Literature.* Chapel Hill: University of North Carolina Press.

Robertson, Jennifer. 1998. *Takarazuka: Sexual Politics and Popular Culture in Modern Japan.* Berkeley: University of California Press.

Shim, Doobo. 2008. "The Growth of Korean Cultural Industries and the Korean Wave." In *East Asian Pop Culture: Analysing the Korean Wave*, edited by Chua Beng Huat and Koichi Iwabuchi, 15–32. Hong Kong: Hong Kong University Press.

Yano, Christine R. 2004. "Letters from the Heart: Negotiating Fan-Star Relationships in Japanese Popular Music." In *Fanning the Flames: Fans and Consumer Culture in Contemporary Japan*, edited by William W. Kelly, 41–58. New York: State University of New York Press.

Part IV
Image

9
Idols: The Image of Desire in Japanese Consumer Capitalism

Patrick W. Galbraith

> Death is not desired, but what is desired is dead, already dead: images.
>
> —Gilles Deleuze and Félix Guattari[1]

The idol as image

On 22 November 2010, fans across Japan rushed to purchase *Tomochin!!*, a collection of photographs of Itano Tomomi, a member of the popular female idol group AKB48. Of the 148 pages in the book, 64 were manga; drawings of Itano and a fictional story about her accounted for 43 percent of a photo book bearing her nickname and presenting her to fans. While the reaction was not entirely positive, it is interesting that such a conflation of images could occur at all. This was not an isolated incident. Just a few months earlier, the members of AKB48 began appearing as characters in their own manga series. As *Tomochin!!* makes clear, for some perhaps uncomfortably so, fiction is part of the makeup of an idol. The association of real and fictional images exposes how idols are made up and how they are imagined.

This chapter focuses on the production and circulation of female idols as images, and consumption of and interactions with these images among enthusiastic male fans in Japan. Idols appear in magazines and on TV, in "image videos" (*imēji bideo*) and "raw photographs" (*nama shashin*), in manga and anime. Considering these and other examples, the chapter will interrogate the libidinal and material economy of images. Idols are not only associated with the commodities that they promote, but also become the image of those commodities. The image of the idol gathers and focuses desire, and becomes a commodity in and of itself. As Gabriella Lukács (2010, 47) points out, the entire

185

market (media and beyond) is organized by the movement of these "image commodities." In Japan, it is entirely possible for an idol to perform across genres and media outlets simultaneously, with all these images playing off one another. Constantly present and exposed, the idol becomes "real," the basis of feelings of intimacy among viewers, though this is independent of "reality." John Fiske (1987, 116) describes the situation as "inescapable intertextuality," where all texts refer to one another and not to any external reality. This is not to say that reality does not exist, but rather that what is accessible in cultural products is a construction of reality, which must be understood on its own terms. "Images are made and read in relation to other images and the real is read as an image" (Ibid., 117). The meanings of images, however temporary, are made (or negotiated) in interaction with images.

To demonstrate this point, Fiske offers an example. Most people have not physically experienced a car chase, but when a car chase appears in a movie or on TV it can be understood in relation to familiar scenes of car chases encountered in the media. By this logic, even if someone is involved in an actual car chase, they make sense of it by turning it into images, which are read intertextually. Just so for the fan who encounters an idol at an event, for example those held to build up feelings of intimacy (Aoyagi 2005). Having likely never met the idol before, the fan reduces the idol to an image that is understood in relation to other images encountered in the media. Images lead to more images, not to a "real" person. Indeed, there is growing awareness in Japan that images can operate independently of referents, specifically of identifiable human bodies. For example, in an exhibition on idols held in 2007, portraits of anime, manga, and video game characters were displayed alongside portraits of idols, indicating continuity between them as images (Amano 2007). Fictional characters and idols occupy the same conceptual space; like a mascot, an idol appearing in a marketing campaign in Japan is called an "image character" (*imēji kyarakutā*).

This chapter emerges from an apparent contradiction: the idol is a fiction that has very real effects/affects. This is not confusion about the distinction between fiction and reality, but rather valuing fiction as such.[2] The need for the idol to be an "absolute existence" (*zettai-teki na sonzai*) that is unchanging and outside the everyday, providing a source of security and unwavering support for fans, has been noted in the literature (Ōgawa 1988, 122–123; Sasakibara 2004, 50). What remains less explored is how the idol is imagined, is made an image, to that end. This tendency seems most prominent among enthusiastic fans, called "*otaku*" in Japan. Clinical psychologist and Lacanian psychoanalyst Saitō Tamaki (2007, 227) defines *otaku* as those with an affinity for "fictional contexts" (*kyokō no kontekusuto*). They are sensitive not only to the text itself, but also to how it relates to other texts and contexts. "When enjoying a work, the *otaku* takes pleasure in straddling all the levels of these layered contexts" (Ibid., 227). They recognize that texts are constructed (or personalities are managed performances), but see them as "layered," allowing for reality somewhere (Gamson 1994: 163).³ That reality is accessed through, and understood in relation to, media. Images of the idol refer to other images, not to a "reality" beyond them. *Otaku* are attracted to the fictional contexts of images in and of themselves.

This chapter takes up the example of *otaku* not only because they are a force in the idol market (Kitabayashi 2004), but also because general consumers in Japan are increasingly being positioned as *otaku* affectively attuned to images (see Chapter 3 in this volume).⁴ The *otaku* orientation towards images allows us to consider the "perversion" at the heart of media and consumer culture. By perversion, I mean only that pleasure is not contained in the genitals and sex is not reproductive, or even with another human being. When speaking about intimate relations with images, or what Thomas LaMarre calls "a world of sex without actual women" (LaMarre 2009, 241), we are speaking of perversion. Attachments are only loosely organized and continue to wander and multiply; anything can be an object of desire. This is, I argue, one of the tenets of capitalist society: consumptive pleasure suspended from (re)productive functions. I will explore this through the example of *otaku* consuming and interacting with images. As Saitō sees it, *otaku* are unique in that they take fictional characters (from manga, anime, and games) as sexual objects.⁵ However, the spread of idolatry seems to suggest otherwise.

Narrativizing idols

Nakamori Akio (2007, 9) tells us that the 1980s heralded the "death" of stars and triumph of the idol system in Japan. This chapter is concerned with this system. Given the importance in recent years of female idol groups such as Morning Musume and AKB48, it seems appropriate to begin with their predecessor: Onyanko Club. Formed in 1985, this group was comprised of 52 girls. The original members were selected from guests on the TV program *All Night Fuji: High School Girl Special*, based not necessarily on singing ability or good looks, but rather on how interesting they were. Not only were they given their own idol group, but also their own TV show, *Yūyake Nyan Nyan* (Sunset Meow

Meow) (1985–1987), which achieved cult status despite being comprised of nothing more than the girls playing "childish and frivolous" games and answering inane questions (Kinsella 1995, 235). The popularity of Onyanko Club was such that it inspired numerous imitators and a "high school student boom" (*joshi kōsei būmu*) in Japan (Okada 2008, 93). Like many idols before them, Onyanko Club was produced by a man, Akimoto Yasushi (who would go on to produce AKB48), but, unlike those that had come before, the group specifically targeted a male audience (Kimura 2007, 259). This is clear not only from their logo—a pussycat bent over flashing her bloomers—but also in their use of the phrase "*nyan nyan*" (meow meow), which was at the time slang for sex (Kinsella 1995, 225). They embodied a tension between the pure and sexual, which proved to be extremely compelling. Though as a chorus they sounded only slightly better than caterwauling, their first single, "Sērāfuku o Nugasanai de" (Don't Take Off My School Uniform), was a top five smash hit.

The rise of idol groups with many members—52, 14, 48!—requires comment. As it becomes increasingly difficult to predict consumer tastes, producers put up a wide selection of idols in the same group for fans to choose from. A large fan base can be cobbled together from the small fan groups of individual idols, and these groups compete with one another to boost their idol's popularity. This is actually the structure of the entire idol industry, in which numerous groups and individuals compete with one another (even though they might be from the same agencies, which reap the benefits of staged rivalries) for the support/money of fans.[6] The meaning of the individual idol is determined in relation to the group, and the group in relation to the larger idol market. This is nothing new. It resonates with Francesco Alberoni's discussion of the traditional Hollywood star system, which "never creates the star, but ... proposes the candidate for 'election', and helps to retain the favour of the 'electors'" (quoted in Dyer 1979, 19). To return to the example of Onyanko Club, the major qualification for being a member was a difference from the other members that fans could respond to and rally around. The mass-production and standardization of idols is masked by "pseudo-individuation" (Adorno 1991, 87, 303). In the end, a lack of talent not only makes an idol replaceable, but also encourages fan support, empowering them to become involved in the idol's growth, development, and success (which they experience vicariously). In the case of Onyanko Club, this was valorized in the aesthetic of "nonability" (*hijitsuryoku*), or innocence and inexperience that made them somehow cuter and more "real."[7]

In line with the general trend towards consumption as a way to connect to larger networks of meaning in the 1980s (Ōsawa 2008), idols
were informational. Each of the members of Onyanko Club represented
a distinct set of statistics, measurements, and personality points, which
fans memorized and shared. Further, the members were mechanically
assigned numbers, which they used to identify themselves to audiences.
These numbers should give us pause, as they suggest an underlying
order. In his discussion of "narrative consumption" (*monogatari shōhi*),
Ōtsuka Eiji (2010, 107) draws attention to precisely this phenomenon
of ordering in the 1980s, and makes no distinction between idols
and fictional characters. As Ōtsuka sees it, the pleasure of consuming
both a set of idols and a set of anime character stickers comes from
(re)constructing the "narrative" of the whole by collecting its parts.
The consumer accesses the "grand narrative" (or underlying system)
by consuming "small narratives" (the pieces or episodes); a commodity gains value due to the grand narrative that it holds in partial form.
Speaking of anime, Ōtsuka (Ibid., 107–108) points out the tendency
to desire information about the grand narrative, worldview or underlying system, which manifests in the form of supplementary materials.
It seems clear that the same process is at work with idols, who are constantly introduced and interviewed in magazines and on TV, all of which
provides more information about them (fleshing out their grand narrative). Ōtsuka is touching on an important development of the Japanese
"media mix" model, which Henry Jenkins (2006, 95–96) describes as
"transmedia storytelling," or stories that "unfold across multiple media
platforms, with each new text making a distinctive and valuable contribution to the whole." Though this is not Jenkins' intention, perhaps
it is possible, in dialogue with Ōtsuka, to consider the possibility of
transmedia storytelling about groups or personalities, which promotes
consumption across commodity forms. The drive could be for reasons
of intimacy, wanting to know and possess the idol more fully.[8] It could
also be to know and possess the grand narrative (or underlying system)
more fully, gaining the ability to create small narratives or even new
pieces that expand the set while maintaining its order (Ōtsuka 2010,
109–111). This would mean understanding the idol system and gaining
the power to produce original copies (the basis for fan-produced virtual
idols; see Chapter 10 in this volume). What Ōtsuka is suggesting is that
the reality of the idol is no different from that of the fictional character. The images and objects contain parts of the narrative and take on
intertextual meanings, but in the end refer to one another and their
internal reality, not to external "reality."

Idols and the "fiction game"

As more and more idols were produced in the 1980s, often irrespective of ideologies of authenticity or talent, they became part of a "fiction game" (Grassmuck 1990). That is to say that idols began to play with the boundary between fiction and reality, drawing attention to themselves as "idols" and performing "idol-ness." For example, Koizumi Kyōko released a single titled "Nantettatte Aidoru" (Idol All the Way) in 1985. Some idols engaged in a form of self-parody, drawing attention to their own produced artificiality. Take, for example, Moritaka Chisato, most famous for the 1989 song "17-sai" (17 Years Old). This was a remake of the hit song that launched the career of Minami Saori, one of the foundational idol figures of the 1970s. Even as Moritaka rose to the pinnacle of the idol industry (Minami reborn, or rather recycled), she released an album titled *Hijitsuryoku-ha Sengen* (Non-Ability Proclamation) (1989). The album not only showcased Moritaka's proclaimed lack of singing ability, but even contained a song called "Hijitsuryoku-ha Sengen" (Non-Ability Proclamation) wherein she literally states that she has no ability, never did, and does not want or need it. Not even Onyanko Club was so brazen! Despite what might seem like a slap in the face to fans (and an affront to the system by calling attention to its mechanisms), in fact the song was extremely popular. Fans were not surprised, because they had never been "duped" by Moritaka, her producers, or the industry in the first place. As idol fans, they were enjoying playing the fiction game (recall *otaku* taking pleasure in straddling layers). The fact that "Non-Ability Proclamation" was released the same year as "17 Years Old," and that both appeared on the same album, makes it hard not to consider Moritaka as a parody of the category of idol (from Minami to herself). We note continuity between the outrageous costume Moritaka wears on the *Hijitsuryoku-ha Sengen* album cover and the one she wore while performing "17 Years Old." In every conceivable way, Moritaka draws attention to herself as an idol and as a fiction, and she is not alone in this. The 1980s is replete with similar examples of album covers and song titles referring to the fantasy or fiction of idols, and the decade is characterized by the excessive number, style, and performances of idols.[9] (Figure 9.1).

Looking back to the 1970s, we can see the foundations of this fiction game. For example, when idol photography gained popularity, manga magazines were among the first to realize that these images could be used to increase circulation and sales. Okada Toshio (2008, 92) notes that there has been an idol on the cover of every issue of *Shōnen*

Figure 9.1 Cover of Moritaka Chisato's 1989 album *Hijitsuryoku-ha Sengen* (Non-Ability Proclamation).

Magazine since number 52 in 1972, when Minami Saori appeared there. Today, almost every manga magazine has an idol on the cover, and contains at least one section of glossy "gravure" (*gurabia*) photographs of idols in swimsuits. In these magazines, ostensibly dedicated to serializing manga (and targeting both boys and men), drawings of "fictional" women appear right beside photos of "real" women. The crossover is clear, for example in *AKB49: Renai Kinshi Jōrei* (AKB49: The Prohibition Against Love), a manga about AKB48 serialized in the pages of *Shōnen Magazine* starting in 2010. This became possible partly because of the way idols have been presented in such "boys' magazines." Historically, one of their emphases was collecting, categorizing, and controlling information about objects of interest. In this sense, idols fell in line with bugs, gadgets, and imaginary creatures. These magazines catalogued idols, providing pictures, measurements, and biographical statements for fans. Taking the manga magazine as a microcosm of the larger system, it is clear that idols underwent mechanical reproduction as images, were associated with fiction, and were fragmented and datatized (marketed and memorized in terms of parts). It is not surprising, then, that in the 1980s it became something of a fad to depict idols in anime as well, or that many of these animated characters, voiced by "real" idols, went on to become idols in their own right.[10]

The end of the 1980s to the early 1990s is a time referred to as the "idol ice age" (*aidoru hyōgaki*) or "winter time of idols" (*aidoru fuyu no jidai*). The mass culture of idols suffered due to market saturation, scandal, and competition from other types of music (see Chapter 1 in this volume). The idol became a form of kitsch with her colorful, frilly costumes and childish flouncing. And yet she persisted, and continues to persist, as an object of desire that is also a known fiction. In 1996, Horipro, a major agency for female idols, debuted Date Kyōko (a.k.a. DK-96), the first example of a "virtual idol" (a failed experiment that foreshadowed a later boom). In 1997, the hit idol group Morning Musume was formed, largely due to fan response (the five original girls launched a grassroots campaign and sold 50,000 copies of a demo in four days of promotion). For their producer, Tsunku, and perhaps for the fans, the appeal of the group was a return to the "golden age of idols" (*aidoru no ōgon jidai*) in the 1980s—that, and resistance to the chaotic street culture of the 1990s, where girls had become too "self-possessed" for all the media attention (Tsunku specifically mentions the high school student boom) (Tsunku 2000, 98–99).[11] In Tsunku's estimation, Japanese men were losing confidence and needed idols, or rather a very specific kind of idol (Ibid., 99). At the height of his influence, the producer wrote a book (some 219 pages long) describing in excruciating detail his preferences for girls; he develops a typology by discussing members of Morning Musume. Tsunku spends much of the book explaining why he prefers girls who are not naturally beautiful or talented. His rationale is as follows: on the one hand, the less beautiful and talented girl tries harder and is easier for fans to approach and get behind; on the other hand, she has more room to grow and does not resist being produced. It is this potential for an "image change" that most captivates Tsunku. What matters, he writes (to female readers?), is finding one thing to focus on and develop a "character" around. This might be size, personality, or style—anything that sets a girl apart from the crowd (or group, in the case of idols). Because girls cannot see what that they need to focus on, they need a producer. The ideal idol candidate must be "obedient" (*sunao*) (Ibid., 53). She must lack a strong sense of self and give her agency over entirely. "In sum, take the value system of someone outside yourself into yourself" (Ibid., 51–52). That is, allow Tsunku to decide your image, draw out your character, and produce an idol from your raw material (which both is and is not you). As a man and a fan, Tsunku knows what constitutes an "idol," and communicates that idol to other men and fans with and through the idol but to a certain extent irrespective of the girl.

Fast-forward a decade later to 13 June 2011. On the cover of *Weekly Playboy* is Eguchi Aimi, a new member of AKB48, who is to appear along with the group in a television commercial for Glico ice cream. The article infuriates fans, as it is revealed that Eguchi, whom they have never seen or heard of before, was given the coveted "center position" (*sentā pojishon*) in the commercial over favorites such as Maeda Atsuko and Ōshima Yūko. Fans of the group say that she is not even a real idol. It was later revealed that they were right, in a way: Eguchi was a virtual idol, constructed from the digitalized facial features, body parts, and characteristics of the AKB48 girls to be an "image character" (*imēji kyarakutā*) for Glico. Given this, it is interesting that her producer, Akimoto Yasushi, called her the "ultimate" (*kyūkyoku*) idol.[12] Her creation was a publicity stunt, but it made clear just how produced all the members of AKB48 really are. When the commercial was aired on 20 June 2011, Eguchi looked, for lack of a better word, natural standing next to Maeda Atsuko and the others.[13] For Akimoto, Eguchi did not lack the essential qualities of an idol. She provoked visceral responses from supporters and detractors, who importantly positioned her as an idol in relation to other idols (and therein lies the source of their anger). Or, rather, her *image* provoked visceral responses and was positioned against *images* of other idols, taking on a sense of reality. Though she moved less than the other AKB48 idols (in the sense that she was confined to the one advertising campaign and not allowed to become an intimate part of everyday life), Eguchi was open to reproduction. On the Glico website, fans could make their own "Eguchi Aimi" from parts—the "best" parts or the parts they liked best—of AKB48 members (Ezaki Glico Co., 2011).[14] Those who did participate in this, a very limited example of the much larger trend of creating virtual idols in Japan today, were not confused about the distinction between reality and fiction. They simply played the fiction game and took pleasure in the idol, in the image and its movements.[15]

Capitalism and perversion

The importance of image is well documented in the study of stars and celebrities (cf., Dyer 1979, especially part two). What is less understood is how fans interact with images on their own terms. In the case of male fans, psychoanalysis offers compelling clues. Jacques Lacan argues that the formation of Ego is a process of objectification in the "mirror stage." When the infant sees its reflection, the mirror image initiates and then aids the formation of an integrated sense of self. However, it also entails misrecognition of an autonomous and whole self. Humans are constituted by a lack and produce images of themselves as autonomous and whole by latching onto objects. This is related to the structure of male desire. Saitō Tamaki explains:

> Desire directed at the *object a* incarnates desire as an illusion within the symbolic world... The male follows a chain of metaphors directed towards the desired *object a* that he cannot attain. In the process, he constructs the illusion called knowledge. What he tries to possess (e.g., the illusion of the woman) is actually a stand-in for the singular *object a* that perpetually eludes his grasp.
>
> (Saitō 2007, 233–234)

This is why Lacan argues that the woman does not exist, or exists as a "symptom of man" created for his ontological consistency (LaMarre 2009, 236).[16] There is a very appropriate phrase for this in Japanese, *sōzō suru*, which means "to imagine," but is also homonymous with "to create;" imagining is an act of creation, both of the other and of the self. One pursues objects and in possessing them is nevertheless lacking, which feeds further pursuit.[17] Thomas LaMarre points out that the "nonexistence of woman implies that, potentially, any substitution in the shape of woman might do. The path is clear for endless substitution" (Ibid., 241). John Whittier Treat (1993, 364) argues that the idol's purported "lack" is what makes her an interchangeable and disposable commodity that affiliates with the "signifying processes of Japanese consumer capitalism." While Treat is referring to a lack of talent, it seems possible to expand the point: the idol's lack of an autonomous existence makes her an interchangeable and disposable image commodity.

In this vision of consumer capitalism, people chase around images and objects for the pleasure of immediate interaction, without necessarily achieving a stable subject or viewing position. Objects do not necessarily assist in establishing clearly defined subject positions or transitions between them.[18] They are replaced regularly and endlessly, even destroyed only to be recreated, thereby fueling the continuous movement of capital. Attachments are multiple, shifting, and partial.

In this sense, the idol, who appears in myriad media and material forms, fostering deep attachments only to be replaced, is symptomatic of the global phenomenon of open-ended transition and modal consumerism (Szollosy 1998; cf., Ivy 2010). Marilyn Ivy suggests that the two figures most often associated with this in Japan are *otaku* and *shōjo* (girls). What connects the two conceptual figures of *otaku* and *shōjo*, in addition to both being ambiguously between gender and age distinctions, is their association with the "unproductive" (*hiseisanteki*), or consumptive plea-sure suspended from (re)productive functions (Ōtsuka 1989, 18). The *shōjo* consumer emerged in the 1970s, with the nascent *otaku* move-ment soon to follow, accelerating in the 1980s with advances in media and consumer culture, which collided in the form of idols. Men (espe-cially *otaku*) were attracted to the idol as girl (*shōjo*), herself already a fiction of the consumer and of consumable pleasure.

In experiencing the immediacy of images and interacting with them on their own terms, fragmented, multiple, and shifting gazes are possi-ble.[19] A ready example is the idol "image video" (*imēji bideo*). Originally a way for companies to showcase products, the image video was quickly picked up by the idol industry to showcase girls (and notably retains this gender bias). In addition to almost all female idols, even aspir-ing actresses might release image videos; they are common enough to be available for purchase in convenience stores in Japan. These videos began with nudity, but are now a genre of non-nude erotica (*chakuero* or *chiraizumu*).[20] The viewer sees the idol from a first-person perspective (i.e., the camera is positioned to act as eyes), usually alone in a private setting, and often engaged in everyday activities. There is a tendency towards voyeurism and peeping, such as seeing the idol in bed or in the shower. She is seen in (staged) unguarded moments—unpretentious, trusting, and innocent—making the viewing feel intimate. Facial close-ups are common, which tends to increase feelings of intimacy (Dyer 1979, 15–16). The idol speaks to the camera (imagined viewer) directly; a response on behalf of the viewer may appear as text onscreen, or in the form of the camera motioning to nod "yes" or "no." She looks at the camera (imagined viewer), and oscillates between making bedroom eyes and shyly avoiding eye contact. If not already in a swimsuit or under-wear, she strips off her costume down to them as the viewer watches. Each video contains multiple "scenes," set apart by theme, location, and costume (walking on the beach in a bikini, working in the kitchen in a maid outfit, waking up in the bedroom in pajamas).[21] The idol appears almost doll-like, her body unchanging even as her surroundings, appear-ance, and role change compulsively. In each scene, especially while stripping or in swimsuit/underwear, the idol adopts various positions and poses, making sure that there is ample time to see each from multiple angles. Movement is interspersed with repetitious close-ups of isolated body parts—eyes, lips, hands, legs, buttocks, breasts. The camera does not linger too long, focusing in only to be swept out again. Movement of the camera (gaze) and the idol is persistent, as is the presence of (images of) supple flesh.[22]

The image video demonstrates the almost irresistible urge to visualize, a cinematographic perversion that Linda Williams calls the "frenzy of the visible" (Williams 1999), but there are no depictions of genitals, penetration, or ejaculation. There is instead a continuous movement of the gaze, an eroticism that is decentered. As much time is spent looking at the face as at the thighs, almost as if for reassurance or approval. Most of the men I spoke to about these videos stressed that they were about "purity," despite the sexual tone. They seldom referred to idol photographs or image videos as masturbatory material—regardless of whether or not they were masturbating to it. They could get or had pornography for that purpose, and could climax to it much more efficiently; they insisted that idol media were different. Three of the most common descriptions of the pleasure of engagement were: (1) it heals me (*iyasareru*) to be taken out of my stressful day by the idol (often seen in relaxing or exotic environments); (2) it energizes me (*genki ga deru*) to see the young and happy idol (often involved in energetic movement, such as running or jumping, and eating); and (3) it allows me to see the idol's growth (*seichō o miru*), keeping me connected and close to her (a nostalgic consumption of intertextual meanings built up across works over time). Fans describe idols, and by extension their relationships with them, as "pure" (*junsui*).

This purity also implies a sort of chastity or virtue on the part of the idol, which interacts with sexual desire in interesting ways. In order to keep the idol "pure," it is necessary to displace sexual desire from the idol onto other images/objects. The pure relationship with the idol is maintained by replacing her with a series of interchangeable sex objects, or what LaMarre refers to as "soft-porn images of bodies" (LaMarre 2006b, 57). This is encouraged by the presentation of idols in the media—for example, young idols wearing swimsuits in men's magazines beside more mature women in less clothing (perhaps even nude). This splitting of the woman into the pure and the sexual is all too familiar (Ueno 2010, 42–47).[23] While it may seem obvious that a fan might follow an idol and masturbate to pornography featuring different women, it is interesting that the image video offers what appear to be "soft-porn images" of the idol's body, but nonetheless the idol maintains her pure (unspoiled) image. This suggests the possibility of dissociation of images (or fantasies) of the same idol from one another. One might likewise consciously shut down or deny intertextual linkages that threaten the preferred image of the idol. This seems to speak in turn to the desire for (relatively) stable objects that encourage attachment and offer access to safe and known fantasies, which is at odds with the constant movement of capitalism.[24]

Even as interactions and pleasures are immediate and intense, the idol as image evaporates without constant replacements to evoke and ground her. This leads to purchasing photographs, videos, and other goods emblazoned with the image of the idol (and imbued with her "soul").[25] In the form of a physical commodity, the idol can be possessed, handled, displayed, collected. But that is not all. Anne Friedberg (1990, 42) notes an "extra-cinematic identification" with stars, or the need to consume goods associated with them and to keep the connection alive beyond the theater. In a similar way, when images of idols appear on goods, merchandise, and collectibles, attachments become visible and tangible. Consumption serves to anchor and legitimate attachments (Hills 2002, 171). The increased presence in one's life leads to feelings of intimacy. Objects summon up meaning or aid in imaginative work. They lead back to images, hold them in place (if only for a moment), and make them somehow more real.

There is an interesting desire for more "authentic" traces—for example, "raw photographs" (*nama shashin*) or untouched photos of idols taken by fans and sold among them.[26] Such images seem to reveal something more of the idol, something for fans to grasp onto, but are not revealing enough to show that she is human after all (which would undermine her as an idol and absolute existence). This is categorically different from scandal media (see Chapter 2 in this volume). Other examples of "authentic" traces include photographs signed by the idol, kissed by her (marked with lipstick), or sprayed with her perfume—all given away to loyal fans (or with purchase).[27] If the image itself is not enough, then it might be paired with one of the idol's used costumes for serious collectors, or the two can be combined as "costume cards" (*ishō kādo*). Here, a piece of a costume is imbedded in a card-sized printed photo of the idol wearing that costume; an arrow is drawn on the card to indicate where the piece was located. There is a small window cut into the card to see and perhaps touch the imbedded material. As the costume is comprised of a finite amount of material, there are a limited number of cards in the series. Ostensibly, if one owned all the pieces in the set, the costume could be reassembled, adding a material basis to the image, which by then would have multiplied a hundred times over. In the end, however, the idol as image cannot be possessed; feelings of closeness are paired with infinite distance, completion with infinite deferral. This is why it is actually much better that there is no climax (pornography), as the foreplay and fetishizing can continue endlessly (image videos). The unobtainable image continues to seduce in commodity form. There is no point of culmination or external end, only a continuous movement that requires ever more images, pieces of images, objects and traces. This movement of perversion/proliferation seems to be precisely the movement of consumer capitalism (LaMarre 2006a, 385) (Figures 9.2, 9.3, 9.4, and 9.5).

Conclusion

This chapter has focused on the production, circulation, and consumption of idols to interrogate the libidinal and material economy

Figure 9.2 Inside of a store selling photographs of AKB48 members, located right behind the stage where they perform live shows in Akihabara, Tokyo. Photo by author.

Figure 9.3   Advertisement for a store in Akihabara selling "raw photographs" of AKB48 members. Photo by author.

of images. Equating idol and image, concentrating on the production and consumption of images rather than idols themselves, risks being complicit with the systematic denial of female agency. That is not the intention. Women do exist and idols do have agency, but there is an economy to producing and reproducing them as images. Fantasy making in Japan is big business, as the object can never be fully possessed, the climax is indefinitely deferred and the continuation or serialization of interaction can be sold as harmless fantasy to both children and adults (Allison 2000, 150). The idol oscillates between an unreachable ideal (the pure) and infinitely available material (the sexual), which I have discussed in terms of a movement between lack and object. In approaching desire this way, we see that the idol is a symptom not just of man, but also of consumer-capitalist society. However, contrary to Lacan's theory of the subject, an analysis of enthusiastic fans of idols—or idol *otaku*—suggests that interactions with images do not necessarily assist men in securing ontological consistency. In the world of images, subject and viewing positions constantly emerge and are undermined, even as the idol is real but draws attention to her own

200

Figure 9.4 Example of "perfumed pictures" of AKB48 members given away to *Shōnen Sunday* readers.

Figure 9.5 An example of a "costume card."

fiction. One of the results is that attachments are loosely organized, orientations are multiple, and one experiences the immediacy and intensity of images. This may well describe aspects of perversion, but such movements and desires, which we might call *otaku*, are facilitated and exploited by consumer capitalism.

Notes

1. See Deleuze and Guattari (1977, 337).
2. This is something that I was confronted with while doing fieldwork in Tokyo. A longtime idol enthusiast, 34, male, told me quite bluntly that the definition of idol is "image" (*gūzō*) and said, "I don't care what the real person is doing" (Galbraith 2009, 24). This is not unique to Japan, or to fans of idols. In his classic analysis of religion and society, Émile Durkheim argues that "the images of the totemic being are more sacred than the totemic being itself" (Durkheim 2001, 104).
3. If we take up Joshua Gamson's categorization of celebrity watchers, *otaku* show some of the characteristics of "second-order traditionals," whose awareness of the production system helps them validate a truth that they seek out, and "game players," who play with images and issues regardless of authenticity (Gamson 1994, 146–147).
4. See also Chapters 4 and 8 in this volume for examples of how women of all ages are forming intimate relationships with idols as distant or even imaginary entities, which was once thought to be the sole province of *otaku*.
5. As if channeling *otaku*, Gilles Deleuze suggests that "sexuality reaches its goal much better and much more promptly to the extent that it ... addresses itself directly to Images" (Deleuze 1990, 313).
6. Consider, for example, groups produced by Akimoto Yasushi in the new millennium. First, in 2005, came AKB48, a female idol group comprised of three teams (A, K and B) of 16 girls each. They are based in the Akihabara neighborhood of Tokyo, where they have a stage and perform live shows daily. Fans can "meet" them, or at least develop a similar feeling of intimacy. Strong bonds are formed; rivalries between members and teams are crucial to bringing in fan support and dollars. As they became more famous, Akimoto spun off a variety of other groups. SDN48, or Saturday Night 48, took on idols deemed too old for AKB48, whose ranks were replenished with young "trainees" (*kenkyūsei*), also grouped into performing teams. The phenomenon then spread across Japan—SKE48 (based in the Sakae neighborhood of Nagoya), NMB48 (based in the Namba neighborhood of Osaka), and HKT48 (based in Fukuoka)—adding local involvement and pride to the competition. In 2011, Akimoto went international, auditioning girls for JKT48, based in Jakarta, Indonesia. Also in 2011, he produced "official rivals" (*kōshiki raibaru*) for AKB48, a group called Nogizaka 46, based in another Tokyo neighborhood. This external multiplication is matched by internal processes: AKB48 spins off a seemingly endless line of subunits comprised of its members, who enter into new relations and take on new meanings for fans.
7. Non-ability is a particularly capitalist fantasy, in that it is diametrically opposed to the constant struggle to perfect one's self and skills and succeed in the neoliberal market. For example, in their often uncoordinated and unpolished dances, idols seem to be having fun; this is a "performance of pleasure" or "show of enjoyment" that is "not directed towards mastery" (McDonald 1997, 288–293). They are imagined to be in a place where (and a time, "youth," when) excellence is not demanded. While idols do exert effort, for example when on stage or preparing for concerts, this is always

presented as their own choice (i.e., they want to work, often as part of the group), and they are shown to receive benefits. In this way, idols present a fantasy of unalienated labor. The realities of fierce competition and strict control are minimized or disavowed.

8. The idol might also be brought to life by narrativizing acts of consumption. Consider the example of Elvis. With each act of consumption, the fan references an "archive" of images and memories (often mediated); Elvis is evoked through consumption (Hills 2002, 165). Matt Hills refers to this as "performative consumption," in the sense that fans are "performing" Elvis, mentally and sometimes physically. But when we consider that idols such as Onyanko Club are produced and consumed by men, an interesting gendered dynamic emerges: the female idol performed by men. This suggests the possibility of identification with the object of desire and the creation of a zone of indiscernibility with women (consider male fans performing karaoke of favorite female idols), an issue that will be taken up in future research.

9. The example of Haga Yui makes abundantly clear the fact that idol fans are aware of, and take pleasure in, the fiction game. Produced as a joke, Haga Yui debuted in 1990 and never revealed her face; her voice was a playback recording. For this reason, practically anyone could have been this idol, as was revealed when three different girls appeared (unmasked) at a fan gathering and were introduced as Haga Yui (Grassmuck 1990). Fans could essentially choose which "version" of Haga Yui they preferred. What is interesting is that the joke of Haga Yui became a serious idol phenomenon, or fans were serious about joking. While Japan is not the first or only place to develop virtual idols, the enthusiasm for play with the boundaries of reality, or awareness of the reality of fiction, makes virtual idols in Japan quite different from The Archies (1968–1973) or Gorillaz (1998–). In general, *otaku* seem particularly cognizant and positive about their love affair with media and technology, focused and grounded by the idol/imaginary woman. For example, in the animated work *Megazone 23* (1985), the protagonist discovers that the world he knows is an illusion managed by a computer, which projects an idol singer as its avatar. Quite contrary to *The Matrix* (1999) scenario, the idol, or rather the machine producing and projecting this image, is not trying to enslave humanity, but rather to save it from war by recreating the happy excess of Japan in the 1980s.

10. Two examples are Lynn Minmay (voiced by Iijima Mari) from *Super Dimensional Fortress Macross* (1982–1983) and Morisawa Yū (voiced by Ōta Takako) from *Creamy Mami, the Magic Angel* (1983). The careers of both real idols overlapped with the fictional idol characters that they performed. It comes as little surprise that *seiyū*, the people who provide the voices for anime and game characters, are one of the most vibrant sources of idols today. Their voices are associated with characters, which are imbedded in networks of meaning, and unembodied, fuel imaginative possibilities as they leap arrhythmically from character to character across media platforms. *Seiyū* performing "character songs" at live shows present fans with an interesting "layering."

11. Tsunku further criticizes "gals" (*gyaru*), or high school girls associated with the fashionable consumer space of Shibuya, and a moral panic about teenage prostitution (*enjo kōsai*) in the 1990s (Tsunku 2000, 18). Just like the high

school student boom before them, these "bad girls" were a media phenomenon. Indeed, did not the interest in (idolization of) high school students in some way lay the groundwork for the arrival of gals—girls who were aware of their market value and capitalize on it? As Sharon Kinsella phrases it, gals were "performed" by and for men who produced and consumed them in the media (Kinsella 2006). In a description that foreshadows the arrival of virtual idols, Kinsella points out that girls on TV were "disguised with screen pixilation and voice synthesizers. The girls appeared as blurred and shifting impressions of flesh with squeaky computerized voices and autonomous naked legs" (Kinsella 2002, 226–227).

12. This statement was made in the 13 June 2011 edition of *Weekly Playboy*, though it circulated widely in official and alternative media. In full, Akimoto said, "She's the 'ultimate' " (*kanojo koso "kyūkyoku"*), emphasizing Eguchi as an idol above others (by use of the marker *koso* in Japanese) and drawing attention to "ultimate" (and perhaps also the way idols are evaluated) by placing it in scare quotes.

13. The commercial can be viewed online at http://www.youtube.com/watch?v=Z0fU3O8ynTE (accessed 2 April 2012).

14. It is interesting to note that many AKB48 fans were aware that Eguchi was a composite before the mainstream media announced her as such. They not only identified the parts of the story that seemed constructed, but also recognized the parts of their favorite idols from which Eguchi was constructed (mouth, eyes, hair, body, etc.). On online bulletin boards and blogs, they took great pleasure in speculating about what part came from which AKB48 member. This recognition of their idols (or rather parts of them), and of the system that produced Eguchi and the commercial, was a way for fans to assert authority and get involved in the fiction game (cf., Jenkins 2006, 25–58).

15. One might also consider virtual contact with idols via computers beginning in the mid-1990s. Interestingly, in his ethnographic fieldwork, Hiroshi Aoyagi did not encounter fans who were worried about whether it was actually the idol responding to them in relay chats (Aoyagi 2005, 212–213). This opens a path for potentially anyone to perform the idol, for example an assistant or producer. The other way around, the consumer performs the idol when interacting with the computer, imagining a woman beyond the screen and summoning her up to engage in a play of surfaces.

16. As Saitō Tamaki sees it, the woman who does not exist is "possessed" through fictionalization, or creating information and knowledge about her. This seems to fit well with *otaku*, who at times display a sort of "information fetishism" where their idols are concerned (Grassmuck 1990).

17. Further, for Lacan, "surplus enjoyment" becomes a site for the accumulation of capital (Lacan 2007, 177). Note that enjoyment here, *jouissance*, is an "imitation" that is "produced by our industry" (Lacan 2007, 80–81). There is an inversion of "real" *jouissance*, which is the realm of the Real and cannot be symbolized.

18. Object relations theory has been applied to the study of media personalities, for example to argue that the androgynous male idols preferred by girls and young women serve as "safe" or practice objects to assist transition into sexuality (Karniol 2001). However, this approach assumes that one grows out of the need for such objects, which is belied by the prevalence in Japan

of "safe" objects for adults, be they androgynous male idols or infantilized female idols.

19. For Azuma Hiroki, what Lacan meant by "castration" was "to abandon a direct tie to the image (the direct gratification of desire) and come to recognize one's own gaze" (quoted in Ivy 2010, 7). What then if *otaku* were not "castrated," or did not abandon the world of images?

20. The eroticism of the clothed body is certainly not unique to Japan, as Roland Barthes demonstrates: "[I]t is intermittence, as psychoanalysis so rightly stated, which is erotic: the intermittence of skin flashing between two articles of clothing (trousers and sweater), between two edges (the open-necked shirt, the glove and the sleeve); it is this flash itself which seduces, or rather: the staging of an appearance-as-disappearance" (Barthes 1975, 10).

21. Recall John Fiske, in the sense that each scene is a mediated fantasy referring to other scenes encountered in the media. The "walk on the beach" works much like "the chase."

22. The camera here seems to be reproducing something like what Laura Mulvey calls the "male gaze" (Mulvey 1989), particularly through the fragmentation of the female body, if not also the fetishization of the star. We need to be aware that sexual subjectivities are not easily or totally overcome. The image video is, after all, almost without exception men looking at women. However, as Thomas LaMarre argues, stable subject and viewing positions are "perverted" by the movement of the fracturing, multiplying, shifting gaze. There are moments when subject and object are not necessarily gendered, even when the boundaries between the subject and object blur. In contexts where bodies are not necessarily mimetic of humans—for example, manga, anime, and games—we do see an enormous amount of gender ambiguity, in terms of both the subject and the object of desire. The most recent iteration of this is "boy-girls" (*otoko no ko*), used to describe not only fictional characters, but also actual men so attracted to female characters that they embody and perform them (quite independently of sexual orientation).

23. One other pleasure of seeing idols in this context might be eroticizing them by association or indulging the imagined possibility that they are after all the same as "other women." There is always the chance that the pure girl will transform into the sexy woman. Some will want to see that moment (hence the market for scandal, and the high prices paid to idols to appear in pornographic films), though fans tend to want to preserve the idol as a pure/absolute existence.

24. A good example of how idols address this desire is the AKB48 song "Everyday, Kachūsha" (2011). The lyrics beseech a girl not to remove her *"kachūsha,"* or the band of cloth holding her hair up. The idols of AKB48 all wear the specified *kachūsha* while performing the song (oddly, singing as the boy/man in love with the *kachūsha* girl/woman), making them appear as the arrested image of the girl, who is absent (or never existed). That their *kachūsha* image can be accessed every day accounts for the title of the song. If only for one song, there is a sense of stability and unchanging-ness in contrast to a field of compulsive change. In a similar way, the image video is a record of the idol at a given moment, where she is frozen in looped scenes and motions and "can meet [you] anytime" (*itsu demo aeru*). Object relations theory has been applied to understand dangerous fan behavior stemming from the desire to

control the idol and make him or her into a petrified image (Hills 2002, 96–99). In Japan, the animated film *Perfect Blue* (1997) depicts fans obsessed with stopping an idol singer from transitioning into an acting career. The real threat to these fans, the movie implies, is that the idol might grow out of her image and into a real woman (LaMarre 2006a, 382).

25. LaMarre offers an explanation for the ability of the image to move from the screen to objects, albeit in an ostensibly different context. He argues that, due to visual flatness and limited motion, characters in animated television shows have become "soulful bodies," where "spiritual, emotional, or psychological qualities appear inscribed on the surface" (LaMarre 2009, 201). Pushing movement to the surface of the image "conjures from within it a portable animus, an image of the soul that can attach itself to anybody or anything" (LaMarre 2009, 206). For evidence, one need only look at the power the animated image character or idol has to enchant an endless string of commodities, as her image moves from one surface to another, transferring and localizing soul. Though it may seem unfair to compare the idol as image to the animated character as soulful body, recall that for Barthes all photography is spirit photography (Barthes 1982, 14). It captures what is not there, what has already passed, conjuring up a spirit or "soul." The notion of soulful body alone is certainly not enough to explain the idol's capacity for affect. The idol is not propelled solely by residual energy/momentum from live performances or internal movements pushed to the surface. Her energy is renewed by fans, who infuse the static image with their own energy and channel its affects through bodily intimacies. Internal movements are drawn out by fans, who are moved by the image. The idol is brought to life and put into motion—is animated—by the dreams and desires of those interacting with the image. The idol as image is "dead" and yet "alive" with the affective force of its movement, layered contexts, and embedded social relations.

26. This market is forbidden by agencies, which try to totally control the movement of the idol's image and have their own official photographs for sale (and even store locations to sell them).

27. For example, manga magazine *Shōnen Sunday* ran a campaign giving away "perfumed pictures" (*kaori-tsuki shashin*) of AKB48 members with its February, March, and April 2011 issues. This sort of thing is likely to become more common. When it was announced on a technology website in June 2011 that soon it would be possible to "smell" in addition to see images on TV, the immediate imagined application was idol image videos (*Gigazine* 2011).

Works Cited

Adorno, Theodor. 1991. *The Culture Industry: Selected Essays on Mass Culture*, edited by J.M. Bernstein. London: Routledge.

Allison, Anne. 2000. *Permitted and Prohibited Desires: Mothers, Comics, and Censorship in Japan*. Berkeley: University of California Press.

Amano, Tarō. 2007. "Idol Exhibition at Yokohama Museum of Art: 'IDOLS!' Understanding Contemporary Portraiture Through the Depiction of Idols."

Trans. Suda Takahisa. *High Fashion: Bimonthly Magazine for Women and Men* 313 (1 February): 261.

Aoyagi, Hiroshi. 2005. *Islands of Eight Million Smiles: Idol Performance and Symbolic Production in Contemporary Japan*. Cambridge: Harvard University Asia Center.

Barthes, Roland. 1975. *The Pleasure of the Text*. Trans. Richard Miller. New York: Hill and Wang.

———. 1982. *Camera Lucida: Reflections on Photography*. Trans. Richard Howard. New York: Hill and Wang.

Deleuze, Gilles. 1990. *The Logic of Sense*. Trans. Mark Lester. New York: Columbia University Press.

Deleuze, Gilles and Félix Guattari. 1977. *Anti-Oedipus: Capitalism and Schizophrenia*. Trans. Robert Hurley, Mark Seem and Helen R. Lane. New York: Penguin.

Durkheim, Émile. 2001. *The Elementary Forms of Religious Life*. Trans. Carol Cosman. Oxford: Oxford University Press.

Dyer, Richard. 1979. *Stars*. London: British Film Institute.

Ezaki Glico Co. 2011. "AKB48 Oshimen Mēkā." http://www.icenomi.com/oshimen/index.html (accessed 21 June 2011).

Fiske, John. 1987. *Television Culture*. London: Methuen.

Friedberg, Anne. 1990. "A Denial of Difference: Theories of Cinematic Identification." In *Psychoanalysis and Cinema*, edited by E. Ann Kaplan, 36–45. London: Routledge.

Galbraith, Patrick W. 2009. *The Otaku Encyclopedia: An Insider's Guide to the Subculture of Cool Japan*. Tokyo: Kodansha International.

Gamson, Joshua. 1994. *Claims to Fame: Celebrity in Contemporary America*. Berkeley: University of California Press.

Gigazine. 2011. "'Nioi ga Deru Terebi' Kaihatsu-chū, Aidoru ya Joyū no Kaori mo Saigen Kanō ni." 22 June. http://gigazine.net/news/20110622_tv_screen_smell/ (accessed 1 July 2011).

Grassmuck, Volker. 1990. "'I'm alone, but not lonely': Japanese *Otaku*-kids Colonize the Realm of Information and Media: A Tale of Sex and Crime from a Faraway Place." http://www.cjas.org/~leng/otaku-e.htm (accessed 1 June 2011).

Hills, Matt. 2002. *Fan Cultures*. London: Routledge.

Ivy, Marilyn. 2010. "The Art of Cute Little Things: Nara Yoshitomo's Parapolitics." In *Mechademia 5: Fanthropologies*, edited by Frenchy Lunning, 3–30. Minneapolis: University of Minnesota Press.

Jenkins, Henry. 2006. *Convergence Culture: Where Old and New Media Collide*. New York: New York University Press.

Karniol, Rachel. 2001. "Adolescent Females' Idolization of Male Media Stars as a Transition into Sexuality." *Sex Roles* 44, no. 1/2: 61–77.

Kimura, Tatsuya. 2007. "History of Japanese Idols: From the Silver Screen to the Internet Via the Living Room." Trans. Suda Takahisa. *High Fashion: Bimonthly Magazine for Women and Men* 313 (1 February): 259–260.

Kinsella, Sharon. 1995. "Cuties in Japan." In *Women, Media, and Consumption in Japan*, edited by Lise Skov and Brian Moeran, 220–254. Honolulu: University of Hawai'i Press.

———. 2002. "What's Behind the Fetishism of Japanese School Uniforms?" *Fashion Theory: The Journal of Dress, Body & Culture* 6, no. 2: 215–237.

———. 2006. "Minstrelized Girls: Male Performers of Japan's Lolita Complex." *Japan Forum* 18, no. 1 (March): 65–87.

Kitabayashi, Ken. 2004. "The *Otaku* Group from a Business Perspective: Revaluation of Enthusiastic Consumers." Nomura Research Institute. http://www.nri.co.jp/english/opinion/papers/2004/pdf/np200484.pdf (accessed 1 June 2011).

Lacan, Jacques. 2007. *The Seminar of Jacques Lacan, Book XVII: Other Side of Psychoanalysis*, edited by Jacques-Alain Miller. Trans. Russell Grigg. New York: Norton.

LaMarre, Thomas. 2006a. "*Otaku* Movement." In *Japan After Japan: Social and Cultural Life from the Recessionary 1990s to the Present*, edited by Tomiko Yoda and Harry Harootunian, 358–394. Durham: Duke University Press.

———. 2006b. "Platonic Sex: Perversion and *Shōjo* Anime." *Animation: An Interdisciplinary Journal* 1, no. 1: 45–59.

———. 2009. *The Anime Machine: A Media Theory of Animation*. Minneapolis: University of Minnesota Press.

Lukács, Gabriella. 2010. *Scripted Affects, Branded Selves: Television, Subjectivity, and Capitalism in 1990s Japan*. Durham: Duke University Press.

McDonald, Paul. 1997. "Feeling and Fun: Romance, Dance, and the Performing Male Body in the Take That Videos." In *Sexing the Groove: Popular Music and Gender*, edited by Sheila Whitely, 277–294. London: Routledge.

Mulvey, Laura. 1989. *Visual and Other Pleasures*. Bloomington: Indiana University Press.

Nakamori Akio. 2007. *Aidoru Nippon*. Tokyo: Shinchōsha.

Ōgawa Hiroshi. 1988. *Ongaku suru Shakai*. Tokyo: Keisō Shobō.

Okada Toshio. 2008. *Otaku wa Sudeni Shinde-iru*. Tokyo: Shinchosha.

Ōsawa Masachi. 2008. *Fukanōsei no Jidai*. Tokyo: Iwanami Shinsho.

Ōtsuka Eiji. 1989. *Shōjo Minzokugaku: Seikimatsu no Shinwa o Tsumugu "Miko no Matsuei."* Tokyo: Kōbunsha.

———. 2010. "World and Variation: The Reproduction and Consumption of Narrative." Trans. Marc Steinberg. In *Mechademia 5: Fanthropologies*, edited by Frenchy Lunning, 99–117. Minneapolis: University of Minnesota Press.

Saitō, Tamaki. 2007. "*Otaku* Sexuality." Trans. Christopher Bolton. In *Robot Ghosts and Wired Dreams: Japanese Science Fiction from Origins to Anime*, edited by Christopher Bolton, Stan Csiscery-Ronay Jr and Takayuki Tatsumi. Minneapolis: University of Minnesota Press.

Sasakibara Gō. 2004. "*Bishōjo*" no Gendai-shi. Tokyo: Kōdansha Gendai Shinsho.

Szollosy, Michael. 1998. "Winnicott's Potential Spaces: Using Psychoanalytic Theory to Redress the Crises of Postmodern Culture." *Psyche Matters*. http://psychematters.com/papers/szollosy.htm (accessed 23 June 2004).

Treat, John Whittier. 1993. "Yoshimoto Banana Writes Home: *Shōjo* Culture and the Nostalgic Subject." *Journal of Japanese Studies* 19, no. 2: 353–387.

Tsunku. 2000. *Rabu Ron*. Tokyo: Shinchōsha.

Ueno Chizuko. 2010. *Onna-girai: Nippon no Misojinī*. Tokyo: Kinokuniya Shoten.

Williams, Linda. 1999. *Hard Core: Power, Pleasure, and the "Frenzy of the Visible."* Berkeley: University of California Press.

10
The Virtual Idol: Producing and Consuming Digital Femininity

Daniel Black

Idols exist primarily as a carefully constructed mode of performance. While, of necessity, this mode of performance is most commonly generated by a living body, dependence upon a physically present performer is not inevitable. Originating in Japan but also experimented with elsewhere, the virtual idol is a media performance which exists independently of the referent of any living performer. While the virtual idol is a native inhabitant of the digital media world in which all idols primarily operate, it perhaps remains the case that a lack of living materiality limits her capacity to emulate traditional forms of media celebrity; at the same time, however, this media image's independence from any single living body provides an opportunity for a new kind of relationship between idol and fan to appear. This new kind of relationship, being overwhelmingly one between an artificial woman and a male consumer, crucially depends upon the commodification and mass-production of a certain kind of femininity.

The claim that music stars are just one more highly planned, mass-produced, demographic-targeted industrial commodity is hardly a new one. Even the prospect of a music producer realizing that he isn't dependent upon the living bodies of performers as the raw material for star production isn't new: Don Kirshner, the musical Svengali who created The Monkees, was responsible for the biggest number one hit pop single of 1969 when another of his creations, The Archies, a band made up of animated cartoon characters, released the song "Sugar, Sugar." Of course, Kirshner, like the architects of most subsequent attempts to replace the bodies of pop stars, was unable to do away completely with living performers: media technologies allowed the circulation of pop star personae independent of living bodies, and animation even allowed bodies to be manufactured without living models, but living performers remained necessary to sing the song and play musical instruments. Nonetheless,

Kirshner had already intuited that, while the entertainment industry was in the business of capturing traces of the human body which could then be mass-produced and sold, media production technologies might—at least to some extent—be capable of simply manufacturing such commodities *ex nihilo*, producing traces of bodies which had never really existed. Fully realizing this capability, however, would require both the means to artificially generate *all* aspects of pop performance (including the sound of the performing body) and an audience willing to develop a powerful relationship with a pop star despite that pop star's lack of living, physical reality.

Traces and representations

The entire media industry is built around the commodification and circulation of traces and representations of the human body. Even before paparazzi and the Hollywood star system, women's bodies were commodified, circulated, and consumed, for example, through the nude in western painting, and *ukiyo-e* images of famous actors and geisha in Japan. However, while the consumption of visual traces of the human body has a long history, it has not been so easy to consume traces of the human voice. Although modern photographic, printing, and video technologies were necessary before the trade in the body's visual traces could attain the massive scale of today, it is nevertheless the case that traces of the human form have been captured and prized since before history. Capturing the sound of the human body has a much shorter history: it was not until the phonograph appeared in the late nineteenth century that it was possible to trade in the human voice (Kittler 1990, 231–233).

Inevitably, the commodification of the human voice initially traded on the idea of fidelity, as reflected by the famous "His Master's Voice" logo of the dog attending to a gramophone's reproduction of its owner's speech. However, while technologies of visual reproduction have maintained "realism" as a key benchmark,[1] in the popular music industry this ideal rapidly lost currency. There may be some residual myth of authenticity in popular music, but the fact remains that musical recordings are no longer believed to truthfully capture some singular performance. As noted by Edward Kealy, the popular music recordings which appeared in the United States after World War II were not understood as accurately capturing some temporally and geographically specific instance of musical performance, as with earlier recordings (Kealy 1990, 211–213); the natural performance space of popular music was not the concert hall, but the recording studio. The pop song might be performed live for an audience, but today the live performance is more likely to be understood as a reproduction of the original studio recording, rather than *vice versa* (cf., Gracyk 1996, 37ff.).

Pop music is generally understood to be highly artificial in its production. Denigrating accounts of pop music have tended to focus on its status as contrived, produced through cynical pandering to a mass audience; the singer a visually appealing mouthpiece spouting lyrics written by someone else, whose lack of genuine talent is masked using technological trickery. But even those who enjoy pop music are unlikely to understand it in vastly different terms; they simply don't evaluate pop music according to a myth of artistic genius and authentic sincerity in musical performance, and so don't find it wanting. At the same time, the obsolescence of authenticity does not render the commodification of particular human bodies redundant—it is just that the body becomes a highly artificial product.

The Japanese idol industry is well known for its capacity to manufacture carefully produced performers who can be utilized in a variety of media settings (Aoyagi 2005, 3–4). Live performances are highly constrained and contrived, while recordings remain traces of bodily performances, but bodily performances that never actually took place. It is the tension between recording technology's simultaneous reliance upon and independence from the human body that underlies its appeal: it can produce fantasies of embodied performance by capturing performances that never did and never could actually occur. Disconnecting the human voice from the human body promises the possibility of creating artificial fantasy voices that can then be attached to artificial fantasy bodies, imbuing them with a sense of authenticity and life.

One of Thomas Edison's first ideas for marketing the phonograph to a mass audience was a talking doll, which could recite nursery rhymes and baby talk through machinery hidden inside its body (Wood 2002, 118–163; Hillier 1988, 93–94). This immediately tied sound reproduction to the commodification and industrialization of female bodies in two ways: first, through the mass production of the strange, perforated metal anatomy of the (female) babies; and, second, by creating a female workforce engaged in the labor of speaking infantile pronouncements into recording equipment in Edison's factory. The voices of these women became a resource that was harvested from their bodies and reproduced on an industrial scale.[2]

Hadaly, the automaton created by the fictional Thomas Edison of Auguste Villiers de l'Isle-Adam's novel *Tomorrow's Eve* (*L'Ève future*), expands upon the idea of the talking doll, rendering the imperfect living woman upon whom she's modeled redundant through her capacity to speak using two phonographs encased in her chest:

> The songs and words of the Android will forever be those that your lovely friend will have dictated to her—unknowingly, without ever laying eyes on her. Her accent, her diction, her intonations, down to the last millionth of a vibration, will be inscribed on the discs of two golden phonographs ... perfected miraculously by me to the point where now they are of a tonal fidelity ... practically ... intellectual! These are the lungs of Hadaly. An electric spark sets them in motion, as the spark of life sets ours in motion.
>
> (Villiers de l'Isle-Adam 1982, 79)

The ability to use language was what, according to Descartes, sepa-rated the ensouled human being from the mere *bêtes machines* of the animal kingdom (Descartes 1988, 44–45), so it is unsurprising that there have been numerous attempts to create a machine which could—if not actually prove him wrong by mastering language—at least entertain an audience by *seeming* to do so by speaking words (Bedini 1964, 38; Riskin 2003, 617, 619). The performance of music was also a favored task for androids, such as Jacques de Vaucanson's flute player and other musi-cians (Fryer and Marshall 1979), and the Jacquet-Droz clavecin player (Voskuhl 2007, 296–297).

Today, this fascination with the artificial production of the voice and musical performance is still apparent. In the twenty-first century, Yamaha has created the Vocaloid software technology, which allows machines to sing, while at the same time the use of auto-tuning effects to make human singers sound like machines (especially in hip-hop and R&B) is common (James 2008). At the CEATEC technology exhibition in Japan in 2009, an HRP-4C robot called Miim put on a musical per-formance utilizing Vocaloid software, as well as a wig and costume, to impersonate the Japanese pop idol Hatsune Miku (*CEATEC News* 2009). Ironically, the pop idol this technological creation was impersonating was herself only a technological creation: the "real" Hatsune Miku is not a living body at all, but exists only as software, computer animation, and an array of official and fan-produced texts (Figures 10.1 and 10.2).

The virtual idol

The idea of the virtual idol has been around for over a decade now. The turn of the twenty-first century was a time when advances in

Figure 10.1 Hatsune Miku.
Source: Copyright Crypton Future Media, Inc., 2010. Reproduced with permission.

computer-generated animation led to various musings on the possibility of replacing living entertainers with digital simulations. The bodies of Humphrey Bogart, James Cagney, and Louis Armstrong were digitally reanimated to appear in a Diet Coke commercial in 1992,[3] and the film *Final Fantasy: The Spirits Within*, adapted by Japanese company Squaresoft from their successful *Final Fantasy* video games at great expense in 1991, had been hoped to demonstrate the viability of "synthespians" (La Ferla 2001), synthetic thespians able to compete with—or perhaps even supersede—living actors. In 1996, Japanese talent agency Horipro unveiled Kyoko Date, the first virtual idol, in a similar attempt to remove living women from the industrialized commodification of bodies while leaving the lucrative chain of representations which sprang

Figure 10.2 "Miim" the HRP-4C android engaged in cosplay as Hatsune Miku.
Source: Copyright CEATEC JAPAN Organizing Committee, 2009. Reproduced with permission.

from them intact. Various other virtual idols followed in Japan and elsewhere, meeting with varying degrees of success (cf., Black 2006; 2008), but ultimately neither virtual idols nor synthespians demonstrated the ability to compete with living performers.[4] Using Chris Rojek's categorization of celebrity types, virtual idols are "celeactors," a sub-category of "celetoids," a term which in turn refers to a figure less stable and enduring than the fully fledged celebrity (Rojek 2001).

Celebrity construction and presentation involve an imaginary public face. In the case of celeactors, there is no veridical self, and the public face is entirely a fictional creation. The audience's connection with celebrities, celetoids, and celeactors is dominated by imaginary relationships. The physical and cultural remoteness of the object from the spectator means that audience relationships carry a high propensity of fantasy and desire (Rojek 2001, 25–26).

All celebrities rely on the fabrication of artificial public personae and the formation of imaginary relationships with an audience, but the virtual entertainer's capacity to inspire a deep fascination is perhaps limited by its high level of predictability and lack of autonomy. As noted some time ago by Richard Dyer, the highly managed public persona of the living celebrity exists in constant tension with the "real" person to which this persona has been attached, and which anchors the artificial persona in physical reality:

> Stars are, like characters in stories, representations of people... However, unlike characters in stories, stars are also real people... Because stars have an existence in the world independent of their screen/ "fiction" appearances, it is possible to believe... that as people they are more real than characters in stories. This means that they serve to disguise the fact that they are just as much produced images, constructed personalities as "characters" are. Thus the value embodied by a star is as it were harder to reject as "impossible" or "false", because the star's existence guarantees the existence of the value s/he embodies.
>
> (Dyer 1998, 20)

The public fascination with celebrity rests largely on those moments when representation and "real" person come unstuck from one another, providing a glimpse of the latter behind the former. Marital infidelities, drug-fueled crack-ups, racist or misogynist rants—those moments when control is lost over the public persona—are exactly when celebrities are most intriguing to the public, and a whole industry has developed around capturing such slips. As a result, while these constitute relationships between consumers and media representations which are independent of the living bodies of performers, additional value and fascination are brought to them by the celebrity persona, and this celebrity persona requires an autonomous human agent to be present at the origin of the chain of representation. The virtual idol is clearly unable to provide this aspect of celebrity fascination.

However, the marketing of the virtual idol Yuki Terai (who appeared in 1997) held out the possibility of a mode of consumption particular to the digital performer, rather than simply derived from that of the living celebrity. While Yuki was commodified through conventional consumer products—such as music videos, CDs, DVDs, and in print—she was also commercialized in a form impossible for living performers, being sold as the digital data used to produce these consumer products (Black 2006). Yuki Terai was originally created by Kenichi Kutsugi in Shade, a 3D modeling package published by eFrontier. eFrontier then went on to market Yuki as a virtual idol in various conventional media, but also "sold" Terai as a package for use in Poser, an application by Smith Micro Software specifically designed to produce realistic 3D images and animations of simulated bodies. Consumers of Yuki Terai in this form, therefore, do not simply acquire fixed, preproduced traces of Terai similar to those of living performers and celebrities; rather, they purchase the digital raw material necessary to produce their own traces of her. An important part of idol fandom is the consumption of *aidoru guzzu*, or idol goods (merchandise), and the sale of the virtual idol's digital data effectively collapses the distinction between idol and idol goods—the virtual idol is herself already a form of merchandise, which can be bought and sold on a mass scale.

Producing and consuming digital femininity

This mode of interaction with the virtual idol is quite different from the traditional relationship between entertainer and audience. It is less mainstream, although it clearly fits into the larger context of a cultural shift towards audiences as "prosumers" who produce, modify, or personalize media in various ways to produce mash-ups, remixes, and so on. Of particular relevance to such a relationship between idol and consumer is the connection between idols (virtual and otherwise) and Japanese *otaku*.

The *aidoru otaku* (Aoyagi 2005, 205ff.) is an idol fan who displays an obsessive loyalty to the idol or idols of his choice (and the idol–*otaku* relationship is overwhelmingly one between a male fan and female performer). The place of idols in *otaku* culture makes the logic of the virtual idol clear, as she stands at the intersection of several different streams of *otaku* desire relating to technology, femininity, and the recycling of media fragments.

Firstly, the virtual idol very clearly ties together the *otaku* obsession with computer technology, animation technology, robotic or otherwise artificial bodies, and the kind of femininity represented by the living idol. This connection is readily apparent elsewhere in *otaku* culture, given its concern with *bishōjo* (pretty girls), and the tendency of these pretty girls to take the form of simulated bodies, for example in animation, computer games, or figurines. Furthermore, the division between simulation and living body is blurred by the *saibā bijin* (cyber-beauty), a girl whose beauty results from its conforming to the aesthetic of anime and computer games (Miller 2006, 121). Turning the female body into a technological artifact also gathers it into the kinds of relationships based on ownership and control apparent in the *otaku* interest in computers.

If the virtual idol can satisfy fan desires in ways the living idol cannot, this power unmistakably arises from the virtual idol's existence as digital data. The contrast between virtual idol as digital data and conventional idol as living body should not be overstated: living performers and entertainers exist for consumers primarily as commoditized digital data, or physical or analog products which have been created out of digital data; at the same time, the virtual idol—while obviously independent of living biology—is an entity whose appeal rests on her ability to reference living biology by simulating certain attributes of the living body. Nonetheless, while both therefore situate themselves at the intersection of the digital and the biological, the virtual and the material, there remain significant differences between them, and it would be a mistake to make easy assertions regarding the virtual idol as Baudrillardian simulacrum (Baudrillard 1994, 1–42) given the degree to which this entity exerts a fascination dependent on the tension and interplay between biological and digital bodies, rather than the collapsing of a distinction between them. While the living idol's commodification and circulation crucially depend upon her translation *into* digital data (digital audio, video, images, etc.), the virtual idol exists as *nothing but* digital data. While the consumption of celebrity might rely on the tension between the celebrity as digital persona and "real" private individual, the virtual idol gains certain advantages even as she is limited in certain ways by the lack of such articulation with the physical world.

Both the digitally mediated bodies of living idols and the digitally produced bodies of virtual idols can be seen as digitally encoded bodies. Digital technology is characterized by the "technical capacity to encode, digitize, and transcode various 'things' from the real world (including other media objects)" (Thacker 2004, 9), and, with the living idol, certain attributes of the living performer are captured and encoded as digital information, but the virtual idol represents the translation of living body into digital information in a more general sense. She is an attempt to capture less individuated qualities of the idol persona and female body and translate them into a digital form that does not seek to faithfully reproduce any particular instance of these things. As a commodity custom-made to appeal to its consumers, the digital body of the virtual idol can be assembled from a "database" (see below) of components which reference earlier commodities and have an established resonance and appeal, and those components in turn make a selective reference to real, living bodies.

Translation always plays on a tension between similarity and difference. Any kind of translation is a process of replacing something with something other than itself, which is nevertheless understood to be equivalent in some crucial sense. For this to occur, there must be a consensus on what attributes will provide a criterion for this equivalence. In translating a sentence from one language to another, the translation is considered a success if the meaning of that sentence is the same, even if every other attribute of the original sentence is lost. In translating a sound into digital data, more complex criteria must be used regarding which frequencies and how many samples qualify as having satisfactorily captured its auditory qualities. The value of translation lies in both its difference and its sameness relative to the original: the valued qualities remain, while undesirable qualities (e.g., unintelligibility and lack of reproducibility) are lost and desirable new qualities arise from its new format. (With digital formats, these are most often related to storage, manipulability, and transcodability.) In the words of Eugene Thacker,

What is of interest in the process of encoding is that, on the one hand, it implies a significant difference constituted in part by the materialization of data, that there is literally a 'difference that matters' between, say, a photographic print and a digital image on a computer screen. On the other hand, encoding's main reason for being is to overcome this difference..., and in the process facilitate a separation between essential data and material substrate.

(Thacker 2004, 17)

The virtual idol is a digital translation of a woman's body, and her value therefore lies in her ability to capture certain attributes of femininity while losing others and replacing them with new attributes particular to her digital format.

The commodification of femininity is a key feature of *otaku* culture. Hiroshi Aoyagi (2005, 73–85) identifies idols with *kawaii* (cute)[5] and a sense of being endearingly imperfect ("life-sized" as opposed to "larger than life"): "Japanese idols ... typically depict images that are fairly standard: appearance, ability, and charm that are above average, but not so much as to alienate or offend the audience" (67). The carefully constructed idol persona that appeals to the idol *otaku* is therefore one that evokes youthful innocence, vulnerability, and meekness, and a lack of remoteness or self-sufficiency. These qualities are endearing in their lack of threat and suggestion that the idol is dependent upon the support, encouragement, and indulgence of her fans.

At its most extreme, the kind of femininity prized by *otaku* (simultaneously infantilized and sexualized, endearingly nonthreatening and subservient) is unlikely to be satisfactorily embodied in any living human being; thus, it exists most clearly in media such as animated characters and figurines. The living idol can stage a performance of this femininity, but the virtual idol is *nothing but* such a performance. Female biology in itself can compromise the clean, nonthreatening "cuteness" of such femininity (Black 2008, 39–41), but this biology is discarded in the translation of woman into digital entity. What the idol's body *gains* through translation, on the other hand, are the qualities of digital data, most obviously an availability for manipulation and modification, appropriation and control.

As reflected by its very name, the virtual idol illustrates the larger shift towards virtualization, "the cultural perception that material objects are interpenetrated by information patterns" (Hayles 1999, 13–14; 1998, 69), where "[p]attern tends to overwhelm presence" (Hayles 1996, 267). This shift of focus from the physical to the virtual is a complex phenomenon whose power comes precisely from its tying together of a number of different strands of thought and experience and its continuity between numerous technological phenomena. At the same time, however, key to its spread has been the amenability of digital data to circulation and commodification. Once a commodity exists in a purely digital form, mass production is no longer even necessary, as each instance of that commodity can spontaneously produce a limitless number of identical instances of itself (as opposed to copies). Even where some digital commodities remain vestigially tied to the mass-production of physical product (e.g., the dwindling production of CDs and DVDs), this physical production has little or no relationship to the value of the product.

This transformation is a double-edged sword, of course, and the replicability and transferability of digital products allow them to slip easily from the grasp of producers, leaving them without the ability to limit and thus profit from their replication. Intellectual property rights holders are often simultaneously seduced by the scale of production and distribution digital formats promise, and frightened by the threat they pose to their control over this process. However, there are also cases of intellectual property rights holders strategically ceding a large measure of control to consumers and subsequently profiting from the unpaid labor of loyal fans. In all kinds of ways, digital formats have made consumers the owners and controllers of digital texts in a way not previously possible, and this is clearly key to the satisfaction idol *otaku* can gain from their relationships with virtual idols.

An idol which exists only as digital data which the fan can "own" and manipulate holds the promise of a more intimate relationship than is possible with a living idol. Celebrities more generally tend to be remote and unattainable, leaving fans straining to catch a glimpse of their real selves through the keyhole of the media. The living idol is seemingly more proximate and attainable, being less intimidating and remote and creating a sense of dependence upon her fans, but of course the *otaku* fan remains, in reality, just one of many feeding off a simulation of genuine closeness and interaction. When the idol can be owned as digital data, however, she becomes unequivocally dependent upon the consumer and under his control.

The appeal of the video game *THE iDOLM@STER* (and its sequel) by Bandai Namco clearly utilizes the capacity of digital idols to fulfill a desire for control. In these games, the player takes on the role of a music producer who must manage the career and control the performances of a stable of idols. The game thus caters to fantasies of ownership over idols, reflecting the real-life gendered power relations between male music producers and the disposable, commodified young girls in which they deal. In playing the game, the fan consumes a fantasy of production: rather than being cast as consumer of the idol text, the fan experiences a fantasy of being the privileged Svengali who directs idols to produce texts for the consumption of others. Of course, the producer figure also enjoys consuming the resulting text, and the fantasy experience is created by consuming the mass-produced text of the game itself, but with *THE iDOLM@STER*, as with other *otaku* texts, this source material can be cannibalized to produce a limitless number of further, fan-produced texts, like "MAD movies"—videos created by editing together fan-selected scenes from across various anime or video games.[6] The practice of harvesting data from digital texts in order to combine and present them in novel ways is widespread, and Hiroki Azuma (2009, 53–54) understands it to express a fundamental attribute of *otaku* culture, namely "database consumption," which he illustrates with the consumption of virtual women in so-called "beautiful girl games":

In this way, the consumers of [these] games can be characterized as having two completely different inclinations toward the surface outer layer (the drama) and toward the deep inner layer (the system) of a work. In the former they look for an effective emotional satisfaction through combinations of [affective] elements. In contrast, in the latter they want to dissolve the very unit of the work that gives them such satisfaction, reduce it to a database, and create new simulacra.

(Azuma 2009, 84)

"Beautiful girl games," like *kisekae* games (Hamilton 1997) and a variety of more recent and technologically advanced 3D games, revolve around the mastering and sexual enjoyment of virtual girls or women. Because the game element restricts the player's access to the sexual payoff, requiring the correct series of in-game actions or the demonstration of certain skills, it is common for players to leverage their own or others' computer skills to hack the games, thereby attaining direct access to the pornographic material and complete mastery over the simulated women.

Azuma cites such practices as illustrative of *otaku* database consumption, in which the texts consumed and produced are a surface layer spread over a repository of components, which can be arranged in different combinations to produce a near-infinite variety of further texts. The key resource being consumed here is the affective charge generated by the endearing attributes of female fantasy figures; thus, these endearing characters and their stories can be endlessly created through the rearrangement of a stock of fragments extracted from the digital files within video games and elsewhere.

Yuki Terai's digital body, which can be purchased and manipulated in the Poser software package, provides tremendous scope for such a project. As a piece of manipulable technology, there are endless opportunities for her upgrading or modification. The body of Yuki Terai comes as a package that can be purchased, but this digital body is also equipped with sliders that can "morph" her body shape and face, and her skin, hair, and eye color also can be altered.[7] There is also a vast selection of further body morphs, clothes, hairstyles, poses, movements, and much more that can be purchased from various digital marketplaces.[8] There is even a trade in the genitalia, which such bodies lack "out of the box."[9] While the traditional idol industry might itself function by endlessly presenting variations on a set of cute and endearing feminine attributes, the Poser software allows fans to undertake this work themselves and to work outside the constraints of physical or biological reality. They can amass a library (or database, in Azuma's terms) of commodified fragments of physical appearance, accessories, and styles of movement, and then assemble them into whichever combinations are considered most satisfying.

The reduction of idols' bodies to a collection of digital fragments to be reassembled in new configurations is illustrated in a slightly different way by the figure of Eguchi Aimi. Aimi was abruptly introduced to the idol troupe AKB48 in a mid-2011 television commercial for Ezaki Glico's "Ice no Mi" frozen sweets, but was soon after revealed to be a virtual idol created as a publicity stunt. Her hair, body shape, face shape, eyes, eyebrows, and nose were selected from living AKB48 members, then mapped onto Aimi's face to create a "perfect" amalgam, which was then equipped with the voice of a further AKB48 member (*Tokyo Hive* 2011). Following the revelation of her origins, a publicity website for "Ice no Mi" featured a web application that allowed visitors to create their own virtual AKB48 performer by combining physical features from a selection of 47 living members (Ezaki Glico Co. 2011). Eguchi Aimi highlights the permeability of the division between living idol and virtual idol, as living idols directly supplied the "database" from which her data were drawn. The largely digital existence of the living idol[10] allows her to be utilized as a resource from which digital fragments can be harvested to be used as raw material for the virtual idol.

The voice as digital commodity

While these technologies and practices clearly create bodies that can be owned, manipulated, modified, and circulated, they nonetheless only offer visual attributes. When Yuki Terai was launched as a virtual idol, for all the cutting-edge technology behind her she was just as dependent upon living bodies for her voice as Kirschner's animated band of 1969: a traditional process of Japanese idol selection took place to find a living singer whose voice would be grafted onto Yuki's digital body. However, the prospect of liberating digital bodies from the living voice was raised in 2004 with the release of Yamaha's Vocaloid software technology. Vocaloid is a software synthesizer which allows a library of generic voice recordings to be shaped into words and matched to notes of the user's choosing, producing a novel vocal performance in response to the manipulation of a user interface. While this technology is not entirely independent of the human body—the libraries of generic sounds must initially be recorded from living performers—the fact remains that these sounds can then be mass-produced and used to create vocal performances that have never passed the lips of any living human being.

In 2008, the original Vocaloid software was superseded by Vocaloid 2, which improved its usability and performance and increased its popularity. A key attribute of both Vocaloid versions, however, is their dependence upon specific voice packages. The Vocaloid software only manipulates a library of sounds; crucial to the particularity of the performances it produces is, of course, the actual voice used to create each library. As a result, the human body remains in the chain of commodification, as its living vocal attributes are harvested for mass-production in a way similar to those of the eighteenth-century women who provided the voices for Edison's talking dolls. However, while those women, like the singers who provided the voices of The Archies, Kyoko Date or Yuki Terai, gave up their vocal performances so that they could be attached to the bodies of simulated performers and marketed in their absence, their vocal performances nevertheless remained at least fragmentary records of actual, unique performances that had passed their living lips. Their performances might have been manipulated after the fact, but they still remained linked to their bodily origin at some fundamental level. What Barthes (1985, 273) referred to as the "grain" of the voice, the "friction" produced between music and language in a particular act of singing, remains in these performances. The Vocaloid technology, however, seeks to break the vocal performance down into components smaller than those of the digitally recorded performance, turning the live singer him- or herself into a kind of machine, a set of "bellows" (Barthes 1985, 272) producing raw material to be shaped by a computer. Once extracted from the human body, this raw material can then be used to create entirely new performances independently of the body from which it was originally collected. The words and expression are provided by the owner of the computer software, who turns the generic, mass-produced raw material of the voice to whatever end he or she desires.

Companies can license the Vocaloid software to play back libraries of audio samples they produce; British company Zero-G was the first to begin producing these libraries, which largely took the form of generic, representative voices appropriate for a particular style of music,[11] which a music producer could insert as backing vocals, for example. On the other hand, Crypton Future Media, a Japanese company, has taken a different approach to its creation of Vocaloid packages. Among Crypton's offerings is the "Vocaloid Character Vocal Series," which presents Vocaloid voices as manga-style characters. The most famous and successful of these is Hatsune Miku, a blue-haired, futuristic idol. Despite being a fictitious character, Miku is attributed her own age, height, weight, and musical tastes (Crypton 2010), and, in a manner analogous to the visual customization of Poser characters, she has spawned an *otaku* movement based around the production and consumption of her vocal performances.

More conventionally, Miku has sung theme songs for anime titles, appeared in a video game, and even performed a "live" concert before 25,000 fans.[12] However, her fame (and financial value) rests primarily on user-generated content. While the Vocaloid technology was initially a niche resource, and the first-generation Vocaloid packages sold a sum total of 3,500 copies, Miku (only one of the second-generation packages) alone sold 35,000 copies in the six months following her release (Lee 2008). The Internet has been flooded with fan-produced Miku performances, and one fan has created a software application called "MikuMikuDance," which allows users to create music videos by choreographing a 3D Miku model.[13] With the Hatsune Miku Vocaloid package and MikuMikuDance, all aspects of idol performance can be created by the fan—Miku can sing a song she has never before sung and do a dance she has never before performed at the behest of her *otaku* owner.

While Miku does appear in conventional, "professional" performances, therefore, her popularity is clearly based most importantly on the fact that she can become an *otaku's* own, "personal" idol. Certainly more so than the living idol, and even more so than previous virtual idols such as Yuki Terai, Miku can be owned and controlled by each fan individually.

While she may never intrigue her fans by becoming embroiled in behind-the-scenes controversy (something which in any event would only sully her *kawaii* purity in the eyes of *otaku*), her very lack of a "real life" or true self independent of her fans allows a kind of all-encompassing relationship with consumers impossible for a living idol. Her existence as nothing but digital data allows her fans to personalize her and orchestrate the production of new performances according to their own particular desires.

Conclusion

While the virtual idol is a product of a time in the 1990s and early 2000s when new technologies inspired attempts to create artificial media stars, more recently there has been an important shift in the production of such stars. Originally conceptualized as a new way to create performers whose careers would nonetheless follow the logic of traditional, living media stars—centrally managed and disseminated to consumers as fixed, mass-produced texts—they have evolved towards inviting forms of consumption that leverage the advantages of their origins in digital data. While their lack of physicality and agency in some ways limits their capacity to create satisfying relationships with audiences in the mode of living performers, their freedom from questions of agency, originality, and exclusive ownership and control makes them more amenable to appropriation and manipulation. For an *otaku* audience eager to both consume and produce a technologized, artificial, endearing, and seductive fantasy of femininity from fragments of digital information, an idol such as Hatsune Miku promises a relationship which is in at least some ways superior to that offered by a flesh and blood performer.

While the virtual idol lacks an autonomy which might generate novelty and scandal or a unique biological body which could serve as an anchor for her media performances, the very fact that no part of her exists outside flows of commodities and digital texts enables relationships with fans that are far more intimate and all-encompassing than those available with a living star. No part of the virtual idol lies beyond the reach of the *otaku* fan, who can manipulate and modify her to produce an endless series of texts for further consumption. The appeal of this relationship for a subculture devoted to the consumption and production of a commodified, technologized, artificial femininity is clear; whether such a mode of consumption can make further gains against a celebrity culture still crucially concerned with the articulation of media persona and living body remains to be seen.

Notes

1. I wouldn't want to suggest that visual realism itself is a straightforward or unproblematic concept; however, while what realism is taken to mean and how it is measured might be dependent upon context, the appeal to realism, and the idea of some kind of fidelity to nonrepresentational reality, remains. Even the hyperrealism of much CGI imagery is dependent on a concept of visual realism in a way that most of the sounds in popular music do not depend on a concept of aural realism. The singing voice is perhaps the only exception to this, as it remains directly attributed to the body of an individuated performer, and the alteration of this relationship through technology is one of the primary concerns of this chapter.

2. Heavy and expensive, and in its first iteration with an amplifying trumpet projecting from the top of its head, Edison's talking doll was, however, a commercial failure.
3. Available at http://www.youtube.com/watch?v=A5K7fvv1sG8 (accessed 2 April 2011).
4. Most famously, *Final Fantasy: The Spirits Within* was a disastrous commercial failure.
5. See also Kinsella (1995) and McVeigh (1996).
6. See, for example, "THE iDOLM@STER MAD World Service" at http://idolmaster.tdiary.net/.
7. Yuki Terai is only one of a selection of such Poser models available for purchase at Content Paradise (http://www.contentparadise.com/), as well as further bodies, which are modifications of those originals, although she is the only one to exist as a virtual idol with an elaborated character.
8. See the websites of Content Paradise (http://www.contentparadise.com/), DAZ 3D (http://www.daz3d.com/), and Renderosity Marketplace (http://market.renderosity.com/).
9. See Renderotica at https://www.renderotica.com/xcart/home.php?cat=262 (accessed 2 April 2011).
10. Bearing in mind the greater proximity of acts such as AKB48 to their fans.
11. Although one of Zero-G's libraries, Vocaloid Miriam, sought to mass-produce the vocal performance of a particular session vocalist, Miriam Stockley. See http://www.zero-g.co.uk/index.cfm?articleid=805 (accessed 10 December 2011).
12. Her animated image was projected onto a giant screen.
13. See the Vocaloid Promotion Video Project at http://www.geocities.jp/higuchuu4/index_e.htm (accessed 10 December 2011).

Works Cited

Aoyagi, Hiroshi. 2005. *Islands of Eight Million Smiles: Idol Performance and Symbolic Production in Contemporary Japan*. Cambridge: Harvard University Asia Center.

Azuma, Hiroki. 2009. *Otaku: Japan's Database Animals*. Translated by Jonathan E. Abel and Shion Kono. Minneapolis: University of Minnesota Press.

Barthes, Roland. 1985. *The Responsibility of Forms: Critical Essays on Music, Art, and Representation*. Trans. Richard Howard. New York: Hill and Wang.

Baudrillard, Jean. 1994. *Simulacra and Simulation*. Ann Arbor: University of Michigan Press.

Bedini, Silvio A. 1964. "The Role of Automata in the History of Technology." *Technology and Culture* 5, no. 1: 24–42.

Black, Daniel. 2006. "Digital Bodies and Disembodied Voices: Virtual Idols and the Virtualised Body." *Fibreculture Journal* 9. http://nine.fibreculturejournal.org/fcj-054-digital-bodies-and-disembodied-voices-virtual-idols-and-the-virtualised-body/

———. 2008. "The Virtual Ideal: Virtual Idols, Cute Technology and Unclean Biology." *Continuum: Journal of Media and Cultural Studies* 22, no. 1: 37–50.

CEATEC News. 2009. "Yamaha Corporation Live Performance by Self-Playing Piano and Singing Robot." http://www.ceatec.com/2009/en/news/webmagazine_detail.html?mag_vol=019&mag_type= (accessed 19 June 2011).

Crypton. 2010. "What is the 'Hatsune Miku' Movement?" http://www.crypton.co.jp/mp/pages/prod/vocaloid/cv01_us.jsp (accessed 19 October 2010).

Descartes, Rene. 1988. *Descartes: Selected Philosophical Writings.* Trans. John Cottingham *et al.* New York: Cambridge University Press.

Dyer, Richard. 1998. *Stars.* London: British Film Institute.

Ezaki Glico Co. 2011. "AKB48 Oshimen Mēkā." http://www.icenomi.com/oshimen/index.html (accessed 19 June 2011).

Fryer, David M. and Marshall, John C. 1979. "The Motives of Jacques De Vaucanson." *Technology and Culture* 20, no. 2: 257–269.

Gracyk, Theodore. 1996. *Rhythm and Noise: An Aesthetics of Rock.* Durham: Duke University Press.

Hamilton, Robert. 1997. "Virtual Idols and Digital Girls: Artifice and Sexuality in Anime, *Kisekae* and Kyoko Date." *Bad Subjects* 35. http://bad.eserver.org/issues/1997/35/hamilton.html

Hayles, N. Katherine. 1996. "Virtual Bodies and Flickering Signifiers." In *Electronic Culture: Technology and Visual Representation*, edited by Timothy Druckrey, 259–277. New York: Aperture.

———. 1998. "The Condition of Virtuality." In *The Digital Dialectic*, edited by Peter Lunenfeld, 68–94. Cambridge: The MIT Press.

———. 1999. *How We Became Posthuman: Virtual Bodies in Cybernetics, Literature, and Informatics.* Chicago: University of Chicago Press.

Hillier, Mary. 1988. *Automata & Mechanical Toys: An Illustrated History.* London: Bloomsbury.

James, Robin. 2008. " 'Robo-Diva R&B': Aesthetics, Politics, and Black Female Robots in Contemporary Popular Music." *Journal of Popular Music Studies* 20, no. 4: 402–423.

Kealy, Edward R. 1990. "From Craft to Art: The Case of Sound Mixers and Popular Music." In *On Record: Rock, Pop, and the Written Word*, edited by Simon Frith and Andrew Goodwin, 207–220. London: Routledge.

Kinsella, Sharon. 1995. "Cuties in Japan." In *Women, Media and Consumption in Japan*, edited by Lisa Skov and Brian Moeran, 220–254. Richmond: Curzon Press.

Kittler, Frederich A. and Michael Metteer. 1990. *Discourse Networks 1800/1900.* Stanford: Stanford University Press.

La Ferla, Ruth. 2001. "Perfect Model: Gorgeous, No Complaints, Made of Pixels." *New York Times*, 6 May.

Lee, Mike. 2008. "Meet Japan's Virtual Idol." *AsiaOne.* http://www.asiaone.com/print/Digital/Features/Story/A1Story20080513-64968.html (accessed 25 October 2010).

McVeigh, Brian. 1996. "Commodifying Affection, Authority and Gender in the Everyday Objects of Japan." *Journal of Material Culture* 1, no. 3: 291–312.

Miller, Laura. 2006. *Beauty Up: Exploring Contemporary Japanese Body Aesthetics.* Berkeley: University of California Press.

Riskin, Jessica. 2003. "The Defecating Duck, Or, the Ambiguous Origins of Artificial Life." *Critical Inquiry* 29, no. 4: 599–533.

Rojek, Chris. 2001. *Celebrity.* London: Reaktion.

Thacker, Eugene. 2004. *Biomedia*. Minneapolis: University of Minnesota Press.

Tokyo Hive. 2011. "The Truth about AKB48's Eguchi Aimi Revealed!" http://www.tokyohive.com/2011/06/the-truth-about-akb48s-eguchi-aimi-revealed/ (accessed 29 June 2011).

Villiers de l'Isle-Adam, Auguste. 1982. *Tomorrow's Eve*. Urbana: University of Illinois Press.

Voskuhl, Adelheid. 2007. "Motions and Passions: Music-Playing Women Automata and the Culture of Affect in Late Eighteenth-Century Germany." In *Genesis Redux: Essays in the History and Philosophy of Artificial Life*, edited by Jessica Riskin, 293–320. Chicago: University of Chicago Press.

Wood, Gaby. 2002. *Edison's Eve: A Magical History of the Quest for Mechanical Life*. New York: Alfred A. Knopf.

Index

Lightning Source UK Ltd.
Milton Keynes UK
UKOW06n0705030816

279848UK00010B/220/P